D0221083

Visual Consumption

How do images communicate? How do images circulate in consumer culture? What does the production and consumption of images mean for marketing and society? What can a visual approach bring to consumer research?

A key characteristic of the twenty-first century economy is "the image." Products are advertised via images, and corporate image is critical for economic success. This book draws from art history, photography, and visual studies to develop an interdiscplinary, image-based approach to understanding consumer behavior.

The book focuses on four themes: representation, photography, images, and identity. It presents a theoretical perspective on visual consumption, providing wide-ranging examples from advertising, the Internet, photography, design, theater, and tourism. The author also discusses the importance of the Internet in bringing visual issues into the mainstream of strategic thinking, and spurring research into perception and preference of visual displays.

This book provides an unparalleled guide to the visual consumption processes necessary for understanding and succeeding in today's market.

Jonathan E. Schroeder teaches Marketing and Design in the Department of Industrial Economics and Management at the Royal Institute of Technology in Stockholm. He is also a research affiliate of the European Center for Art and Management, Stockholm. He has published widely in marketing, psychology, design, and law journals.

Routledge interpretive marketing research

Edited by Stephen Brown
University of Ulster, Northern Ireland
and Barbara B. Stern
Rutgers, the State University of New Jersey, USA

Recent years have witnessed an "interpretative turn" in marketing and consumer research. Methodologists from the humanities are taking their place alongside those drawn from the traditional social sciences.

Qualitative and literary modes of marketing discourse are growing in popularity. Art and aesthetics are increasingly firing the marketing imagination.

This series brings together the most innovative work in the burgeoning interpretative marketing research tradition. It ranges across the methodological spectrum from grounded theory to personal introspection, covers all aspects of the postmodern marketing "mix", from advertising to product development, and embraces marketing's principal sub-disciplines.

The Why of Consumption
Edited by S. Ratneshwar, David Glen Mick and Cynthia Huffman

Imagining Marketing
Art, aesthetics and the avant-garde
Edited by Stephen Brown and Anthony Patterson

Marketing and Social Construction
Exploring the rhetorics of managed consumption
Chris Hackley

Visual Consumption
Jonathan E. Schroeder

Also available in Routledge interpretive marketing research series:

Representing Consumers
Voices, views and visions
Edited by Barbara B. Stern

Romancing the Market
Edited by Stephen Brown, Anne Marie Doherty and Bill Clarke

Consumer Value
A framework for analysis and research
Edited by Morris B. Holbrook

Marketing and Feminism
Current issues and research
Edited by Miriam Catterall, Pauline Maclaran and Lorna Stevens

Visual Consumption

Jonathan E. Schroeder

London and New York

First published 2002
by Routledge
11 New Fetter Lane, London EC4P 4EE

Simultaneously published in the USA and Canada
by Routledge
29 West 35th Street, New York, NY 10001

Routledge is an imprint of the Taylor & Francis Group

Typeset in Sabon by Exe Valley Dataset Ltd, Exeter
Printed and bound in Great Britain by
Biddles Ltd, Guildford and King's Lynn

British Library Cataloguing in Publication Data
A catalogue record for this book is available
from the British Library

Library of Congress Cataloguing in Publication Data
Schroeder, Jonathan E., 1962–
Visual consumption / Jonathan E. Schroeder.
p. cm.
Includes bibliographical references and index.
1. Consumers–Research. 2. Visual communication.
3. Advertising. I. Title.

HF5415.32. S363 2002
658.8′342–dc21 2001049110

ISBN 0–415–24424–2

To Janet Borgerson

The capacity to perceive the expressive qualities of things inheres spontaneously in the human mind. It is found most purely in children, at early stages of civilization, and in persons of highly developed intuitive sensitivity, such as artists. It is hampered by a civilization that favors practical utility in a purely physical sense and hesitates to acknowledge the existence of phenomena that cannot be measured or counted.

(Rudolf Arnheim, *The Dynamics of Architectural Form*, 1977)

Each of my works originates from a simple desire to make people aware of their surroundings, not just the physical world but also the psychological world we live in.

(Maya Lin, *Boundaries*, 2000)

Contents

Preface

My first professional presentation was at the Association for Consumer Research conference in Honolulu, Hawaii. I was nervous and excited – the conference locale made quite an introduction to the conference circuit. As I struggled over my presentation, producing several versions of my talk, poring over my overheads to get them just right, I wondered who I would be speaking to – my first audience. On the day of my talk, I eagerly headed down to the room to get ready for my debut. A few of the other presenters were there, but by the time the session was scheduled to begin, the room was fairly empty – there seemed to be more presenters than audience members. "Where is everyone?" I asked my advisor. "Out sightseeing," he replied, with a knowing grin. Perhaps it was then that I learned the power of visual attractions – my talk went fine, but I learned that places like Hawaii often make poor sites for an academic conference – there are too many sights outside the conference hotel that lure colleagues away from intellectual discourse. That day, at least, visual consumption handily beat out theoretical speculations about consumer behavior.

As I was completing this book, I traveled to the Swedish island of Gotland, 50 miles out into the Baltic Sea. Gotland was a medieval seat of the Hanseatic League, a historical precursor to the current European Union. There, in the museum, I saw dozens of "picture stones" – huge stones engraved with pictures and runic inscriptions from previous civilizations. The stones were interesting, but the images meant little to me on first seeing them. I traveled around the island for awhile, and happened to meet someone whose father studied the picture stones, which were created over a span of about a thousand years, including the Viking age. She arranged for me to meet her father, a retired professor of archeology at Uppsala University, in the same museum that I first encountered the picture stones. During his illuminating lecture, he carefully laid out the history of picture stones – which provide compelling evidence of Scandinavian culture via their representation of mythical figures, boats, animals, and people. He told me about the Roman influence on picture stones, their role in Viking culture, and their importance as an artistic form unique to Gotland. I began to see the stones differently. They began to speak to me from the distant past. With the proper context, some motivation, a little background information, and an expert lecturer, what had been interesting pictures on some old rocks transformed into impressive icons of an entire cultural tradition. After this brief, informative introduction, the stones began to call forth an entire cultural way of life. An indistinct stimulus was transformed into a deep, resonant expression. This is what I am trying to do, too. Thank you Bertil Almgren.

For encouragement, support, and advice, I want to thank many colleagues, including Pierre Guillet de Monthoux, Claes Gustafsson, Judith Tolnick, Russell Belk, Morris Holbrook, Gary Bamossy, Janeen Costa, Craig Thompson, Pierre McDonagh, Andy Prothero, Deborah Fain, Dominique Bouchet, Alladi Venkatesh, Fuat Fırat, Laurie Meamber, Dag Björkegren, Emma Stenström, Ann-Sophie Köping, Karin Ekström, Mats Edenius, Charlotte Birnbaum, Daniel Birnbaum, Peter Dobers, Karin Becker, Anette Göthlund, Pauline Maclaran, Linda Randall, Galen Johnson and Detlev Zwick. Some teachers that pointed me along the way include Robert Pachella, Rudolf Arnheim, Franco Nicosia, Christina Maslach, Charlan Nemeth, Jonathan Cheek, and Robin Wiseman.

I also thank James Whiting, Annabel Watson, and Nicola Cooper at Routledge, Michelle Gallagher, formerly with Routledge, and Colin Morgan at Swales & Willis. To Stephen Brown and Barbara Stern, I am deeply indebted for guiding this publishing series; their support of my work has been instrumental to completing this project.

Part of chapter 4 appeared as a review of Orvar Löfgren's book *On Holiday: A History of Vacationing* published in the *Journal of Macromarketing*, June 2001: 99–101. I thank the editor Sandy Grossbart and the book review editor Roger Dickinson for permission to include it here. Part of chapter 6 appeared in *Imagining Marketing: Art, Aesthetics, and the Avant-garde*, edited by Stephen Brown and Anthony Patterson and published by Routledge.

I am fortunate to be part of a remarkable technical university whose motto, *Vetenskap och Konst* – Science and Art – signals a broad interest in the intersections of science, technology, and art. I also thank the Wesleyan University Center for the Humanities for welcoming an interloper from the business school world. In Stockholm, the European Center for Art and Management provides a unique research environment, conducive to disparate pursuits. I also want to acknowledge financial support from the Swedish Foundation for International Cooperation for Research and Higher Education, the Wenner-Gren Foundation, and the University of Rhode Island.

Jonathan Schroeder
Stockholm
May 2001

Part 1
Consuming representation

1 Introduction

A visual approach to consumer research

We are exposed to hundreds of images every day. Not in church, or at museums – but all around us in advertising, on the Internet, on television, in newspapers, on billboards, magazines, buildings, radio, cable, t-shirts, credit cards, shopping carts, and cash register receipts. We live in a visual information culture. In no other time in history has there been such an explosion of visual images. And yet we seem to pay little attention to them, we do not always "understand" them, and most of us are largely unaware of the power they have in our lives, in society, and how they function to provide most of our information about the world.

This book is about visual consumption. By visual consumption, I mean not just visual-oriented consumer behavior such as watching videos, tourism, or window-shopping, but also a theoretical approach to the interstices of consumption, vision, and culture, including how visual images are handled by consumer research. Visual consumption is a key attribute of an experience economy organized around attention. We live in a digital electronic world, based on images designed to capture eyeballs and build brand names, create mindshare and design successful products and services.

How do images communicate? How do people decode and understand images? How do images circulate in a consumer society? In other words, what are the conceptual and historical foundations of consuming visual culture? What can a visual approach to consumption bring to consumer research? Contemporary consumption involves looking, watching, spectatorship, seeing sites, gazing, window shopping, browsing, perusing, traveling, viewing, surfing the Web, navigating the Internet, and many other visual processes. These consumer behaviors rely on images, including brand images, corporate images, artistic images, and digital images. My goal is to understand how visual images function within a cultural system of meaning influenced by advertising, consumption, marketing, and mass media.

My perspective is multidisciplinary. I am not anchored to a particular academic discipline or interpretive school. This approach reflects the interdisciplinary roots of consumer research. I draw on several streams of research and scholarship, including consumer behavior, marketing, art history, and visual studies to develop the concept of visual consumption as a way of thinking about, understanding, and researching consumer behavior. Four themes flow throughout the book: vision, images, photography and identity.

I do not intend to argue that visual consumption is inherently distinct from consumer behavior, instead I want to articulate and conceptualize visual aspects of consumption from an interpretive perspective. The topics and examples I discuss are meant to be illustrative, not necessarily representative or typical instances of visual consumption. I have proceeded much like a photographer who makes a contact sheet from a roll of film's negatives – an image made from the negatives' *contact* with photographic paper – and then uses the contact sheet to quickly scan the roll of exposed film. Some images are marked for enlarging and cropping, others are crossed out as unusable or poorly exposed. Often, only one or two images are then enlarged and subjected to further scrutiny. This book, then, is like a contact sheet of visual consumption; a few aspects are selected, enlarged, and inspected to represent interesting or illuminating ideas. Most are left as possibilities for the future – indicators of how things appear through the lens of visual consumption. Further, it is my "camera" that has produced this contact sheet, and I have made editorial choices in what to enlarge and expand upon. I leave the contact sheet for others to look at, they may see potential in the images I have captured.

The visual consumer

The information technology revolution of the past twenty-five years revolutionized marketing. Computers, the World Wide Web, mobile telecommunications, and audiovisual technology have had a profound impact on management practices, the structure of the market, and society at large. Whereas technology was the primary source of innovation and strategic advantage in the twentieth century, information is becoming the key ingredient for success in the twenty-first (Castells 1999). At the center of this shift is what I call the production and consumption of images.

A key characteristic of the twenty-first century economy is the image. Brands are developed based on images, products are advertised via images, corporate image is critical for managerial success (Chajet 1991). Marketing is fundamentally about image management: "in marketing practice that is most likely to succeed in contemporary society, image is primary and the product is treated as merely a variable that attempts to represent the image" (Fırat *et al.* 1995: 46). As consumer theorist Susan Willis states:

> In advanced consumer society, the act of consumption need not involve economic exchange. We consume with our eyes, taking in commodities every time we push a grocery cart up and down the aisles in a supermarket, or watch TV, or drive down a logo-studded highway.
>
> (Willis 1991: 31)

If we understand that the market is based on images – brand images, corporate images, national images, and images of identity, then we realize that vision is central to understanding management in the information society. Visual consumption starts with images.

The awareness that global consumers are enthusiastic consumers of images, that brand image, corporate image, and self-image are critical economic and consumer values, and that global market culture is largely the construction of symbolic environments makes visual consumption critically important for understanding contemporary consumers. In the turbulent world of the twenty-first century, the real skill of marketing management and consumer research may shift from problem solving to problem recognition, from the production of goods to the production of images.

How do we develop an appreciation for visual consumption? Marketing scholarship will be well served by expanding its domain to include the most profound explanations of human and market behavior. As my former Dean at the University of California Berkeley Haas Business School stated: "We may come to see the search for themes, patterns and metaphors in literature and the arts as a source for hypotheses to explain the increasingly complex global economy" (Miles 1989: 3). This book brings a visual perspective to bear on consumption issues, and provides disparate, wide-ranging examples of how this interdisciplinary enterprise leads to recognition of novel patterns and unique solutions.

Following the interpretive turn in management and marketing scholarship, my research on the production and consumption of images draws from art history, photography, and visual studies to develop an interdisciplinary, visual approach to understanding behavior in the consumer society. I focus on the image and its interpretation as foundational elements of visual consumption. I turn to an array of research from disciplines concerned with image and representation to build a multidisciplinary approach to visual consumption. In addition, visual communication and images are central to my pedagogical philosophy, and I have developed a visual curriculum for management students to stimulate their critical thinking skills, visual literacy, cultural capital, and a more sophisticated understanding of the image-based economy.

An image serves as a stimulus, a text, or a representation that drives cognition, interpretation, and preference. As psychologist and art historian Rudolf Arnheim argues, "one must establish what people are looking at before one can hope to understand why, under the conditions peculiar to them, they see what they see" (Arnheim 1977: 4). I draw upon several image theorists to develop a way of understanding images for consumer researchers. One of my goals is to make visible particular possibilities of meanings relative to certain images. Images function within culture, and their interpretive meanings are subject to change. The goals of this study are interpretive rather than positive; my aims are to show how images can mean, rather than demonstrate what they mean. As art historian Richard Leppert suggests:

> To talk about an image is not to decode it, and having once broken its code, to have done with it, the final meaning having been established and reduced to words. To talk about an image is, in the end, an attempt to relate oneself to it and to the sight it represents.
>
> (Leppert 1997: 7–8)

Image interpretation is never complete, or closed. Interpretations are meant to be contested and debated. Visual consumption of images is an important, but by no means comprehensive approach to understanding consumers. Rather, by focusing on visual issues in consumer behavior, we place consumption more fully within the realms of other disciplines that engage with images.

Overview of book

This book is focused on how visual representation works within a cultural system of meaning influenced by marketing, the Internet, and mass media. I offer theoretical reflections about consumption that integrate work from disparate areas of visual theory in a way that links marketing as a visual representational system that produces meaning to visual consumer behavior theory. In part 1, "Consuming representation," I present a theoretical perspective on visual consumption from the point of view of the consumer. My interest in what I call visual consumption encompasses touring, watching, viewing, and other seemingly non-use activities that to me are indeed consumption.

Chapter 2 "Visual representation and the market" deals with the concept of representation. Representation remains a central concept within the humanities but it is not well researched within consumer behavior and marketing (cf. Stern 1998). When I talk about representation, I am thinking of it as a system that produces meaning through language. The conventional view of representation, from Plato, held that representation is a copy-like process that creates clear, one-to-one meanings about the things that exist in the material and natural world. These things have natural and material characteristics that have a meaning outside how they are represented. Representation, in this view, is only of secondary importance, it enters the picture only after things are fully formed and their meanings constituted.

In another, emerging social constructionist view, however, representation is conceived as entering into the very constitution of things. Culture is conceptualized as a primary or constitutive process, as important as the economic or material base in shaping social subjects and historical events – not merely a reflection of the world after the event. In this view, eloquently and forcefully articulated by Stuart Hall, one of the founders of cultural studies, representation research falls into two broad approaches: the semiotic approach, which is concerned with the how of representation, that is how language produces meaning. The discursive approach is more focused on the effects of representation, the consequences and political ramifications (Hall 1997).

For my purposes these two approaches to representation correspond roughly to the interest in understanding how marketing creates things like brand images, customer satisfaction, product identity on one hand, and more macro issues such as the role of marketing in society, ethics, and consequences of consumption. Chapter 2 focuses on three interrelated visual consumption issues: representation, identity, and advertising. I discuss implications of an approach that takes representation seriously. I introduce art historical concepts for understanding visual consumption, and I draw on consumer research, social psychology, cultural studies, and advertising to build a model of visual representation's place in the market.

If we agree that products are marketed via visual images, then we need to think carefully about what this implies economically, managerially, psychologically, and politically. One logical conclusion that this implies a rethinking of competition. From a consumer point of view, competition need not be constrained by standard industrial classifications, product categories, or corporate discourse such as the Pepsi vs. Coke wars. If we consume images, then products may reflect fitting in, being cool, and belonging. In what I call a hyperaffluent society such as ours, we no longer buy necessities as necessities. For example, most of us have many shoes. If we truly understand how consumers and marketers alike build brands psychologically, it may force us to reconsider how we think about competition. Shoes may compete with other clothes, watches, compact discs, or haircuts – each might contribute similarly to a consumer's image and each may be marketed as products or services that exemplify desired lifestyles. Current discussion about competition often reflects a modernist, rational, physical product-based view of the market that is at odds with the way the consumption really works.

In chapter 3, "Through the lens: reflections on image culture," I present a theoretical discussion of photography as a vibrant, essential visual information technology. Image culture concerns how people understand and decode them, as well as how images circulate in culture. The image concept is important to strategic marketing issues – brands, corporate communication, advertising, and investment information depend on images. Photography is the foundation for corporate communication and advertising. Technology often subsumes previous forms, photography used the camera obscura, film developed from still photography, the Internet adopted earlier audiovisual technologies. Photographic images – scanned, digitized, and incorporated into Web pages as graphic elements – helped transform the Internet from a text-based communication network into the image-dominated World Wide Web.

Photography is an information technology that is part of everyday life. As a photography dealer observes: "the impact of photography in today's world is relentless. We are a photographic-picture generation" (Sotheby's Philippe Garner, quoted in Suder 2001). Chapter 3 reviews historical conceptions of the image, and draws upon current thinking in photography to articulate how the image functions in consumer culture. Several examples of photographic-based consumer research are presented to illustrate its potential as well as point to the underestimation of photography's role in consumer behavior and marketing communications. Consumption is inherently visual, yet consumer researchers have seemed reluctant to embrace art history and visual studies as critical fields for study. I discuss reasons for this neglect, sketch some remedies, and prepare the way for research that incorporates visual aspects of consumption.

Consumers can be compared to tourists; they are "sensation-seekers and collectors of experiences; their relationship to the world is primarily aesthetic; they perceive the world as a food for sensibility – a matrix of possible experiences ..." (Bauman 1998: 94). In part 2, "Consumption domains," several arenas of visual consumption are discussed to demonstrate the visual approach's potential for consumer research. This section demonstrates the usefulness of the visual approach to consumer research via three case analyses that provide readers with tools and insights into the visual domain of consumption. Photography, the World Wide Web, architecture, and advertising design represent visually varied yet related domains that well serve the goal of explicating certain processes of visual consumption. Each are examples of a language, or a system of representation that interacts with consumer behavior in important ways.

Current marketing communications promotes Kodak as your memory deliverer – "keep all your photos on line, to be ordered and viewed when you want them!" Chapter 4, "Photography as a way of life," frames photography as a key consumer practice. Photography is one of the central ways that consumers understand the world, yet few consumer research studies specifically address photography as a separate domain. Why do people spend so much time taking pictures? Travel and tourism provides answers to how people consume visually. Furthermore, travel is a convenient metaphor for analyzing global issues of identity, economic power, and marketization. Travel and photography are intertwined – pictures, postcards, travelogues, and now the World Wide Web have put a world before consumers' eyes, a world in which "the ability to visualize a culture or society almost becomes synonymous with understanding it" (Fabian 1983: 106). This theoretical point is reflected in a popular guide to travel photography: "If the photographer's attitude is open, frank and friendly, all barriers will come down and he will capture on film his impression of a person, a people, and a nation" (Time-Life Guide to Travel Photography 1972: 199). Tourism, then, is a powerful metaphor for consumption. Spectacular consumption sites offer visual experiences to consumers, art museums promote their gift shops as much as their collections, virtual reality promises travel without movement. Travel writing and travel have become central to postcolonial studies; travel often invokes economic, ethnic, and social inequities and the gaze of the conqueror or tourist (e.g., Clifford 1997; Desmond 1999; Pratt 1992; Torgovnick 1991). I analyze several photography guides that reflect an optimistically progressive and liberating mindset to investigate how photography functions in consumer practice.

In chapter 5, "E-commerce, architecture, and expression," the World Wide Web's role in visual consumption is addressed via a close look at how financial institutions visualize consumer values. The colossal California financial conglomerate Wells Fargo Bank's 1999 Annual Report announced that "the basic financial needs of our customers, however, do not change that much. They want to borrow, invest, transact, and be insured. They want convenience, security, trust and dependability" (Well Fargo Annual Report 2000: 4). The Internet has fundamentally altered banking and financial services, yet basic customer desires continue to rest on stability, security, and strength. These psychological needs were often symbolized with architectural form: "banks adopted the canons of classical architecture as appropriate forms to house their functions, the less tangible (psychological) attributes of strength, security, and stability characterize them as a distinguishable building type" (Chambers 1985: 20). Although space and time are transfigured within the information-based electronic world of contemporary commerce, architecture and design remains a viable method for communicating corporate values.

Chapter 5 builds upon several assumptions about visual communication. First, architecture is a visual language as well as a functional art. That is, buildings signify – they communicate cultural, economic, and psychological values. The architectural style known as classical is a particularly powerful example – classical temples were used by the Ancient Greeks to house their gods, classical style was revived during the Renaissance for church, state, and the elite citizens, and classical buildings played important roles in the United States and its rise to world power. Furthermore, Western banks adopted the classical style for their often-imposing headquarters – thus, the image of a bank has come to resemble a Greek temple. In the age of the Internet, how does this visual form survive? Chapter 5 shows that classicism is alive and well on Internet banking sites, and discusses the role that earlier visual forms play on the current Web scene.

Chapter 6, "Marketing identity, consuming difference," examines advertising imagery in much the way an art historian treats pictures and proceeds to analyze an illustrative example through classic art historical analysis techniques: description, interpretation, evaluation, and theorization. I claim that greater awareness of the connections between the traditions and conventions of visual culture and the production and consumption of advertising images leads to enhanced ability to understand how advertising works as a representational system and signifying practice. Contextual matters are brought to bear in the analysis through application of race, gender, and sexual orientation issues. My focus shows how a visual approach illuminates advertising elements infused with visual, historical, and rhetorical presence and power.

An art historical approach grounds my analysis of advertising images, focusing attention on how the human figure has been represented in Western art, a source for many conventions in contemporary advertising. Scholars in the humanities provide advertising researchers with a variety of useful techniques and terms with which to analyze and interpret images in advertising such as the male gaze – the acknowledgment that much imagery is produced by men for men, image analysis and historical insight.

The concept of *consuming difference* is introduced to theorize how gender and multicultural identities are represented in contemporary advertisements. Our identity guides much in our consumption patterns, and the interaction of consumption and identity in a society such as ours signals the power of marketing. In a visual consumer society, our consumer choices reflect our values, both in a psychological sense and at a very practical level. Once consumers have a wide choice of goods, preference between items takes on a social and psychological meaning. Furthermore, all products are marketed to specific groups of consumers, identified through marketing research, and linked via specific psychological, social, and behavioral attributes.

No discussion of visual consumption would be complete without a consideration of sexuality. In chapter 7, "The fetish in contemporary visual culture," I discuss fetishism – the erotic reification of images and objects – from a visual consumption perspective. Fetishism is a useful concept for understanding why visual images create desire. This chapter presents a conceptual framework for conceptualizing how the fetish functions in the image economy. Images are like fetishes – they are worshipped for their almost magical ability to conjure desire and delight. Images, in the form of television, film, and the Internet, often interfere in human relationships (e.g., Kraut, Lundmark, Patterson, Kiesler, Mukopadhyay and Scherlis 1998; O'Guinn and Shrum 1997). Intent pornography represents a highly profitable and growing element of e-commerce. Pornography has also driven many of the technological innovations of the Web, such as video streaming, pay per view, and real-time images. I do not concern myself with pornography here, rather I am more interested in broader issues of how visual images stimulate the imagination. In the image-based world advertising imagery, photography, fetishism, and cultural values intermingle.

The book concludes with some speculations on how visual consumption is influenced by the World Wide Web, and how consumers apprehend visual imagery in a cluttered visual landscape. Chapter 8, "Visual consumption in an attention economy," addresses questions about consumer knowledge and insight into visual images: are consumers visually savvy or conceptually clueless when it comes to decoding visual culture? Like humans, the answers are complex. However, the dominance of visual imagery does not necessarily make for visually literate consumers. Visual consumption often involves mere looking without comprehension, gazing without knowledge, and watching without engagement. This way of thinking about consumption questions traditional models of competition, consumer choice, and branding.

Vision and consumer culture

Vision happens in culture. Central to contemporary life, "this remarkable ability to absorb and interpret visual information is the basis of industrial society and becoming even more important in the information age" (Mirzoeff 1999: 5). Visual culture depends on the modern propensity to picture or visualize experience (Osborne 2000). Historical precedents of this tendency include medicine, which transforms internal bodily functions into scans, sonograms, or X-rays; geography, which maps the world via satellite technology; and the allied biological sciences. Today, we take visual computer displays for granted, but of course, making patterns of 1s and 0s into "desktops," "browsers," and "windows" is a recent development. Furthermore, visual knowledge has often been cast as an inferior mode of knowing; Western civilization has long privileged the written and spoken word over the image (Jay 1993).

Skeptics have long considered images to be ephemeral – inferior to the word in matters of truth and knowledge. There is a long history of speculation about images from Plato forward that points to the ability of images to fool the eye and falsely persuade. The visualization of everyday life does not mean we know what we are seeing. Groups such as interpretive communities, cultural associations, and market segments – often organized around images – develop certain visual conventions. These are often not well understood, or even cognitively available to consumers: "the effectiveness of conventions to some extent lies in the degree to which they manifest themselves as being 'natural'" (Leppert 1997: 8). Visual images "succeed or fail according to the extent that we can interpret them successfully. The idea that culture is understood by means of signs has been part of European philosophy since the seventeenth century" (Mirzoeff 1999: 13). Some argue that consumers have a heightened visual or semiotic literacy today, which makes them resistant to image-based marketing, but I remain doubtful, as I discuss in chapter 8. I contend that the analogy that people know more about images because they live surrounded by them is like claiming that someone who eats a lot knows a lot about cooking. As one writer complains, "I suffer from abundance ... my senses are flooded by images, the difference in value between one image and another becomes as fleeting as my own movement; difference becomes a mere parade of variety" (Sennett 1990: 127). The overwhelming number, variety, and presence of images interferes with the ability to carefully scrutinize and reflect upon individual images, and lulls viewers into believing that seeing is understanding.

Dreamlike images

Shortly after moving to Stockholm I attended a production of August Strindberg's surreal masterpiece, *A Dream Play* (1982/1901). Robert Wilson, the American avant-garde visual artist and theatrical director, staged the play. Wilson transformed Strindberg's elliptical, loose narrative, stream of consciousness story into a dazzling visual experience, illuminated with his trademark elaborate, computer-controlled lighting. *A Dream Play* concerns a character called Indra's daughter, who comes to earth and experiences earthly emotions of love, loss, and longing. Wilson's production, staged for Stockholm's year as European cultural capital, was a resounding success, and it has since been performed in Nice, New York, and London.

Upon telling an American colleague about the play, he stopped me and asked, "did you understand it?" I was a bit taken aback. *A Dream Play*, of course, was performed in Swedish, so I assume he meant did I understand the language, or perhaps was I able to get the gist of the play. But the question is an interesting one – it begs for a closer look. What exactly was the "it" that I was to understand, misunderstand, or not understand? I enjoyed the play very much, and was able to see it in France with French subtitles, which I could read fairly well. By that time, my Swedish had improved a bit, so I could also catch more of the actors' words as well. Yet the experience of the play was primarily visual; each scene was set up like a photograph that slowly came alive as the action unfolded. After reflecting about this central question of interpretation for quite some time, I think I understood a version of the play that struck me deeply – it is one of my favorite theatrical experiences. But I still find the question curious, and important for any project about images and interpretation.

In some way, compared to a friend who reviewed the Wilson production for *Artforum*, I probably got very little out of *A Dream Play*. In his review, he was able to contrast Wilson's production to an important historical genealogy of *A Dream Play* productions, including several by Ingmar Bergman, Sweden's legendary film and theater director (Birnbaum 1999). He noted that Wilson did not draw upon Stockholm imagery for the sets; his settings are much less rooted in time and place, pushing the play into a more international arena. He wondered about the photograph of a house that provided an opening backdrop for the play. The two-story wooden house looked old – solid, yet mysterious. Why did Wilson use this image?

The photographic backdrop provided my hook into the play. I gave a talk on Wilson's *A Dream Play* at a theater conference in Nice in conjunction with its performance in the European festival. In the talk, I concentrated on the photograph that opens up the play as a structural device that unifies the entire work. Later, back in Stockholm, I was talking about *A Dream Play* to a colleague who informed me that that photograph was by an American photographer, Frances Benjamin Johnston. In fact, several of *A Dream Play* sets borrowed from Johnston's imagery of the Hampton Institute, taken for the 1900 Paris Exposition (Johnston 1966). The Hampton Institute was a vocational training school for African-Americans set up during reconstruction to help train and prepare former slaves for life in post-slavery United States. These photographs reflected a central theme in Johnston's work – to emancipate the underprivileged through positive representation. The images, exhibited at the New York Museum of Modern Art in 1966, show serious, well-groomed, hopeful African-Americans and Native Americans, earnestly posing for a famous photographer's camera (Kirstein 1966).

Johnston's *Hampton Album* images supply a spectacular clue to Wilson's enigmatic staging of *A Dream Play*. Page after page reveals his visual inspiration for each scene – the house that begins the play is "A Hampton Graduate's home," a curious scene that involved huge cow figures directly quotes "Agriculture. Sampling Milk," and the penultimate scene in the play – where the cast gathers on steps and unburdens their innermost wishes – comes from "The Post-graduate Class of 1900" (Johnston 1966). Seeing these photographs – months after attending the play – sent a shiver up and down my spine, as if I was seeing my dreams photographed and reproduced in an obscure, 35-year-old book. So the photographs were vitally important themes in the play. I had understood that much, after all.

Sign, symbol, metaphor – living in a visual consumer culture

Marketing is the institution that handles most of the roles that religion, the state, and the family once held: providing meaning in a myth-like way that helps us make sense of our world. Firms attach meaning to the product through a sense of power and personality, and then attempts to connect this to identity of the person who perceives the ad. Even if we as individual consumers purchase very few of the products advertised, the ads still function as meaning producers. Often, we define ourselves by what we do not buy – "I would never wear a Rolex" or "I will boycott Nike" or "You wouldn't catch me wearing those polyester skirts."

Advertising techniques and metaphors have crept into almost every area of life. Political candidates are packaged, their image carefully constructed with marketing and political experts. Singles advertise in personal advertisements, marketing and selling themselves as a bundle of attributes, much like product marketing. We sell our ideas, make a case for our arguments, and so forth. Brands are bought and sold for their image value over and above a firm's physical, intellectual, or organizational assets (see Brown

1995). Internet companies are traded for enormous sums based on their position in the market, rather than sales or profits.

Advertising sells the past to the future via a sophisticated and often misunderstood information technological system (Berger 1972). The world of imagery in ads is directly connected to the visual past – art history. Advertising creates a dream world of images where anything seems possible. Except, that is, advertising places limits on the imagination due to its very purpose. Its cultivation of images is designed with one thing in mind: purchase.

Our identity guides much of our consumption patterns, and the interaction of consumption and identity in a society such as ours signals the power of marketing. The mass media have reshaped how we live our lives, changing patterns of living, how we conceptualize time and space, and how we live in the global village. The rise of the mass media is synonymous with the growth of the global economy – indeed it is inconceivable without advertising and information technology that it supports. In today's economy, consumer choice is infused with psychological, cultural, and political significance. Market segmentation based on consumer identities is a hallmark of marketing strategy.

Propositions about visual consumption in the image economy

1. Advertising is the dominant global communication force. Advertising – and the mass media which it supports – has emerged as a primary societal institution. For advertising is no longer a means of merely communicating information about products, it is the engine of the economy, and a major player in the political sphere. The major technological medium of advertising is photography, which of course, includes still photography, film, and video.
2. The world's photographability has become the condition under which it is constituted and perceived. *No single instant of our life is not touched by the technological reproduction of images* (Cadava 1999: 135). Politics and History are now to be understood as secondary, derivative forms of telecommunications. There has been no significant events of the twentieth century that have not been captured by the camera, indeed photography and film makes things significant.
3. Identity is now inconceivable without photography. The world has taken on what Cadava calls "a photographic face" (Cadava 1999). Personal as well as product identity (already inextricably linked via the market) are constructed largely via information technologies of photography and mass media. The visual aspects of culture have come to dominant our understanding of identity, as well as the institutionalization of identity by societal institutions.
4. The image is primary for marketing products and services. Products no longer merely reflect images – the image oftens is created prior to the

product, which is then developed to fit the image. Many informational, or content, products share this production cycle. For example, films are pitched as ideas – images – first, before they are produced. If they seem worthwhile, then they may attract capital and a production budget. Many products are designed to fit a specific target market; they conform to an image of consumer demand. This represents a shift in the economy towards experience, towards images, towards attention (e.g., Davenport and Beck 2000).

These four propositions create an interdisciplinary matrix for analyzing the role information technology and identity play in the economy. Specifically, they call attention to photography as an overlooked process within the marketplace of ideas and images. This set of propositions directs our gaze to the cultural and historical framework of images, even as it questions the information that feed those discourses.

Photography has emerged as a ubiquitous representational form, "with us from sunrise to sunset, in the privacy of our homes and on public streets, in a format we can hold in our hands and one that towers over us on billboards the size of buildings." As photography curator James Cuno continues, "so familiar has it become to us – more than any other artistic medium – that knowledge of photography is now crucial to our understanding of the terms of the debate about art and culture at the turn of the twenty-first century" (Cuno 1997: 1). Early criticisms of photography as an art form described the new technique as one that directly reproduced reality (e.g., Batchen 1997). However, the disparity between the photographic record and perceptual experience reveals the artistic, political, and representational potential of photography (e.g., Goldberg 1993). The photographic image maintains a privileged place in the pantheon of visual consumption.

Images and inquiry

Why focus on images? Images provide a useful starting place for understanding visual consumption. Specifically, images afford (from Perkins 1994):

- sensory anchoring – interpretation is anchored in the image;
- instant access – references to images can be made and checked in an iterative process;
- personal engagement – images hold and draw our attention. Much interpretation is a blend of passionate encounter and critical concern.
- wide-spectrum cognition – images engage a variety of cognitive processes;
- multiconnectedness – images are rooted in culture.

Moreover, working with visual communication is a effective means to introduce and develop critical thinking – higher-order cognition that is essential for intellectual work. Management scholar John Mingers identifies four different aspects of critical thinking that are central to management education: the critique of rhetoric, the critique of traditional thinking, the critique of authority, and the critique of objectivity (1999).

Critical thinking is most often associated with the critique of rhetoric, logical analysis within a broader skepticism toward statements and rhetoric. This type of critical thinking should be reflective and able to propose alternatives. The second type of critical thinking involves questioning tradition and custom – "the way we do things around here" (Mingers 1999: 7). Thus, the critique of tradition is necessary for changing organizations, questioning long-standing yet perhaps ineffective practices, and developing new knowledge and traditions. The critique of authority operates at a deeper level to foster skepticism of one dominant viewpoint. This aspect of critical thinking is perhaps most difficult for the teacher or manager to foster. In a world of multiple stakeholders and cultural diversity, the critique of authority remains a key attribute of critical thinking. The last aspect of critical thinking – the critique of objectivity – questions "the validity of knowledge and information that is available, and [recognizes] that it is *never* value-free and objective" (Mingers 1999: 8). Particularly in a visual information economy, it is essential to realize that information is not free, cannot be extricated from culture, and is always becoming outdated.

Blind spots: visual issues in marketing research

The visual context of consumption has not been fully explored within marketing and consumer research Too often, research is dominated by an information-processing paradigm which neglects the work of those scholars who deal specifically in the visual realm – art historians. This book seeks to bridge this gap and introduce a way of thinking about consumers and consumption that is uniquely visual. Most of the existing research on visual issues in consumer behavior has focused on images as stimulus material within experimental research, or used photography merely as a data-gathering tool. In contrast, my approach focuses on the image as a basic building block of consumer behavior, and I pay particular attention to photography, which encompasses still photography, film, and video, as a key information technology. Most often, I emphasize still images over moving images, for they constitute the building blocks of video technology. This book is not a comprehensive survey of visual perception, visual marketing communications, or visual aspects of consumption. Rather, a few central issues in visual consumption are taken up, particularly psychological processes of making sense of images and integration via a close look at visual information technologies of photography, architecture, and advertising. Through a sustained look at a few images, it is possible to see them in a new way.

I hope that this book will be useful to advertising, marketing, and consumer behavior researchers; students of consumer behavior theory; and visual studies students and scholars. At present, students of consumer behavior interested in art and visual issues are not well served. Whereas there are several books that link art and advertising (e.g., Messaris 1997), or discuss art within a marketing framework (e.g., Jensen 1994), there is little work that proposes a visual approach to consumption, broadly speaking. In addition, the book will be of interest to researchers in several disciplines who are part of the tremendous growth of cultural studies. Moreover, there is growing concern surrounding visual literacy, visual studies and design. As more scholars from various disciplines become interested in consumption and marketing issues, it is crucial for marketing academics to contribute to the interdisciplinary conversation about visual consumption. With the emergence of the World Wide Web, global advertising, and the growth of worldwide tourism, visual issues have become increasingly important for marketing practice and theory.

Turning to art history, art criticism and visual studies provides well-established theories and techniques for understanding images. Art criticism investigates art and its objects as cultural documents that both reflect and shape the culture that produces and preserves them. Closely linked to the related fields of aesthetics, art history, art theory, and archeology, art criticism requires an understanding of the styles and functions of art, the social and cultural contexts in which artists have worked, and the technical factors that affect artistic execution (Barnet 1997). Issues that art criticism addresses include evaluation, value, classification, identification and comparison (Stokstad 1995). Like literary criticism many interpretive approaches to the subject, the context, the meaning, and the production of art inform art criticism (cf. Stern and Schroeder 1994). The art world of museums, collectors, scholars, and the public has increasingly encompassed "low" forms of art – such as graffiti, advertising, comics, and industrial design – within the realm of fine art, thus focusing critical attention on a wide range of visual communication (e.g., Guillet de Monthoux 2000; Staniszewski 1995).

Most consumer research from a visual-centered approach focuses on advertising – an important, but limited, application of the rich tradition of art history. In contrast, many art historians have discussed broad issues of consumer behavior. Marketing and consumption is a hot topic in many fields right now, from literary studies to anthropology to history. What once seemed beneath the gaze of humanities scholars has emerged as a central site of analysis. Furthermore, the disdain for marketing and popular culture that characterized much humanities-based work of this century, in particular the Frankfurt School of critical theory, has transformed somewhat into a more complex blend of critical inquiry, celebration, and passionate interest.

However, most humanities-based work that I have come in contact with does not engage with marketing scholarship. Examples include Nicholas Mirzoeff's *An Introduction to Visual Culture* (1999), an excellent overview of visual culture from an art history perspective, Arthur Berger's *Ads, Fads, and Consumer Culture* (2000), a contemporary account of American advertising, and Don Slater's *Consumer Culture and Modernity* (1997), a sweeping sociological history of modern marketing. Each of these engages seriously with marketing issues, yet each lacks references to marketing as an academic field that might contribute to the dialog about visual consumption (see Holt 1995b). Furthermore, many humanities scholars underestimate the theoretical work within marketing and often reflect an unsophisticated comprehension of consumption processes. Thus, despite the rest of the academic world waking up and realizing how important marketing and consumption are as institutional and global forces, marketing scholars seem still relegated to second-class status, our work unread, uncited, unappreciated. This book is aimed at providing an accessible entry point for scholars in various fields who are interested in multidisciplinary approaches to consumption and marketing issues.

While humanists are surveying the marketing of art, marketing researchers have been slow to turn to visual issues to analyze consumer processes – even though visuality is a central feature of the culture that art depicts, packages, comments on, and is marketed within. This book will analyze several case studies – consumption domains – to illuminate the visual context of consumption. It will present a way of thinking about consumer behavior that emphasizes the visual – imagery, representation, design, and visual art. The book will not assume a strong background in art history or aesthetics; I endeavor to present basic concepts in a straightforward manner to make the book accessible to a wide audience.

I will not attempt to answer the question of whether advertising is art, or vice versa. My premise relies on the fact that advertising has become the dominant form of visual communication, and that it has incorporated many attributes of fine art. Advertising often refers – directly and indirectly – to art: "when an advertising art director sought to create an aura of style around a product ... he was likely to turn to high art for the desired association" (Marchand 1985: 140). The traditional separation of art and commerce is a false one, for art as we know it has much in common with advertising (cf. Schroeder and Borgerson 1998). Art, like advertising, often celebrates wealth, power and the *status quo*. Indeed, art is a product in many respects, to be consumed through auction and gallery sales, museum patronage, reproductions, commercial art, and so forth. The line between art and commerce is a blurry one; many artists specifically produce things to be sold, artists' letters from the past are full of references to monetary matters, and advertising has incorporated the techniques, look, and producers of art. Advertising agencies, photography studios, and design firms are full of people with art history training. Furthermore, the world of advertising represents a popular art form that is often represented in fine art museums (Schroeder 1997a). Thus, it seems reasonable to turn to art history – a field that has been analyzing images for hundreds of years – to expand our knowledge of advertising images.

Art history has developed many different critical interpretative stances – iconology, iconography, social history, Marxist, feminist, biographical, psychoanalytic (Barnet 1997; Minor 1994). Each offers tools grounded in a theoretical discourse to focus on particular issues of aesthetic objects (see Stern 1989). A full discussion of these schools of criticism is beyond the scope of the book – which draws largely from semiotic approaches that emphasize the importance of cultural context in understanding visual consumption. A foundational point is that art does not speak for itself: paintings, photographs, and other art works require interpretations to place them within art history, cultural movements, and theoretical frameworks. Images represent differently than words:

> It is all too easy, and utterly false, to imply that paintings are simply nonverbal substitutes for what might otherwise be expressed or communicated in words – ironically, the vast body of writing *about* art confirms nothing more than that words often fail miserably to "account for" the communicative and expressive power of images.
>
> (Leppert 1997: 5–6)

Visual images demand verbal explanations.

Images in art and advertising play a powerful role in how we view the world. In the words of one art historian:

> Despite our resistance and growing cynicism, we remain to one degree or another caught in the light of what we see – what we are shown. Images show us *a* world but not *the* world [...] When we look at images, whether photographs, films, videos, or paintings, what we see is the product of human consciousness, itself part and parcel of culture and history.
>
> (Leppert 1997: 3)

Advertising, like Western art, traditionally excludes much of society. In the last twenty years or so, art criticism has focused increasingly on exclusion and misrepresentation in the canon of Western art (e.g., Stokstad 1995). It is this scholarship that I find useful to interpret advertising, especially advertising that involves representations of diverse cultural identities. Specifically, photographic criticism provides a rich discourse of analytic material and theoretical tools that contribute to marketing and consumer research.

Art and visual consumption

Art history often points to specific connections to current representational systems. The visual past provides a vocabulary of representation that is with us today. One technique that I find valuable is to develop genealogies of visual representation – uncovering historical forms, conventions, and styles of visual expression that inform contemporary images. Arnheim embraces this approach as useful starting point for understanding visual communication: "the 'ostensive' method of arguing with the index finger by pointing to perceivable facts, making comparisons, and drawing attention to relevant relations is a legitimate way of furthering understanding by common effort" (Arnheim 1977: 7). For example, many photographic conventions, including advertising photography, can be traced to Dutch art of the Golden Age, a period that art historians consider crucial in the history of Western art. By a method of close observation, art historical research, and basic analytic techniques of comparison, one gains a fresh perspective on current photographic practice by looking to Dutch art.

Vermeer and many other Dutch artists portrayed regular people in scenes of everyday life, playing music, reading, and cleaning, for example. One recurrent pictorial theme was reading letters – a typical painting showed a young woman intently gazing at a precious letter from one who was away. Countless art historians have contemplated the deeper meanings of these images, invoking themes of literacy, adultery, alienation, and subjective worlds to discuss these enigmatic paintings. In an article I wrote with Barbara Stern, we analyzed Paco Rabanne's famous 1970s man-in-bed ad from a humanities perspective (Stern and Schroeder 1994). In that ad, a man lies in bed, talking to what seems to be a lover on the telephone. We drew many parallels between its composition and signification system and that of Dutch genre art. One example concerns the setting – telephones have largely supplanted letters as a means of personal communication.

Dutch art often appears to show simple scenes, without the trappings of Renaissance or Byzantine art. In other words, meanings seem readily apparent – the subjects of the paintings are often easily recognizable. However, as Simon Schama points out, Dutch art quivers with visual signification:

> surprisingly then, Dutch art invites the cultural historian to probe below the surface of appearances. By illuminating an interior world as much as illustrating an exterior one, it moves back and forth between morals and matter, between the durable and the ephemeral, the concrete and the imaginary ...
>
> (Schama 1988: 10)

Comparisons with advertising are apt – for advertising too, seems to exist in the moment, an ephemeral visual form that merely illustrates product or lifestyle images.

There are many connections between Dutch art and contemporary visual expression. Much like advertising, Dutch art offers both a window and a mirror to society. Cultural and economic resonances include a flowering of consumer culture, exemplified by a growing international economy that celebrates wealth, a concern for cleanliness and keeping a nice house, and economic speculation, such as the famous tulip bulb craze (Schama 1988). The Dutch art market that emerged during the 1600s is highly reminiscent of today's image culture. Dutch families collected scores of paintings for their homes, much the way contemporary consumers generate photographs that fill albums, frames, and refrigerator doors. Finally, we celebrate "Golden Ages" our representational system picks and chooses as referents – we rarely see links to the tarnished years before the Dutch Golden Age, or mention of modern Greek society, for example. There are also specific visual referents between Dutch art and current visual forms, especially advertising photography.

Golden Age Dutch art shows a world constructed, posed, groomed, and carefully represented to portray a vision of the secular good life. Like advertising images, Dutch paintings portray consumer lifestyles, filled with friends, lovers, consumer goods, and entertainment. Dutch art is often seen in moral terms – the images provide instructions on how to live a good, pious life. Advertising delivers instructions on how to live a good, prosperous life. The style of Dutch art has also influenced painting, and in turn, advertising. Dutch art relied on a realist style; the domestic scenes were not dramatized, and made little use of mythical or religious iconography. Dutch art showed recognizable people in realistic settings (see Schroeder and Borgerson 2001). I suggest that this realistic style has exerted a profound influence upon the way photography was received as a technology for realistically representing the world. The interior genre scenes of Dutch art encapsulate a way of seeing and representing the world, a world in which interior space signifies privacy, seclusion, withdrawal, and escape. Many Dutch paintings are of interiors, and present a vision of a single family home, a women's domestic space, and a way of life that included orderliness, possession, and display. Contemporary advertising is filled with this kind of scene, now called the *slice of life*, that reify the everyday, the vernacular, the lost moment, and the consumer lifestyle.

In chapter 6, I discuss the relationship between another Dutch art form and contemporary visual culture – the group portrait. It, too, resonates through the centuries as a powerful visual convention. Group portraits establish and commemorate identity through visual inclusion or exclusion. In Dutch art, however, identity rests on production – group portraits were often of guilds that controlled the production and sale of gold, silver, or other commodity. In current representational practice, groups are linked via consumption, such as those portrayed in consumer catalogs, slice of life ads, and significantly, the CK One campaigns. The visual codes that exist within the portrait's context include ideas about identity, appearance, and its relationship to identity, and existential questions of who we are and how our physical body interacts with our mental and spiritual being. Moreover, portraits are often products for sale or specifically commissioned, or self-generated. Photographic technology allowed the mass-market access to portraits and later, self-representation, altering the notions of identity (Rugg 1997). I believe that art history exerts an overall influence on current representational practices – in statistical terms, both a main effect (Dutch art, for example, is still quite popular and well represented in museums and broader visual culture) and interaction (via generations of artists, photographers, and advertising art directors who draw on prior periods). It is not necessary for all consumers to be aware of these historical precedents in today's visual domains: "The processes and institutions that make up the global economy [...] are reflective of more idiosyncratic desires of ours, desires which we take so much for granted that we are unaware of their existence" (McGoun 2000: 51). The conventions that Dutch art developed influence how we consume representation, how we understand visual images, and what we think of as the good life.

Visual consumption and strategy

Several lines of evidence reveal that interest in visual consumption is growing. First, and foremost, there is a burgeoning awareness of the critical importance of design for Internet sites. Web design has brought visual issues into the mainstream of strategic thinking, and spurred research and thinking about perception and preference of visual displays. Second, there is a growing interest in visual theory in basic fields, such as philosophy, literary studies, and communication. Third, the interdisciplinary field of visual studies is becoming established as an academic discipline, complete with conferences, journals, and degree programs. Visual studies grew out of cultural studies and art history, and maintained a critical approach, often at odds with managerial concerns.

The World Wide Web is driving a visual revolution in marketing in which "everything from the structure of the book to the layout of pages, distribution of images such as photographs, illustrations or digital backgrounds, and use of typography are brought to bear on conveying the company's image" (Murray 2000: 5). The Web mandates visualizing almost every aspect of corporate strategy, operations, and communication. Moreover, the requirements and potentials of the Web have profoundly influenced the dissemination of financial analysis and corporate reports. Corporate competitive advantage relies to a great extent on how effectively such visual information is presented. From the consumer perspective, the Web is primarily a visual phenomenon. The navigational aesthetics of the Web depend upon clear pages that involve viewers, blending coherence and interest in an easily navigable site; consumers "prefer environments in which they can make sense of what they perceive and in which they can learn more" (Kaplan and Kaplan 1982: 194). However, the rapid expansion of the net, combined with a still emerging understanding of how to design sites, has made Web navigation often difficult, messy, and frustrating. One commentator contends that Web designing "comes down to a simple problem: how to make navigating the Web a more visual experience" (Wagstaff 2001: 25). I discuss several aspects of Web visuals in chapters 3, 5, and 8.

In today's economy, brands and brand management have become cornerstones of success in attracting and maintaining a profitable customer base. Brand management has grown to challenge traditional models of product management and industrial production. Brands often compete on brand image, driven by marketing strategy to differentiate brands via marketing communication and competitive advantage. Technical expertise and technological innovation remain important, of course, but the market demands more. Buyers – both industrial and consumer – expect products to work effortlessly, a consequence of over a hundred years of industrial engineering progress. But in what I call a hyperaffluent economy, more is needed. Products can no longer just function well – they must function with style. The dot.com turbulence of 2000 has reminded us that business plans that produce revenue are critical for success – but a business plan alone is not sufficient. Companies need brilliant execution, customer relationship management, and demonstrated product or service quality and an attractive brand image. The Internet has made integration of core management functions – research and development, product design, logistics, and customer service – not only possible, but also necessary for efficient management. Design, in particular, depends upon visual understanding. As management theorist Tom Peters, in his inimitable way, says:

> You can't be a leader in the next five years and not be totally into design. Design specs are the double helix DNA that sets the tone of the culture and establishes the operating ideas that embody the economy. They are your distinguishing characteristics, your brand's brand.
>
> (Peters 2001: 134)

Visual consumption of design – of products, Websites, advertising, tourist destinations, retail environments – is a critical component of contemporary visual culture.

The firm is largely responsible for communicating core benefits and competitive advantage to consumers via information technology dependent media. Marketing communication – which includes advertising, corporate communication, Websites, customer service information, product manuals, and packaging – is often critical for success in a competitive marketplace. How can complex technological products be efficiently and attractively communicated to potential customers? Complex, sophisticated, high-tech products are often difficult to explain and market visually. Furthermore, many consumers have little expertise or time to judge product quality, construction, or even function. How can invisible technologies such as broadband, wireless applications, or microprocessor speed, be visually represented? In the global marketplace, corporate communication requires cultural understanding as well. Many battles of the brands take place in the visual domain – knowledge of visual consumption processes is necessary for understanding and succeeding in today's market.

2 Visual representation and the market

Consumption is inherently visual, yet consumer researchers have seemed reluctant to embrace art history and visual studies as critical fields for study. This chapter is part of a larger call for inclusion of art historical issues within the marketing research canon. I present theoretical concepts about representation and introduce art as a key visual representational system. I then discuss identity as a critically important issue that connects consumption and representation, and conclude with a set of propositions that reflect a more image-based model of consumption, and its consequent effects on notions about competition. Three streams of thought are developed: (1) representation and semiotics as tools for understanding visual consumption, (2) the connections between art and advertising via a focus on the image, and (3) implications for consumer theory and competition derived from taking images seriously as a driving force of consumer behavior. These three streams are woven together to develop a model of visual consumption, informed by art historical, psychological, and cultural issues.

Marketing research often treats visual issues solely as an information-processing variable even though, as one consumer theorist points out, "[i]t is chiefly the visual aspect of the advertisement that conjoins the world and object between which a transfer of meaning is sought" (McCracken 1988: 79). Furthermore, advertising research generally focuses on the internal content of advertisements, by looking at the design of the ad, what it claims, and how it links the product to consumer benefits. These are substantial issues, but advertising also acts as a representational system that produces meaning outside the realm of the advertised product (e.g., Belk and Pollay 1985; Ritson and Elliot 1999; Stern and Schroeder 1994; Venkatesh *et al.* 1993). To more fully understand how images work it is necessary to link perceptual and cognitive processes to larger social and cultural issues via a semiotic approach to visual consumption.

The visual representational system of advertising

Marketing scholarship has turned to the concept of representation for insight into diverse market-related phenomena, including advertising imagery (Schroeder and Borgerson 1998), war propaganda posters (Hupfer 1997), research methods (Stern 1998), and photography (Schroeder 1998). As representation refers to meaning production through language systems (cf. Stern 1998), how that language is used is central to creating that meaning. Using representation as an analytic tool, recent studies have emphasized how cultural practices – such as laws, rituals, norms, art, and advertising – contribute to meaning production within marketing (e.g., Hirschman 1986; Messaris 1997; Pearce 1999; Schroeder and Zwick 1999; Scott 1994a). Conventional views of representation hold that things, whether object, person, or consumer, exist in the material and natural world, and that their material characteristics define them in perfectly clear terms; representation, according to this view, is of secondary importance in meaning making.

Meaning produced or constructed by social and cultural forces would suggest that representation is of primary importance, however. In this view, representation enters into the very constitution of things, since an object's or idea's meaning is shaped by the very process of representing it by way of language or images. For example, representations of "islanders," stoked by tourist marketing brochures, colonial literature, and advertising imagery, help construct an islander identity that may bear little resemblance to actual people who live and work on tropical islands (Borgerson and Schroeder 1997). Research using this approach has been characterized as falling into two categories, semiotic and discursive (Hall 1997). Semiotic research, or the *poetics* of representation, is concerned with how representation produces meaning. Discursive research, or the *politics* of representation, stresses effects or consequences and connects representation to power and culture (du Gay 1997). Both types of research – at times overlapping, at times discrete – are necessary for a full examination of representation as meaning producer. For my purposes these two approaches correspond roughly to the interest in understanding how marketing creates things like brand images, customer satisfaction, product identity on one hand, and more macro issues like the role of marketing in society, ethics, and consequences of consumption.

Often, advertising research focuses on the internal content of advertisements – what the ad claims, how it links the product to consumer benefits, or the design of the ad. These are important considerations. However, advertising also acts as a representational system that produces meaning outside the realm of the advertised product or service. As McCracken observed:

> Advertising is a kind of conduit through which meaning is constantly being poured in its movement from the culturally constituted world to consumer goods. Within advertising, old and new goods are constantly giving up old meanings and taking on new ones. As active participants in this process, we are kept informed of the present state and stock of cultural meaning that exist in consumer goods. To this extent, advertising serves us as a lexicon of current cultural meanings.
>
> (McCracken 1988: 79)

This meaning production contributes to advertising's status as representation (cf. Nava *et al.* 1996).

Advertising, a pervasive form of communication and representation, both reflects and creates social norms. As one critic believes:

> The ways in which individuals habitually perceive and conceive their lives and the social world, the alternatives they see as open to them, and the standards they use to judge themselves and others are shaped by advertising, perhaps without their ever being consciously aware of it.
>
> (Lippke 1995: 108)

This *seeing* of "lives and the social world" is intensified and magnified by the information technologies of photography – which include still photography, video, film, and digital imaging – and representation today depends on photographic imagery to accomplish its many tasks (e.g., Solomon-Godeau 1991). Sociologists Goldman and Papson point out the close interconnected relationship between advertising and photography:

> [t]he power of advertising lies in its ability to photographically frame and redefine our meaning and our experiences and then turn them into meanings that are consonant with corporate interests. This power to recontextualize and reframe photographic images has put advertising at the center of contemporary redefinitions of individuality, freedom, and democracy in relation to corporate symbols.
>
> (Goldman and Papson 1996: 216)

In addition, the information technology of photography is central to understanding how advertising produces meaning within a circuit of production and consumption.

Photographic representations of the advertising process ripple through the culture, circulating information about the social world, even the world itself has taken on "a photographic face," according to Cadava (1999). What emerges as a significant rippling effect is how these cultural translations become key concerns of visual consumption. Although photography – encompassing still, video, film, and digital photography – is arguably the most pervasive form of communication in the world, most of us have had little formal training in the historical background of photography, the processes of photographic production, or the function of pictorial conventions. Advertising, like photography, seems to present a world that just is, even though photographic images are cropped, selected, edited, and circulated for consumption. A fully developed art-centered research program will include issues of film theory and criticism, graphic design, prints, and artistic production, to name a few. I will discuss photography in greater detail in chapters 3 and 4.

Advertising is linked to the good life. Ads once focused on products, providing information about how to incorporate new items into one's lifestyle:

> Advertising addressed both production and consumption domains: while creating demand to solve the problem of overproduction, advertising would simultaneously persuade workers that the satisfactions not available in the workplace were available in consumption.
>
> (Leiss *et al.* 1990: 31)

Advertising today concentrates on the social and psychological meaning of consumption. Older ads used text to guide viewers' interpretation of the visual image. Advertising now provides its own codes, as well as drawing upon cultural referent systems. "Ruled by its overriding imperative to communicate quickly, advertising first raids the ceremonial practice in our daily existence for its material, and then returns them to us in exaggerated forms, accentuating many of their least attractive features" (Leiss *et al.* 1990: 218). All ads:

- create positive associations for the product, service, or organization,
- are as carefully constructed as art,
- are aimed at a specific "target audience,"
- must dwell in the future,
- propose that their product or service is part of the good life,
- influence, construct, and reflect consumer identity.

Semiotics

Semiotics – the science of signs – provides a framework for understanding both the construction and decoding of meaning within advertisements and the overall process of commodification that characterizes the market (cf. Goldman and Papson 1996). Semiotic analysis centers around the sign, made up of a signifier – the sign's perceptual component – and the signified – the concept to which the signifier "points." David Mick suggests succinctly that "semiotics analyzes the structures of meaning-producing events, both verbal and nonverbal" (1986: 197). Semiotics need not be relegated to deconstructing meaning, however, for semiotics also describes the process of constructing meaning. Goldman and Papson argue that semiotics provides interpretive conventions for advertising via the logic of the commodity form, which consists of three elements: abstraction, equivalence exchange, and reification. Abstraction refers to the process of removing an action or relationship from its context. Equivalence exchange is the process of making something universally exchangeable – money, for example, is perhaps the ultimate exchange agent. Reification centers around imparting human attributes onto objects. I will use bananas – a major symbolic stumbling block between US and European trade laws – to illustrate the intertwined processes of semiotics and commodification.

Bananas were abstracted via colonization and industrial agriculture techniques that transformed a locally occurring food source into an international commodity that fueled much colonization of the Western Hemisphere. Once bananas became commercially cultivated and distributed, they entered the arena of commodities – a realm where prices linked to agricultural products are bought and sold via a thriving, complex futures market. Bananas were originally marketed as an exotic and novel fruit that signified tropical life. Banana advertisements also abstract the fruit from its neocolonial production arrangements, promote an exchangeable sign value of fun and authenticity, and reify the banana through characters such as the animated "Chiquita banana" that sings and dances. Furthermore, companies like Banana Republic – which originally sold adventure clothes, but now focuses on dressy casual clothing lines – incorporate the banana's symbolic lifestyle value and colonial signifier. Of course, customers may relate more to the plantation master than the native workers. The banana remains a potent signifier of economic relationships between colonizer and colonized, modern and primitive, and the US and Europe. Thus semiotics provides a theoretical perspective to understand two powerful historical forces that underlie the contemporary consumer culture, the rise of mass produced commodities and advertising's emergence as the engine of the economy (see Slater 1997).

Aesthetic appropriation

Through what has been called "the logic of appropriation," advertising turns culture into consumer signifiers by drawing on symbolic referent systems (Goldman and Papson 1996). First, advertising imagery colonizes and appropriates existing referent systems from literature, art, science, or other cultural discourses. For example, Nike, of course, existed first as a Greek god. In Scandinavian countries, the Norse myths are routinely drawn from to provide vivid corporate imagery. Telia, the huge, recently privatized Swedish telecommunications company, took its name from the ancient Icelandic word *telia*, to narrate or reveal, as used in the mythical sagas that are part of every Swedish child's reading. Second, advertising creates its own referent systems. This contention is controversial – many scholars believe that advertising can only reflect culture, not create values and beliefs. It is not my desire to resolve the reflection or creation of values debate here, I will only point to the long-running DeBeers diamond campaign that first established diamonds as the standard engagement ring stone, and then created a cultural belief that an appropriate amount to spend on such a gift is "two months' salary."

Clearly, advertising is capable of producing beliefs and creating cultural values, partially due to the source effect – we often remember "facts" but not where we learned them. Further, ads are *intertextual* or self-referential – they refer to other ads, brand names, and advertising itself, in a "continuous process of taking meanings from one context and placing them into the advertising framework where they become associated with another meaning system" (Goldman and Papson 1996: 15–16). An example is a recent Pepsi television spot that refers to Coke's famous "Mean Joe Green" ad in which the imposing American football star Green gives his sweat-stained jersey to an awestruck young fan who offered him a drink of Coke. In the more recent Pepsi ad, the scenario has shifted to soccer, the fan asked for a player's jersey, only to use it to clean off the can and hand it back. Understanding this ad doesn't rely on an awareness of the older ad, rather it deepens the connections and complicates the meaning. Third, advertising taps referent systems to generate image value, turning signs into a kind of myth designed to sell lifestyles (Goldman and Papson 1996). Advertising often positions products as authentic, or the path to individuality, selling badge-like images to subcultures, consumer target markets, or even offering products to resist consumer values.

Identity and consumption

Ads depict our consumer society as a fountain of personal freedom and satisfaction, where citizen and consumer are almost interchangeable expressions of identity. Through appropriation, ads turn controversy, hardship, and oppression into consumable spectacles. For example, ads regularly use images of inner-city life – the "hood" – as a sign of coolness or authentic toughness. Often ads use counter-positioning – suggesting what a product or brand is *not* as a key to understanding its sign value. These themes will be explored in chapter 7's examination of the CK One campaign.

Ads hail the viewer by promoting a personal connection between viewer and sign. This *signwork* is a key to understanding the visual landscape of contemporary society (Goldman 1992). As consumers, we cannot connect with every ad – or even most ads. Only a few brands and products puncture our awareness and match our lifestyle goals, psychic longings, or bank account. Thus, most of us are not deeply affected by most advertising we see. Furthermore, ads provide reasons not to buy products more often than not – we create our own images by what we don't consume as well as what we do consume.

Consumption "is crucially about the negotiation of status and identity – the practice and communication of social position" (Slater 1997: 30). What is the relationship between our things and our identity? Russell Belk has written extensively on this question, pursuing answers of consumer behavior and existence (1988, 1990, 1995). He presents several lines of evidence of the rich connections between possessions and identity.

1 *Consumption and self-perceptions.* Belk finds that people often incorporate their possessions into their version of the self-concept. Our body, and its internal processes, ideas, experiences, and those persons, places, and things that we feel some control over, or attachment to, all are examples of possessions that people consider part of themselves. This brings up important philosophical questions relating to the mind/body distinction. For example, we usually say "I have a tan" instead of "I have a tanned body." But we also say "I am tired" rather than "I have a tired body."
2 *Loss of possessions.* Typically, when someone loses their possessions in a fire or other disaster, they report that they miss their photographs the most. They often feel as if they lost a part of their self – their home, their possessions. Institutions often enforce this diminishing of self, such as the military issuing uniform haircuts, dress, and titles.
3 *Investing objects with identity.* We often make things our own through ritual, alteration, or customization. People report investing psychic energy into their favorite possessions, especially ones that require time and effort to maintain. In many cultures, the dead are buried with their possessions or a significant possession. Recent auctions of celebrity estates show how much of a person is thought to be invested in their objects – from Andy Warhol's cookie jar collection to Jacqueline Kennedy Onassis's fake pearls.
4 *Possessions and personal history.* I have a watch that I inherited from my Grandfather Schroeder that reminds me of him each time I wear it. Our sense of the past – our memories, our heirlooms, our scrapbooks – are critical to our identity. Objects are a useful way to "store" meaning – a souvenir reminds us of a trip, a photograph represents a important accomplishment, a dog-eared paperback signifies an important book. Our collections reflect the identities we are constructing. We display things that are pleasing or valuable, and those that give us a connection to the past in a way that is similar to museum display of a shared culture. Much is left out, edited, and hidden from view. We rarely find photographs of ourselves in our bad moments, unsure, unhappy, or worse.
5 *Collections.* As the spectacular success of the online auction house eBay demonstrates, collecting is popular and often profitable. EBay started out as a giant flea market, connecting individuals with stuff they wanted to sell to others who might be interested in acquiring treasures. Our collections, which often require vast amounts of time, money, and energy, often reflect totems, or favored animals, favorite activities such as music or shell collecting, or intellectual pursuits. What we collect and how we organize our collections are closely linked to our identity (Belk 1988, 1995).
6 *Money.* Money, the last taboo, plays a complex and powerful role in the self-concept. In this society, to have more is better, to be wealthy

seems to be an end goal, and many people experience money as the ultimate identity marker. Money is exceedingly exchangeable, yet it is also reified and worshipped for its own sake. Further discussions about money are found in chapter 6.

7 *Gift-giving*. What we give, how it is received, how much it cost all are crucial variables in our relationship with gift-giving. Once again, our consumption choices reflect our values and goals. The gift-giving concept has expanded in recent years to include so-called "self-gifts" – those items we buy ourselves for reward, retail therapy, or just because "we deserve it." Gift-giving is a useful way to problematize competition, for what can serve as a gift is usually competing with a wider variety of possible products than a competitive industry model. For example, traditional gifts to bring to a party include wine, flowers, or candy – fairly disparate product categories that end up competing for the gift-giver's money. Framing consumption within a gift-giving approach makes clear that products serve symbolic purposes, and that image competition is much wider than functional competition, based on industry classification. In other words, wine-makers can be said to be competing with flower-growers in terms of the symbolic meaning the consumer seeks.

Identity, expertise, and quality

Think of your possessions – clothes, watch, pen, shoes, eyeglasses, briefcase – all have been nationally advertised. Most things we buy are heavily advertised: whether we own them or not is a function of the effectiveness of ad campaigns for competing products, and more importantly, competing uses for our time and money. Most items manufactured today are made in such a way that "performance" or "wear" is not an issue. We no longer produce what we consume: we sell our labor for wages and buy goods produced by others. Thus, we are in need of information about goods and services and rely on trust and implicit contracts to live within a consumer society. For example, when I buy a shirt, I am unable, by looking or feeling, to determine whether it will last or how well it is made. Furthermore, in this hyperaffluent society, that is not much of a consideration for me – I own at least twenty-five dress shirts alone, and if one wears out, I can easily wear another.

Consumers have no special expertise about most products that they buy. The vast array of goods that we consume precludes knowing much about their production, construction, or quality – without experiencing them for ourselves. We no longer know much about quality, as measured by longevity of products – quality is often in the mind of the consumer. For example, I have little ability to assess a computer, a car, or a pair of shoes as to their construction (Sirgy and Su 2000). What do we do instead? Well it is important to realize that performance in a hyperaffluent economy refers to how well an item fits into one's lifestyle, or image. Mostly, we consumers wear 20 percent of our clothing 80 percent of the time. Whether or not something is worn a lot is a function of how well it fits in to our identity or image – whether it is psychologically as well as physically comfortable. Thus, performance can refer to how well the item performs a preferred self-image. Most products are marketed to specific groups of consumers, identified through marketing research, and linked to lifestyle indicators – Giorgio Armani, a sophisticated Italian designer, markets his clothing to a different type of person than Levi's Dockers does.

We become aware that different roles and traits are associated with different constellations or groups of products and consumer activities that help define roles. Part of our identity is an awareness of ourselves as we imagine others see us – an image that includes our physical appearance, clothing styles, jewelry, tattoos, car, home decoration, and so forth. Even if we wished others would not judge us by the way we look, we realize that they do, as part of the perceptual processing of our world. Thus, our intentions are not always in line with other's perceptions. Further, even if we intend nothing, we claim to wear things because they are comfortable, other's make psychological judgments just the same. As theater director Robert Wilson says, you cannot help communicating, you cannot help symbolizing even with the way you stand, the way you walk, your posture. Psychologically speaking, all behavior is up for scrutiny.

To sum up, identity guides much of our consumption patterns, and the interaction of consumption and identity in a society such as ours is strong. Our consumer choices reflect our values, both in a psychological sense and at a very practical level. What we spend time and money on becomes important to us. Identity is especially influenced by the representational practices of advertising, which re-emphasizes identity formation – what it means to be male and female, to be beautiful or handsome, to be desirable, to desire, and how to control your body (Schroeder and Borgerson 1998). These practices, in turn, were influenced by the history of art.

Art and consumption

Although the art historical background of advertising would seem to be a natural subject for marketing researchers, it remains poorly developed within marketing and consumer research. I contend that greater awareness of the connections between the traditions and conventions of visual culture and the production and consumption of images leads to enhanced ability to understand how advertising works as a representational system and signifying practice. However, this represents only a small fraction of the potential for work within a visual frame. The traditional separation of art and business, carefully cultivated and maintained by those whose interest it serves, has obscured the potential of studying the art market as *the* exemplar of consumer culture. Art represents another way of knowing, yet:

> However strange and forbidding to the social scientist, there is no choice but for a science of society to begin in art where feelings of society are objectified and discussed. We cannot churlishly isolate social science from the arts when both are bound by an interest in the forms of social life.
>
> (Sandelands 1998: 11)

For it is art that is based on images, value, and identity above all other sectors of the market. Art represents the highest goals of humans, and also the most crass commercialism and speculation. With the rise of the artist as the acknowledged producer of artwork, the art market serves as an extreme example of branding strategy.

Art-centered approaches offer a means of developing unique insights into the image's prominence within visual culture. Art historical techniques help articulate a grammar of visual representation that producers and consumers use to decode advertising's messages (see Scott 1994a). Regardless of intention, advertising, film, and television images often invoke art historical themes, settings, and references that contribute to their meaning – as an advertisement for a particular product, service, or organization – as well as a cultural artifact. As discussed here, meaning in visual communication is not wholly contained within the image itself. Specifically, advertising's success has depended on a way of seeing advertising imagery visually connected to the larger worlds of art museums, movies, and lived experience. Increased sensitivity to visual elements and their social, historical, and cultural contexts is critical to appreciating the power of images for visual consumption.

The world of marketing intersects with the art world in numerous ways. The separation of art and business – into high and low forms of communication and culture – has had a profound influence on how art is viewed by researchers, cultural critics, and consumers alike. An art-centered approach suggests re-framing this research tradition to acknowledge both the commercial mechanisms inherent in the art market and advertising's prominent place in visual culture. Art historians seldom discuss the cultural power of advertising imagery; marketing researchers rarely apply art criticism. This state of affairs can be largely explained by these respective scholars' training and interests. However, framing advertising within a long tradition of persuasive image making impels us to bring art historical methods to bear on images. Via this interdisciplinary enterprise, researchers gain access to an enormous body of accumulated knowledge, techniques, and perspectives to explore meaning construction via visual consumption in contemporary society.

By considering diverse forms of visual representation as information technology, we gain theoretical links between disparate cultural fields such as photography, the Internet, and art. Painting, and other forms of image creation, can be effectively considered information technologies that both directly and indirectly influence contemporary forms of communication. For example, Renaissance art clients usually made several stipulations when commissioning art (Baxandall 1987). First, the form of the work was specified – altarpiece, portrait, fresco, and so forth. Second, the subject matter – Baptism of Christ, Trinity, or secular scenes – was agreed on. Third, contracts were drawn that usually stated how much of the work was to be done in the hand of a particular artist, or if assistants could be used to complete the background, or paint secondary figures. Although the art market works differently today, information technology usage shares many of these stipulations. Advertisements, for example, are created in a similar way. Form relates to media channel selection. Subject matter, and what it conveys, is central to the advertising strategy. Ads are commissioned to ad agencies, certain ad directors, or more recently, artists or photographers.

Art – like marketing – is an important cultural institution that transmits and reflects values, meaning, and beliefs. In the words of an art historian, "social history and art history are continuous, each offering necessary insights into the other" (Baxandall 1972: 12). Studying art historical trends that shaped art and the society that produced it reveals a different perspective on consumer culture. By scrutinizing subtle changes in art, their eventual ramifications, and the rise of art as a commodity, a unique insight is gained into the history of market economies. There are many connections between art and consumption; for example, both can be considered aesthetic activities (see Csiksentmihalyi and Robinson 1990). I contend that by turning to art, and focusing attention on the use of images within the art system, we gain an appreciation of how images function within consumption processes.

Art history and criticism, traditionally outside the realm of consumer and marketing research, add a necessary component to understanding contemporary marketing practice, as well as useful methods for interpreting and analyzing the historical trends in representing, consuming, and celebrating cultural goods (cf. Hirschman 1986). Art historical tools provide a rich picture of the underlying mechanisms driving the evolution of consumer culture. In addition, art is a commodity, subject to market forces and consumer behavior processes (e.g., Jardine 1996; Jensen 1994; Schroeder 1997a, 1997b; Watson 1992; Witkowski 1996). By analyzing content, form, and the uses of art we gain insight into numerous components of consumer culture – consumer behavior, demand, price, and patronage, to name a few. Art, then, offers an excellent, underutilized vehicle for studying and understanding cultural forces in consumption; this study incorporates art historical variables and tools into the marketing research canon.

Art history is the humanities discipline that investigates art and its objects as cultural and aesthetic documents – reflecting and shaping the culture that both produces and preserves them. Closely linked to the related fields of aesthetics, art history, art theory, and archeology, art criticism requires an understanding of the styles and functions of art, the social and cultural contexts in which artists have worked, and the technical factors that affect artistic execution (e.g., Adams 1996; Stokstad 1995; Staniszewski 1995). Art criticism addresses issues including identification, classification, comparison, evaluation, and value (cf. Woodford 1983). Like literary criticism, work in art criticism is characterized by a myriad of schools employing a variety of approaches to the subject, context, meaning, and production of art (cf. Stern 1989).

Art history writing traditionally has been concerned with the form, content, and purpose of a work of art and with the artist's life (Carrier 1991). Today, art historians, as well as research in the closely related fields of visual studies, material culture, and aesthetics, usually take art and other artifacts as an analytical point of departure, but then branch into questions about the original audiences, owners, or users, and the society and culture that produced and received them (Fernie 1995; Prown 1982). Thus, scholarly emphasis falls less on the object itself than on the world in which it was created. Art and artifacts should not used just as passive illustrations of consumer culture, but should be actively engaged as evidence to investigate consumer culture (see Witkowski 1999).

Several art historians have discussed diffuse issues of consumer behavior. For example, Schama discusses many aspects central to consumer research – such as collecting, demand, and luxury goods – in his monumental study of Dutch art (Schama 1988). Others take a market-oriented approach to the art market, demonstrating that art is governed by market forces similar to manufactured goods (e.g., Watson 1992; Goldthwaite 1993; Jenson 1994). Historical scholarship investigating societal trends often invokes art history in discussing consumption or marketing issues (Jensen 1994; Schama 1988; Watson 1992). Thus art historians are studying the marketing of art, yet consumer researchers have largely failed to incorporate art to analyze consumer processes – a central feature of the culture that art depicts, packages, comments on, and is marketed within. A notable exception is Joy's work on the art market's influence in corporate strategy, which dubbed corporate sponsors of art "the Modern Medicis" (1993, 1998).

Marketing communications often depend on the language of painting that celebrates wealth and private property and is often nostalgic, referring back to a golden age. Specifically, advertising uses formal art conventions – pose, symbol, style – as well as techniques borrowed from painting, photography, and film (e.g., Johnston 1997). Direct connections to painting, such as the reproduction of the image itself, the framing of the ad, and "quoting" art historical sources give a certain presence to ads, linking them to fine taste, prestige, and affluence. Art belongs to the good life. Artistic references also suggest a cultural authority superior to crass material interests (Berger 1972). Thus, by referring to art, advertising can denote both wealth and spirituality, luxury, and transcendent cultural value.

Art developed visual conventions that were adapted by advertising. Today, the distinction between the high world of fine art and the low world of commercial image production, including advertising and graphic design, is difficult to trace. Artists engage with the world of advertising imagery, and marketing interacts with the art world via patronage, appropriation, commissions, and sponsorship (see Schroeder and Borgerson 2001). Advertising agencies, photography studios, and design firms are full of people with art history training (Bogart 1995; Lears 1994). Furthermore, the world of advertising represents a popular art form that is often represented in fine art museums (Schroeder 1997b). Conversely, art borrows imagery from the commercial world, including brands, products, logos, packages, and slogans (Belk 1989; Spiggle 1985; Schroeder 1992).

Advertising depends on the language of painting that celebrates wealth and private property and is often nostalgic, referring back to a golden age (Berger 1972). Specifically, advertising uses art conventions of form – genre, poses, symbols – as well as techniques borrowed from painting and photography. Advertising often invokes the world of art. For example, Leonardo Da Vinci's *Mona Lisa* appears often in ads as an icon of portraiture, fine art, value, and as a vehicle for humor. Ads often call products masterpieces, or a work of art, and so forth. Direct connections to painting, such as the image itself, the ad frame, and quoting art historical sources give a certain presence to ads, linking them to taste, prestige, and affluence. Manet's *Olympia,* for example, has been parodied hundreds of times, and often serves as a theme for advertisements (see Schroeder 2001).

In opening up this dialog between art and marketing, I hope to add to the enterprise of research that takes images seriously, both for their power to persuade, and for their pervasive role in visual culture (see O'Donohoe 1997; and Stern 1996). My framework views advertising as a powerful representational system that produces knowledge through discursive practices. I draw on diverse fields of knowledge, spanning the traditional boundaries between them, opening up a space to encounter the contemporary visual landscape, filled with manufactured images.

Decoding images

Visual images are not mere substitutes for verbal language. Images – whether paintings, drawings, photographs, or Web graphics – do not necessarily speak for themselves, rather they make visible a realm of possibilities and potential meanings, many of which are difficult to articulate (Leppert 1997). Thus, interpretation is not a matter of "getting it right" – rather, it is an exercise in coaxing culturally and historically situated meanings from images.

Decoding images – advertisements, photographs, paintings, films – begins with a personal understanding of symbols, conventions, and stereotypes. First, it requires drawing on one's common knowledge, then connecting associations with a broader set of concerns. For example, most of us have some idea, however hazy, about vampires. Vampires are superhuman – powerful undead beings that prey on humans for sustenance. Vampires have fangs, draw human blood, shun daylight, garlic, and crosses, and don't reflect in mirrors. How does one obtain this knowledge? Largely without intention, we gain insight about signs through media exposure and interpersonal interaction. The vampire is a type that shows up in films, cartoons, advertisements, and popular novels from Bram Stoker's *Dracula* to Anne Rice's *Interview with a Vampire*. Thus without studying vampires, most of us have some understanding of the cultural referents or iconography – symbols and meanings – surrounding vampires and their victims.

We could look at a recent ad campaign for Bacardi rum that shows people in various situations enjoying the night, such as "banker by day, Bacardi by night." Several of the ads draw on vampire images, showing people with fangs, dressed in black. We rely on notions about what vampires are and what vampires do to begin to make sense of the ad. For example, there might be a connection between current vampire-related movies such as *Blade*, *Dracula*, and so forth, and AIDS – another bodily "condition" that relates to blood, infection, and often, death. If we do a little reading about vampires, we might learn more about their symbolic relationship to Christianity, sexuality, and diseases like the plague – vampires constitute a cultural code.

We can then apply this knowledge to sorting out the messages in the Bacardi campaign. Some people may know more about vampires and thus bring more to reading the ad than others. The symbols need not seem to be a hidden language or knowledge system, accessible only to the semiotically literate. Images, particularly advertising images, need to make clear associations in order to get their message across. Bacardi, in this instance, seems to desire a connection between their product and the power, danger, and mystery of vampires, thus drawing on cultural conventions of superhuman beings to promote their rum. Vampires, then, are a potent semiotic figure, appropriated, abstracted and applied to other commercial contexts based on a largely hidden referent cultural system of superstitious beliefs about otherworldly creatures.

In Bacardi's ad campaign, like many others, little or no product information is given, nor is any coherent functional or utilitarian product claims made. *Amelia*, a Swedish women's magazine, recently unveiled a campaign that featured a woman with crudely drawn fangs that appear graffiti-like over her teeth, as if someone had doodled on the ad, turning her into a cartoon-like vampire. "Now with more grrrrrr," read the ad, in a typically opaque, difficult to assess claim. Yet much marketing and advertising research and theory clings to the notion that advertising provides product information, and that product claims are central to understanding efficacy or ethical marketing concerns.

Approaching visual representation within consumer research via the interpretive stances presented offers researchers a grounded method that is able to account for political and ethical issues. As art historian Keith Moxey argues:

> semiotics makes us aware that the cultural values with which we make sense of the world are a tissue of conventions that have been handed down from generation to generation by the members of the culture of which we are a part. It reminds us that there is nothing "natural" about our values; they are social constructs that not only vary enormously in the course of time but differ radically from culture to culture.
>
> (1994: 61)

The visual world often seems as if it needs no interpretation, and the logic of many visual forms act against critical reflection and thought. Furthermore, there is a related tendency to regard intensive intellectual effort antithetical to aesthetic or sensory experience (hooks 1994).

Images and the market

Market segmentation produces a world where everything depends on differentiation of products, services, and ideas. Advertising is a key strategic method of target marketing and market segmentation. Marketing campaigns, however, are not just managerial – they are ideological as well. Goldman and Papson outline several sociological features of advertising, conceived as a social institution as well as a managerial tool. Advertising creates discourses that socially and culturally construct a world. They disguise and suppress inequalities, irrationalities, and contradictions. Ads promote a normative vision of our world and our relationships – including our relationships with things. Ads reflect the logic of ownership and the power of capital (Goldman and Papson 1996).

Advertising is often conceptually distanced from the firm, or the theory of the firm – as if advertising campaigns are created independently, away from corporate control. As part of the distancing phenomenon, advertising is often considered to be an art – something that "creatives" invent, whimsical ways of promoting products. Economic theory, particularly, tends to downplay advertising, or defines it in ways that clearly relegate it to information provision or its contribution to irrationality within the marketplace.

Propositions about image-based consumer behavior

My interest in consumption and representation requires a level of analysis that is much broader than a strictly industry-based model. It tries to take into account three interrelated assumptions. First, economics and rational man continue to exert epistemic dominance over consumer research, that is, economic models and thinking completely color how we think about consumers, and economic presuppositions about information, choice, and preferences have led to a unrealistic picture of how consumers consume. Second, this economic influence on consumer theory leads to a production bias – emphasizing production over consumption – and generates epistemological models of competition that are at odds with how products "compete" in the minds of consumers. Products compete within the realm of the image – and advertising has encouraged consumers to think so. Yet economic models rarely take advertising seriously from a consumer point of view. Third, what consumption means to consumers is not well served by these models. Consumer ontology – how consumption relates to life and identity – often does not map on to standard economic or industry-based product classifications.

Concerning the intellectual dominance of economics

Forty years of consumer research has shown that consumers are not the rational "men" of classical economics, yet economic thought exerts a profound and stifling effect on how the consumer is conceived. For example, consumer research is dominated by decision making models that assume consumers make choices informed by information, preferences, and evaluation. Specifically, much consumer research asks research participants to make choices between products within categories, such as cameras, yogurt, or computers. I suggest, however, that most consumers do not allocate money to specific categories, such as "shoes" or "entertainment." These categories are in the mind of the consumer, so for example, a pair of Nike tennis shoes may represent a symbolic affiliative need – which may also be met by watching Seinfield, or other popular television programs, or perhaps organizing a bowling league or singing in a choir.

I believe it is more useful to think of consumption as the allocation of time to activities – activities in which the consumer's lifestyle and identity is constructed, largely via images. This type of thinking about consumption is poorly captured by research in brand switching, which is mostly concerned with changing brands within product categories – from Marlboro to Camel cigarettes, for example. Often consumers make choices between vastly different product categories, or between purchase and postponement – for example, not buying a new car until your present car breaks down, or not buying a new computer due to fears of it becoming quickly obsolete. Furthermore, many consumer choices compete not with similar items, but with opting out of a decision altogether. Thus, a major competitor for live music is staying at home.

Concerning epistemology of competition

Products compete in social-psychological terms, not strictly economic terms. In a hyperaffluent society such as ours, most people own multiple examples of basic items. For example, the same person might own several pairs of shoes, a couple of cameras, several televisions, and many shirts and pants. The idea that we set out to buy one item to satisfy physical needs is of course quaint – but this paradigm remains influential in consumer and marketing research. However, in real life, consumption choices compete along a wide variety of attributes, benefits, and images. For example, a sportscar purchase, fueled by fantasies of glamour, displaced sexuality, and vanity, may be "competing" in the consumer's mind with cosmetic surgery, a trip to the Bahamas or Cape Cod, or a sailboat. Gift-giving also provides insight into consumer-based competition. For example, I regularly bring gifts back to the US. I want something that represents Sweden – something "Swedish." This might be hand-blown glass, gravlax, wooden crafts, vodka, or any number of things that somehow communicate the image of Sweden. The category that I use in this instance has little to do with standard industrial classification systems. If we take seriously the theory of consumer behavior that has been developed in the last forty years, we will realize that competition needs to be problematized, and understood within the representational system of images.

Concerning ontology of consumption

Ontology is the study of being. Being is active, verbal, not simply in the sense of being a speaking out, or voicing of a subjectivity, but related to activity in general – including, of course, consumer activity (cf. Miller 1994). Moreover, consumption categories are psychological. That is, they are often idiosyncratic, based on psychological needs, and not necessarily in line with the standard industrial product classification system. We can demonstrate this via a set theory approach. If we imagine members of the set "soft-drink" we may find Coke, Pepsi, 7–Up, etc. What we are not accustomed to thinking about is that there are many other sets, some with overlapping membership, such as "bottled beverages," and some that are organized on different psychological properties, such as "sociable behaviors" in which consuming heavily advertised soft drinks is a member, or "exercise rewards" in which some drinks may be members along with "buying self a gift" or "renting new video." Thus, the meaning of consumption – its relationship to ontology – becomes critical for understanding consumers (cf. Holt 1995a).

In the spring of 2000, I began to plan for the upcoming summer. I had wanted to study Swedish intensively, so I looked into language programs in Sweden. I was also invited to spend July in Southern France. Another option was to stay in Stockholm and enjoy the short, spectacular Swedish summer. After some information gathering, reflection, and a busy spring, the choice came down to either a Swedish course in Uppsala or renting a house in Southern France – and France carried the day. When I tell people this story, they usually laugh, and remark that it didn't sound like a difficult decision – studying language or lounging in Southern France. However, in my experience of the decision making process, these two choices were both compelling – for different reasons, and both seemed like worthy options at the time. I think these types of choices are much more reflective of how we really make consumer choices – there are few occasions when I am faced with a choice among similar options, and these are usually trivial.

Consuming the image

Consumption characterizes modern life. We live within the logic of the market. Contemporary artist Barbara Kruger captures the essence of this worldview with her famous work "*I Shop, Therefore I Am.*" Fashion consciousness pervades all consumption – clothes, cosmetics, music, film, cars, appliances, furniture, architecture, travel, food, and every other representable aspect of consumption that can be rendered as an image-producing act; "the most effective advertising communication is therefore one that achieves a matched layering of basic self-image, manufactured and mediated image, and product image ..." (Barry 1997: 256).

This shift from product to image profoundly affects product development and marketing communications. Images – or brand identities – are the driving force of the market. When Ford Motor Company decided to compete with Chevrolet's huge, hot-selling Suburban sport utility vehicle, what was important was the *image* of the vehicle. Ford developed the even bigger Lincoln Navigator, which was successful as the biggest of the big. When films are "pitched" it is the image of the film that gains or loses approval. Products no longer merely reflect images, then, the image is the starting point for market communications. An example from the media world illustrates this important principle.

Wallpaper magazine caters to "global nomads." According to *Wallpaper*, global nomads are interested in interior design, entertainment, and travel – "the stuff that surrounds you." Of course, not just any stuff will do – the glossy, thick magazine promotes an affluent contemporary jetset consumer lifestyle that requires ample disposable income for the latest and most stylish stuff. Global nomads seem similar to cosmopolitans, whose "raison d'être is mobility and the pursuit of excitement and novelty" (Thompson and Tambyah 1999: 237), but the term originated with the magazine. *Wallpaper*, bought by Time-Life after its spectacular success in the mid 1990s, is quite articulate about their target market: global nomads – a term coined by the magazine to represent cosmopolitan travelers. Articles on airport design include hints on finding hidden lounges at international hubs, features about hot ski resorts note the trendiest places to stay, food blurbs mention obscure staff favorites from around the world. *Wallpaper*'s success is marked by their advertisers: Guess Jeans, Prada, Chanel, Clinique, Swatch, Hugo Boss, Christian Dior, Cartier all grace the first twenty pages of a recent issue. Like many magazines before it, *Wallpaper* supplies a guide for living; in this case, living life as a global nomad – they are just more self-conscious about constructing their market segment than most other publications. The image of a global nomad came first, then *Wallpaper* set about attracting advertisers, and convincing them that global nomads exist, they are an attractive market segment, and that *Wallpaper* uniquely represents the segment. In this way, *Wallpaper* delivers the global nomad segment to advertisers. Media, then, exist largely to gather a group of consumers for advertising interests.

The market is adept at making it seem as if consumer desires are independently determined, that each consumer has tastes, desires, and wants that are uniquely satisfied by a vast array of consumer choices. The articulation of the marketing concept gave rise to a new way of selling goods; consumer research supported the notion that consumers make decisions (e.g., Schroeder 2000). The market began to address consumers individually, paving the way for future developments in customer relationship management and one-to-one marketing. The consuming subject was born; "generation and maintenance of selfhood become a lifetime task for individuals – an endless series or exercises in self-improvement, personal development, self-expression, mental and physical tone, 'selling oneself,' cultivating approval, 'winning friends and influencing people'" (Leiss *et al.* 1990: 58). The current market revolves around the image, consumers consume visions of a good life, fueled by consumer lifestyle images.

3 Through the lens

Reflections on image culture

The lens is a defining technology of the current era. Images from microscopes, cameras, telescopes, video and film cameras make up what A. D. Coleman calls lens culture (Coleman 1998). Lenses predated photography, but continue to mold vision in ways that are often unnoticed and unacknowledged: "as an instrument of visual communication, the lens is unique in that, for all practical purposes, it is literally as well as metaphorically invisible" (Coleman 1998: 114). Lenses are not seen, but seen through. Technological lens development was fueled by the assumption that the visual domain was potentially unlimited – that with proper lenses, humans can make everything visible. Given the lens's clear influence on visual communication, it is important that "we come to understand the extent to which lenses shape, filter, and otherwise alter the data that passes through them – the extreme degree to which the lens itself *informs* our information" (Coleman 1998: 129). The most ubiquitous lens is found on cameras – from cheap disposable models to exorbitant, sophisticated digital motion picture imaging systems.

In this chapter, I begin a theoretical discussion of photography with a look at images – what they mean, how they communicate, and how people decode and understand them. The concept of the image is found in many marketing and consumer research streams – brand images, corporate images, product images, and image management, for example. Few focus on how people make psychological sense of images, rarer still is the study that concentrates on photography as the information technology that furnishes the bulk of consumer imagery. Photography is the greatest image producer the world has seen; an information technology that unhinged objects from place, revolutionized identity, and continues to shape the world we live in in spectacular – yet often misunderstood and unreflected upon – ways.

Photographic perspectives on the information age

Information Technology (IT) or information and communication technology (ICT) usually refers to complex, sophisticated systems such as mass media, the Internet, telecommunications, or digital satellite transmission arrays. These constitute the basic building blocks of the "information society" – where information is a key corporate competitive advantage as well as a fundamental cultural force. Information technologies exist within cultural, political, and economic arenas: they have a history (Dobers and Strannegård 2001). Technology subsumes previous forms. Photography borrowed from the pre-existing camera obscura; film depended upon still photography; television used radio broadcast techniques; and the Internet developed from earlier forms of audio visual technologies including photography, television, and computers. Moreover, photography remains a key component of many information technologies – digital incorporation of scanned photographic images helped transform the Internet into what it is today. Photography, in turn, was heavily influenced by the older traditions of painting in its commercial and artistic production, reception, and recognition (e.g., Savedoff 2000).

Photographs are ubiquitous in contemporary life. They often appear as if they just *are*, merely visual records of what has happened, how people appear, or where events took place. This quality is one of the most complicated and powerful properties of photography; it often acts like a transparent window on society. Upon reflection, however:

> Photographs do not "show how things look," since there is no one way that anything looks. *What a photograph shows us is how a particular thing could be seen, or could be made to look* – at a specific moment, in a specific context, by a specific photographer employing specific tools.
>
> (Coleman 1998: 57, emphasis in original)

In other words, photographs are subjective, transient images made by a particular person with special equipment at a specific moment in time. Moreover, "all photographs are representations, in that they tell us as much about the photographer, the technology used to produce the image, and their intended uses as they tell us about the events or things they depicted" (McCauley 1997: 63). Photographs and photography have exerted a profound, foundational influence of conceptions of identity and physical appearance, appearance and reality, and vision and evidence. It is now impossible to disentangle photography from identity; photography shapes how we think of ourselves, how we age photographs represent who we are.

Photographs are used so often and so fluidly for scientific, judicial, and civil evidence that it is difficult to keep in mind that photographs are mechanically produced images that exist within shifting planes of meaning and significance. The spectacular trial of the Los Angeles police officers accused of beating Rodney King offers compelling evidence of photography's powerful, contradictory roles in contemporary life. Clearly, the famous videotaped encounter between King and the police meant radically different things to various audiences. The video *seemed* to show King being brutally beaten by several Los Angeles policemen. In the courtroom, however, the photographic "record" transformed into defense exhibit number one. The policemen's defense attorneys showed it over and over, narrating an alternate interpretation reasonable enough to help sway the Simi Valley jury, who voted to acquit. The images of King on the ground, struck repeatedly, linger on in the consciousness of American life. Meaning took on quite significant differences in and outside of court, and its effects reverberated throughout the US.

Though usually less spectacular and controversial than the King incident, images play similar roles everyday in courtrooms, on television, and in the worlds of fashion and celebrity. We rely on images for so much of our information about the world that they now seem natural, a convenient, accurate way to present the world for consumption. Photographic technology has "advanced" enough that it often isn't included in discussions of information technology, the Internet, or marketing strategy. Yet photography remains the key imaging technology, and it forms the basis for the visual displays of most Webpages. Corporate strategy is in the process of being digitized and converted into photographic-based information on the Web – Website design is creating a powerful demand for imaging customer relations, product assortment, hiring practices, and company mission, for example. Furthermore, many marketing campaigns rely on one still photographic image to carry a strategic communication campaign. Photography, too, remains a singular technology of self-representation – for consumers, photography remains closely tied to memory, family, and identity.

Photography, representation, and consumption

Visual consumption encompasses critical ways that people represent themselves. What we see, what we notice, what we photograph are all important consumer processes. Consuming representation refers to engaging with, reading, and responding to signs, symbols, and images (Schroeder 1998, 2000, 2001). In this discussion, consuming representation provides a way of discussing the complex interactions between consuming and producing images. Consuming representation, then, is a perceptual process of making sense and integration.

Photography emerged in the last century as the most powerful and omnipresent technology of representation. In one sense, of course, one might say that the consumer *produces* representation through photography. This apparent paradox – production through consumption – characterizes consumer culture. The framework of visual consumption is an attempt to capture the complex interactions between consuming and producing representations in a visual culture, dominated by marketing images. In chapters 6 and 7, I argue that advertising is the dominant image making global communication force, both for its ubiquity and its support and influence of the vast majority of mass media.

Making sense of images

Viewers make sense of visual images in a number of ways. Furthermore, interpretive work does not imply fixing a particular meaning over time, "since photographs, like any other text, are polysemic, any interpretation the viewer makes will not 'exhaust' the significance that might be attributed to the photograph" (Ball and Smith 1992: 18). Important among these are four processes that tie subject matter to symbolic meaning: resemblance, cause and effect, convention, and signification (Berger 1998). Resemblance refers to how visual representations often look like the objects they depict. Advertisements often use "typical" people in ads for their resemblance to targeted consumers. Cause and effect – or logic – underlies basic inferential processes. Via narrative processes, advertisements rely on cause and effect for many product claims. Art history has developed many visual conventions; certain colors are often associated with holiness, Catholic Saints each have specific items that signal their particular story, visual genres have specific meaning conventions. As mentioned in the previous chapter, slice of life advertisements, which purport to show everyday scenes, draw on conventions developed within genre painting of the Dutch Golden Age (Schroeder 1999). Signification is the process by which one thing signals another, such as a smile signifying pleasure, closed eyelids implying sexual ecstasy, or a classical column signifying stability, status, and high art. Images signify whether they are intended to or not – signification conjoins the image to the world.

Images, according to marketing researcher Gerald Zaltman, "are topographically organized neural representations that occur in the early sensory cortices" (1997: 424). This focus on the sensory basis of images is a bit reductive for my purposes, as it leaves out any connection to higher order cognitive processing, aesthetics, or socio-political dimensions; however, its mention of representation is noteworthy (see Freedberg 1989). Zaltman develops several useful premises about images, including the contentious contention that thought is image based, and the provocative proposal that most communication is nonverbal. His work has shown the importance of metaphor in marketing, and he has turned to photography to help consumers elicit hidden knowledge about their responses to images as well as their preferences (e.g., Coulter and Zaltman 1994; Zaltman and Coulter 1995). Although I think his neurologically based conception of the image detracts from his work, I share his enthusiasm for the power of images.

Poiesz and consumer images

In a review of the image concept, Theo Poiesz identified three approaches to images that he thought were useful for consumer and marketing research.

He described a wide variety of image concepts, which he classified based on what he called an elaboration continuum (Poiesz 1989). A high elaboration approach, such as that employed by Reynolds and Gutman (e.g., 1984), connects product images to consumer identity by probing into consumer choices, and making linkages between product attributes and consumer values. This technique, called laddering, assumes that elaborate meanings are available to consumers, and that they are able to accurately articulate them for researchers. For example, one subject associated drinking wine coolers, which made him less drowsy, with spending more time with his family after work. He found if he substituted wine coolers for beers, he drank less and fell asleep less often. Thus, he made an association between mundane product choice and a higher goal of family life. Critics of this approach point out that there are large social demand artifacts in this research – subjects often rationalize choices for themselves and for interviewers. Furthermore, consumers may be unwilling to divulge negative, socially undesirable, or psychosexual associations – psychoanalysis tells us that many associations are not cognitively available. Poiesz concludes that laddering and other high elaboration methods are more appropriate for products that consumers have thought a lot about. More recent approaches, such as Craig Thompson's existential-phenomenological work, share certain features of laddering research, but are based more in interpretive traditions of the humanities (e.g., Thompson 1996; Thompson and Haytko 1997; Thompson and Tambyah 1999).

Another approach equates images to attitudes, and plugs them into multi-attribute models of attitude formation and attitude change. In this way, consumer images may be high or low on the elaboration continuum, depending on the image/attitude's position in a broader attitudinal network. However, this approach attenuates the image concept, and largely curtails associative processes that are outside the research situation. Thus, attitude model-based research, although internally consistent, is less compelling to those interested in external, real-life conditions of image formation and associational properties of images.

The third approach Poiesz identified "focuses more exclusively upon images as general, holistic impressions or perceptions of the relative position of a brand (product/corporation/store) among its perceived competitors" (1989: 465). This relative position is based on dimensions used to classify and identify the object of interest, derived from research scales or theory, or generated by consumer subjects. Clearly, the focus on marketing images – brand names – circumscribes the image concept in ways that reduce its usefulness. He concludes that this low elaboration approach offers the most parsimonious and useful definition of images, and suggests that researchers avoid "elaboration stimulating research methods for studying behaviors that are characterized by little elaboration" (Poiesz 1989: 468). Unfortunately, this proscription also avoids many consumer behaviors that are interesting, meaningful, and managerially relevant within an image-based, attention economy. Ironically, the "low elaboration" approach seems to be most centrally located within managerially based research. However, its operationalization limits the image concept's usefulness to brand-specific attributes – semiotics apparently offers no insights into the image, and little mention is made of imaging technologies such as photography, film, and graphic arts.

Images are visual. Attitudes, although often visualized, are usually based in cognitive structures, and most often verbally articulated. Attitudes, of course, are linked to images, and like images are infused with emotion. Images, in turn, are not merely associated to brands, products, or corporations. Even within a managerially focused research program, to suggest that the relevance of images is limited in this way severely underestimates the power of images and drastically confines the image concept's conceptual contributions to consumer research. Furthermore, insights into images need not be bound to cognitive behavioral techniques that obscure the historical, cultural, and psychological centrality of the image to thought. In the next section, I introduce several alternative approaches that draw on more complex conceptualizations of the image, and frame the image within a richer intellectual heritage. Images are too important, too complex, and too interesting to be relegated to reductionist cognitive models of consumption focused on comparative analyses of brands. They require a multidisciplinary matrix to call forth meanings via interpretive and theoretical work – not to identify precisely what images mean, but rather to open up possibilities of meaning.

Arnheim and visual perception

The importance of the image places a premium on understanding how images function, what they do, how people respond to them, and why they are so important, psychologically, culturally, and historically. A good starting point is the work of Rudolf Arnheim, a psychologist who wrote extensively about visual information processing, including such classic works as *Film as Art, Visual Thinking*, and *Art and Visual Perception*. Arnheim's approach is uniquely suited to applied social scientists – he elegantly bridges the psychological and art historical realms. His research is based in perceptual properties from the gestalt school, combined with a deep understanding of and appreciation for the expressive, artistic realm. Arnheim provides a perceptual foundation for understanding how people respond to the aesthetic world.

More broadly, Arnheim underscores the role of images in thought and argument. His careful articulation of what images do and how visual perception is linked to understanding builds a persuasive case for visual thinking – the shaping of images – as a basis for intellectual life:

> This union of perception and thought ... is not merely a specialty of the arts ... the remarkable mechanisms by which the senses understand the environment are all but identical with the operations described by the psychology of thinking. This similarity of what the mind does in the arts and what it does elsewhere suggests taking a new look at the long-standing complaint about the isolation and neglect of the arts in society and education. Perhaps the real problem was more fundamental: a split between sense and thought, which causes various deficiency diseases in modern man.
>
> (Arnheim 1969: v)

In Arnheim's work, we gain conceptual connections between images and psychological processes of thought, comprehension, and contemplation, without reducing the image to mere sensation. I return to his perspective in chapter 5 for insights into architectural expression.

Arnheim pointed out that the expressive power of images lies in their *inability* to perfectly represent reality. For example, photography reduces three-dimensional objects into a flat plane, restricts sensory input to sight (and sound in film), delimits the field of vision, and restricts the color range – especially black and white photography. He argued that film makers achieved artistic goals by controlling light, action, movement, size, and angle of view; thus exploiting the gap between film as a medium and film as representing reality (Arnheim 1957). Looking at photographs or watching a movie limits one's ability to choose where to look, when to scan and focus, and when to look away – perhaps to think – or when to shift one's gaze. Film compresses and expands time as well. Photography's power derives from its ability to seemingly represent the real within a convenient, portable, format – one that is also readily reproduced, digitized, and circulated.

Boulding on the image

Kenneth Boulding attempted to develop a science of images, and his work celebrated the image as the key to understanding human life. He stated that "[i]t is the capacity for organizing information into large and complex images which is the chief glory of our species" (Boulding 1956: 25). Boulding identifies several types of images in a typology that makes clearer the complex nature of images, including the spatial image, the temporal image, the value image, the clarity image, the conscious image, the public image, and the private image. For Boulding, like Arnheim, images are a fundamental cognitive entity, but his model also integrates images into a social, temporal, and physical world.

In Boulding's model, the spatial image is an individual's understanding of the space around him or her, and the temporal image that is embedded in the stream of time, and his or her place in it. He also discusses the relational image, the picture of the universe and its laws, and the personal image, a view of the person as an individual within a complex system of groups, roles, and organizations. He introduces valence with his value image, which relates to the ordering of good to bad, in addition to the affectational image – how the image is imbued with emotion. He reminds us that images also relate to conscious, unconscious, and subconscious processes. For each image we perceive we have a dimension of clarity or vagueness, certainty or uncertainty, reality or unreality. Finally, he distinguishes between public and private images – is the image shared by others or is it idiosyncratic? Boulding's work did not result in a new science as he hoped, but his meditations on the image seem especially relevant in the age of the Internet. He expanded the concept of the image, and emphasized the profound influence of the image in knowledge creation.

Photographic images

The ideology of the photograph concerns central issues in representation – representation is now inconceivable without photography. The world's photographic face shapes identity (Cadava 1999). Furthermore, the information technology of photography is central to understanding how advertising produces meaning within a circuit of production and consumption. For many, cameras offer an easy and convenient way of recording noteworthy events, people, and places such that lived experiences are concretized on film. The domain of photography "constitutes images or representations, consuming the world of sight as its raw material" (Tagg 1989: 165).

The context of photographic vision

Vision is historically situated, in terms of the individual, whose visual system develops and diminishes over the lifecourse, and in evolutionary terms, earlier hominids had different visual systems; but also culturally – how and what people see and the importance attached to vision changes over time and from place to place (e.g., Jay 1993; Krauss 1988; Lester 1995; Mirzoeff 1999). The context of vision is critical for understanding perceptual processes, as well as photographic images. Contrary to their promoters' promises, photography and film do not describe nature, they are not neutral, nor are they perfect representations of reality.

Early criticisms of photography as an art form described the new technique as one that directly reproduced reality (Clarke 1997; Goldberg 1996; Newhall 1982; Rosenblum 1994; Szarkowski 1989). The poet Edgar Allan Poe, excited by Daguerre's invention, waxed enthusiastically about photography's capacity to represent the world accurately – he thought photographs would usher in a new way of obtaining truth. Poe wrote: "the closest scrutiny of photographic drawing discloses only a more absolute truth, a more perfect identity of aspect with the thing represented" (Poe 1980/1840: 38). However, the gap between the photographic record and perceptual experience reveals the artistic, political, and representational potential of photography – "it is just these differences that provide film with its artistic resources" (Arnheim 1957: 9).

This is not to imply that photography cannot create realistic images or that there is a real visual world out there that photography cannot capture. Rather, photography is both a critical part of the visual world and an important process of representing identity. Photography represents an important site in the crisis of representation (cf. Benjamin 1968, 1978). Several theorists suggest that photographs may be read like texts (e.g., Barrett 1996; Barthes 1981; Kozol 1994; Scholes 1989). This approach – one of many reflected in the growing academic interest in visual studies (Heller 1996) – is used below to draw links between identity narratives (life as text) and photographic narratives.

CNN Europe has a regular feature called *No comment* that runs unedited film footage – the video feed from around the world – without commentary. Often the video is humorous and it seems to serve a cartoon-like function within the CNN programming. *No comment* also favors violent events, chaos, natural disasters, and showy scenes involving lots of people. On successive days I happened to glance at footage from the Rio Carnival and the Sydney Gay and Lesbian Parade. Both featured spectacular shots of glamorous, gaudy, and giddy revelers. The visual structure of the film footage was remarkably similar; long shots of the participants, close-ups of particularly outrageous outfits and costumes, pans of the gawking crowd. The marchers seemed to keep coming and coming – each more photogenic than the last – and the camera almost seemed to enjoy capturing the lively events. Upon closer inspection, it is easy to distinguish these two events – one celebrates homosexuality, the other clearly is heterosexual. A channel-zapper might have difficult grasping this essential difference – the events photograph in remarkably similar ways. Perhaps at one level the function of these two events is comparable. I was struck, however, by how they were flattened by their inclusion within *No comment*. Photographs alone rendered the respective political and religious significance of the events moot. Furthermore, by appearing on *No comment*, a certain patronizing, distancing tone was effected, making the celebrations seem self-evidently silly or at least humorous. Without interpretive frames, it is difficult to make sense of images.

Interpreting photography

To interpret a photograph is to acknowledge its representational power both as artifact and as bearer of meaning. Many interpretative stances are possible, including psychoanalytic, semiotic, Marxist, feminist, formalist (Barrett 1996). Barthes identified two signifying practices present in all photographs – denotation and connotation – that capture photography's appeal and representational power (1981). Drawing upon semiotics, this system is "basic to any reading of the photographic image and underpin[s] its status as a text" (Clarke 1997: 222). Denotation, the literal meaning or significance of the images and its constituent elements, makes photography a complex medium of representation, for what the photograph shows or depicts has historically been considered a record of reality (Szarkowski 1989). However, a photograph's connotative meanings reflect broad societal, cultural, and ideological codes (see Mick and Politti 1989).

Although interpretations of photographs are difficult to fit into a positivist truth-seeking research framework, the critic "cannot say just anything at all" (Barthes 1987: 81). Rather, good interpretations are resonant, insightful, illuminating, surprising, revealing, and ring true or "take." Less successful ones are strained, "off," unlikely, absurd, or they "stretch it" (after Barrett 1990). Furthermore, personal significance and meaning often elude social confirmation – what a treasured photograph means to me will be personal, subjective, and idiosyncratic (cf. Richins 1994). Photographic collections and albums, posters, and popular culture photos in one's possession also reveal parts of the life story. We select particular photographs – to enlarge, to send as holiday greeting cards, to make into refrigerator magnets, to frame – to represent ourselves to others as well as to ourselves, illustrating our life narrative with photographs. For example, many of the photographic examples I chose to write about here are about travel, which represents an important condition of my life, as I live between Europe and the US. I spend a great deal of time and money traveling – it has become a critical activity in my life story. Chapter 4 discusses travel and photography in greater detail.

Photography's analytic tools

Photography is a process of selection: "it appears that there is nothing more regulated and conventional than photographic practice and amateur photographs: in the occasions which give rise to photography, such as the objects, places and people photographed or the very composition of the pictures" (Bourdieu 1990: 7). Several genres of photography have developed, such as landscape photography, documentary photography, art photography, journalistic photography, and portrait photography. Photography became a central way of representing identity.

The portrait

Portraits, in particular – from the department store photography studio, the instant photo booth, from school, church, the military, and so forth –

represent who we were at various stages of our life, and are perhaps the most straightforward representations of identity. However, the very artificiality of most portraits – smiling, touched up, well lit, posed – demonstrates the gap between the way we are and the way we would like to appear (Barthes 1981; Clarke 1997). In current practice, we are told to smile in order to represent an inner state that may or may not correspond to our own feelings or our desire at that moment in time (Sontag 1977).

The family photograph – an icon of living rooms and holiday greeting cards – is an important item in any discussion of photography as representational practice and ideology (e.g., Belk 1995; Berger 1972). Further, "advertising also relies heavily on images of the family, although rather than following domestic photography it holds out aspirations of how families *should* look, act, and consume" (Williamson 1986: 125). Photographs help construct and constitute childhood memories. They reveal identity, not only to ourselves, families, and friends but also to the state in terms of identification cards, driver's licenses, and passports (Tagg 1989).

Family photographs are important repositories of collective memory, self-presentation, and identity. However, they also represent sites of struggle, conflict, and power. For, as icons of family life, they are subject to domination by one ideal over others. For these and other reasons, Belk contends that "our photo albums are in no way representative archives of family life" (Belk 1995: 152). What is meant by "representative"? What would a representative archive look like? This is a critical question for research using photography. I contend that family photo albums are certainly representative of family life. However:

> The important point is, *whose* memories are being made of this? It is by and large *parents*' memory that family photos represent, since parents took and selected the pictures. Yet children are offered a "memory" of their own childhoods, made up of images constructed by others.
>
> (Williamson 1986: 123)

The crucial question for researchers is, "Which representations are of interest?" A family photo album contains a wealth of information about hopes, values, and tastes, in addition to specific evidence of the life story. I cannot think of a better archive for many questions of identity. It is because photographs are specifically selected for photo albums that they are excellent representatives of family life from a particular perspective (daughter, father, rebel, supporter, and so forth).

Many ads make use of family photography conventions. For example, a print ad from the mid 1990s entitled "The McCooys for Waterman" is an excellent example of how marketers use family photographs to construct symbolic values, such as family togetherness, identity, and personal expression for mass-produced products. Waterman pens are expensive, heirloom writing instruments that are often presented as gifts. Their ad campaigns often revolve around family, and usually use family-style photographs. This particular ad consists of three parts: a black and white photograph of what appears to be four brothers and a sister, some copy about them, and color photographs of five Waterman pens, along with the Waterman name and trademark. To me, the family photo in the ad looks like a Christmas card, or some other posed family portrait. Two brothers on each side in the center, seated on a swing, flank the woman. Each brother is dressed differently, although they have a striking resemblance to one another. Thus, I make a link between the family and a family of pens – each member related, but different. The woman is dressed in white, and is lower in the frame that her brothers. They are posed on a spring or summer day in front of a large white porch, reminiscent of a large family home or cottage. They are all smiling, appear prosperous, and are Waspish in appearance.

My associations involving this ad are many: memories of my family's portraits, my father's fondness for Parker pens, photographs of summer vacations. In addition, I often use this ad in seminars for its demonstration of how marketing campaigns invoke psychological needs for consumer products. For example, affiliation and achievement needs are prominent; belonging to a family, yet being an individual. The photograph also subtly reinforces sex role stereotypes by having the woman supported by a swing, and protected on both sides by her brothers. She also appears smaller in the photograph due to her sitting posture.

This ad makes me think of how concepts like the family and relationships are active constructions; it takes effort to keep them together. The pen as a symbol of writing works to support this interpretation. Writing can be an important way to keep in contact with your family and friends. For an ad for expensive pens, I think this is a reasonable strategy. Furthermore, the link between family photography and product attributes shows many powerful, yet subtle associations between photography and product attributes. Family photography is tied up with social psychological significance for identity, belonging, and togetherness; qualities that are connected to products via marketing campaigns, as well as consumer processes of gift-giving and possession. Photography reveals and memorializes personality; photographic images portray people as well as products.

This *ideology of the portrait* suggests that it serves to remind us of what we are expected to be rather than help remember us the way we were. One of my favorite pictures of myself was taken in Café Pamplona near Harvard Square in Cambridge. I am gazing intently into the lens, briefly interrupted from reading a just-purchased book – it clearly represents (to me) the scholarly part of me. These kind of photos are rare in my family – most of our photo sessions revolved around outdoor activities. Given the importance of reading, cafés, and conversation in my life, this often presents a problem in representing my identity within the context of my family. Family photographs are most closely related to personal experience, but there are many other ways photography touches our lives.

A photographic typology

Terry Barrett describes six types of photographs within a classificatory system based on content, function, intention, and use (1990, 1996). His categories are: descriptive, explanatory, interpretive, ethically evaluative, aesthetically evaluative, and theoretical photographs. This system is useful for both thinking about images, and for utilizing photography for research. Some photographs may fit within several categories, and the classification system depends largely upon the viewer. Barrett's approach emphasizes how photographs are used – it implicates photography in the broader social currents that produce, celebrate, and consume photographic images.

Descriptive photographs record subject matter. Mug shots, X-rays, satellite shots, art reproductions, driver's licenses share a common purpose to accurately describe something. This is not to say that most photographs describe, or that descriptive photographs are not enmeshed in aesthetic, political, and cultural trajectories, but rather to group some photographs into what was one of the bases of photography's promise – to accurately represent nature. *Explanatory* photographs are similar to interpretive photographs, but some photographs offer detailed explanations – such as those used in scientific reports, medical textbooks, or owner's manuals. Most journalistic photographs are also explanatory in nature, although a growing number also serve evaluatory or aesthetic functions. Many product catalogs utilize explanatory photographs – they need to show the product and explain how it looks and/or functions. Barrett's examples include famous photographic studies of how animals and people move, medical monographs, and instructional manuals – each example aimed at showing reality as if through a window. The photographs may be instructive, but often the forum they appear in implicates them in larger issues. In chapter 4, I take up photographic instructional manuals as cultural documents that do much more than describe.

The next categorical group moves well into the aesthetic, subjective realm. *Interpretive* photographs attempt to show how things are – at least to the photographer. Often, photographs appear fictional or dreamlike. Interpretive photographs act as mirrors – they are often personal and subjective reflections of events under control of the photographer. Most artistic-motivated photography – that small percentage of photographs that exist to appear in galleries and museums – belongs in this category. Cindy Sherman probably represents this category as well as anyone, her staged film still photographs traverse the realm of portrait, fine art, and identity statement in ways that have helped make her one of the most important artists of the past twenty-five years (Morris 1999). Interestingly, Sherman is known as an artist, not a photographer – her work, although photographic in material, has merged into contemporary art. Although Barrett doesn't discuss advertising photography much, I suggest that many advertisements fall into the interpretive category. Ads are usually staged; they represent a corporate interpretation of events, people, or products. Earlier forms of advertising photography concentrated around descriptive or explanatory; now advertising photography normally dwells in the more aesthetic realms.

Ethically evaluative photographs make ethical judgments. They are motivated by a desire to condemn or celebrate something. They comment on how things are, or picture how things should be (Barrett 1996). War photographs often fall into this category. Barbara Kruger's explicitly political work exemplifies current ethically evaluative photographs (Kruger 1990). Political photography – the "photo opportunity" – and political advertising routinely make use of ethically tinged images. Advertising campaigns from Benetton, Diesel, and Kenneth Cole share some aspects of ethical evaluation, albeit tempered by inconsistent corporate practices in other areas (see Schroeder and Borgerson 1998). I will discuss Calvin Klein's use of aesthetic photography at length in chapter 7. *Aesthetically evaluative* photographs focus attention on aesthetic issues – what is good or beautiful, what is worth photographing or contemplating. Aesthetically evaluative photographs frequently feature natural forms – the nude, the landscape, still life studies. These subjects appear as beautiful things, beautifully shown, such as Ansel Adams's photographs of the American West, or Sally Mann's probing, provocative family portraits.

Theoretical photographs designate perhaps the most sophisticated, self-referencing photographs. Barrett argues that photographs about photography are theoretical in the sense that they promote reflection about the medium of photography as an artistic, political, and personal tool. Theoretical photographs "speak" to those interested in photography: "they are photographs about films, photographs about photographs, art about art, and can be considered a visual type of art criticism that uses pictures rather than words" (Barrett 1996: 81). Kruger's work, such as *I Shop Therefore I Am*, might be placed into this theoretical category (see Schroeder 1998). I think that much so-called postmodern imagery – including advertising – can be effectively considered theoretical, in that it calls attention to conventions, codes, and categories of communication technology. For example, many ad campaigns refer to advertising conventions of comparison of brand "A" vs. brand "B" in a playful, ironic tone that lets the audience in on the joke and subverts established – old fashioned – marketing ploys.

Barrett's categories might find many uses in marketing and consumer research. First, they provide a useful typology of photographs that contributes to understanding about images. Using the categories requires interpretive work to make sense out of images, as well as comparative analysis to distinguish images from one another. Second, these classifications provide novel perspectives on advertising photography, and a way to connect images in ads to aesthetic issues. Third, the categories explicitly include contextual matters – photographic images are part of image culture, and need to be understood within the external domain of the photograph. Finally, his typology offers a set of propositions about images and how they are interpreted by viewers, the photographer, and perhaps researchers. Each photograph must be interpreted before placement within the six categories, each image requires reflection – a key process of understanding how images influence our world as they do.

The gaze

The *gaze* is one of the most influential concepts in the study of photography. The gaze has been written about from feminist, psychoanalytic, historical, and psychological perspectives (Adams 1996; Olin 1996). To gaze implies more than to look at – it signifies a psychological relationship of power, in which the gazer is superior to the object of the gaze. For example, film has been called an instrument of the male gaze, producing representations of women, the good life, and sexual fantasy from a male point of view (Mulvey 1989). Royalty gaze upon their subjects, viewed as property in the kingdom. Explorers gaze upon newly "discovered" land as colonial resources (Pratt 1992). Interpersonally, the gaze "corresponds to desire, the desire for self-completion through another" (Olin 1996: 215). Photographs represent the gaze through subject matter and its relationship to the viewer and photographer. John Urry extended the concept of gaze in his work on tourism – he calls attention to status differences by referring to the tourist gaze (1990).

The tourist gaze is not a static entity, for:

> The gaze in any historical period is constructed in relationship to its opposite, to non-tourist forms of social experience and consciousness. What makes a particular tourist gaze depends upon what it is contrasted with; what the particular forms of non-tourist experience happen to be.
>
> (Urry 1990: 2)

In his study of Kenyan safari tourism, anthropologist Kenneth Little concludes that:

> The metaphor of the gaze generates the tourist perspective ... mass tourism colonizes the imagination through the construction of the tourist perspective and the consequences of tourist colonialism are no less deep-seated or penetrating than the more familiar economic and political expression of colonialism.
>
> (Little 1991: 149–50)

Recent writers on the gaze urge us to turn the gaze upon ourselves, so that we see ourselves as we gaze, "but to visualize looking is not as easy as it might appear. What might seem to be a purely visual theory, or a theory of pure vision, has become lost in the mysteries of human relationships" (Olin 1996: 218). Gaze, then, relates to the identity of the one who gazes and the object of the gaze. The concept of the gaze connects what is looked at with who is doing the looking, the aesthetic with the political, and the internal contents of photographs with the external world.

Consumer research has turned its "gaze" onto many exotic fields recently, visiting various humanities and social science fields as resources. In previous work, I suggested that consumer researchers are intellectual tourists – we travel through many academic fields in search for methods, concepts, and insights to take home to study consumers (Schroeder 1998). In this way, I also am a tourist in the field of art and photography. I introduce this metaphor as a "travel advisory" for consumer researchers venturing into foreign fields, looking for insights, bringing back new customs and habits.

Mere exposure

Classical microeconomic theory posits a causal relationship between consumers' preferences and action – we prefer what we want, and make choices based on our preferences. Psychological research has found that often preferences are based on "mere exposure" to stimuli – we like what we have already know (Zajonc 1968). The mere exposure effect apparently operates in a wide range of consumer domains: people enjoy pop music because they have heard it before, television characters become both familiar and liked through repetition, advertisements are more effective when repeated *ad nauseam*.

Mere exposure and photography work hand in hand to influence how images look. For example, part of famous, tourist-thronged, appealing cities' allure is that they seem familiar, they are well represented, which makes them appear recognized, known, and celebrated. London, Paris, and New York have appeared countless times in paintings, photographs, postcards, and films. The Parisian sky and streetscapes are so picturesque because, well, because there are so many pictures of them. Our expectations are both shaped and confirmed by our images. I collect records – largely for their covers. I have found that record covers look more desirable when reproduced in books or magazines – I find that even if I thought a cover wasn't interesting or worth having, if I saw it later in a book, its image value increased to the point of irritation. Stockholm is not well known in terms of images – no Eiffel Tower, Big Ben, or Empire State Building. Soon after moving to the Swedish capital, I saw a movie that showed some familiar Stockholm scenes. They looked great on film, they became film-like and worth attending to. Photographic reproduction serves to legitimate and authenticate our consumption choices – in collectibles, travel, clothing, and lifestyle.

Photography and marketing research

The use of photographs and photography in marketing and consumer research represents a departure from traditional information processing approaches that use photographs merely as stimuli or to communicate research techniques. However, the complex nature of photography as a representational practice underscores the problems of relying on traditional methods in representing consumers. Technological advances which allow photographs to be manipulated are making more apparent the fact that photographs depend on context for meaning, and do not necessarily create "objective records of reality." I urge researchers, rather than treating photographs and photography as vehicles to discover "truth," instead turn to photography to complicate and disrupt ways of representing consumers. Part of this turn to photography ought to invoke the critical discourse of aesthetics and art history – the humanities disciplines that investigate art and its objects as cultural documents.

Photographic practice is an essential component of the ways consumers represent themselves. Photographs are an important path into understanding identity, one that is constructed by assumptions and uses of photography that developed along with the medium. In this discourse, photographs can be considered objects that reflect and shape the culture that produces and preserves them, and critical attention can be focused on the social and cultural contexts in which artists have worked and the technical factors that affect artistic execution. Central issues to be addressed include evaluation, aesthetics, classification, identification, comparison, and monetary value. Like literary criticism, art criticism is characterized by a myriad of schools employing a variety of approaches to the subject, context, meaning, and production processes (cf. Stern 1989). Photography and photographs are much more than secondary data – they are crucial issues in consumer identity construction.

In a thorough survey of the use of photography in consumer research, Heisley and Levy describe the way that photographs can serve as data for inquiry into behavioral issues ranging from food consumption to identity construction (1991). They discuss three research methods related to the use of photography: (1) the creation of cultural inventories; (2) projective techniques, or photoelicitation; and (3) examination of photographs as cultural artifacts. The creation of cultural inventories – photographic collections generated by the research subject, researcher, or secondary source – can be analyzed in several different ways. An inventory can serve as a datum for research on its own as the main object of attention (e.g., Heisley *et al.* 1991; Holbrook 1998). For example, the photographs kept in albums, books, frames, and posted on refrigerators can be aggregated and considered an inventory of consumer identity. Although Heisley and Levy concentrate on the creation of inventories by researchers, the research subjects can also participate. Havlena and Holak used such subject participation in a study of consumer nostalgia that explored nostalgic themes in collages made by consumers out of magazine advertisements and photographs (1996).

Identity construction via image management is a central motivating force in consumer behavior. A basic human behavior is to represent oneself through action, word, and image. Photographs may serve as a stimulus onto which consumers project their own wishes, desires, identity, and values. Projective techniques, which assume that meaning is projected through photographs, are a rich source for researchers. Heisley and Levy employed this approach in an iterative photoelicitation study that investigated consumer behavior during the family dinner. They first photographed and audiotaped three families as they prepared and ate dinner. Then sociology students described and analyzed the photographs in terms of family structure and power. The families were then interviewed about their interactions, using the photographs as stimuli (Heisley and Levy 1991).

By means of this rich and multilayered method, Heisley and Levy were able to glimpse this family's gaze – they saw things about themselves of which they were unaware of, such as power relations and roles. Looking at themselves in the photographs, the subjects of the research were caught in a public self-reflective matrix not unlike therapy. The photographic element of the project generated narrativity, enabling the subjects to document their behavior in a way that their own family photographs had not. As Susan Sontag argues, "the images that have virtually unlimited authority in a modern society are mainly photographic images" (Sontag 1977: 153). In providing commentary to the researchers, subjects "corrected" the images, empowered by the fact that "photographs challenge the respondent [to become] projective interpreters of their own actions" (Heisley and Levy 1991: 268). Thus, photographs provided the family members a feedback mechanism for the researchers, themselves, and their families.

This important study represents one of the most sophisticated uses of photography for consumer research. However, it remains focused on internal, personal meanings of photography, and makes little attempt to connect family photographs to broader issues of photography, image making, or the relationship between photography and identity. Furthermore, the photographs under scrutiny were generated for the study, which may create demand artifacts that shape subjects' reactions. Photographs serve as markers of family identity – within the context of the subjects' own families. This, of course, is fascinating, but represents only a fraction of the ways photographs influence consumers. Most photographs we see are not of our family – and for me, family photographs are fraught with a difficult history revolving around how I should appear on film. Photographic representation also includes didactic functions – it delivers instructional information about how we should appear and behave, especially when a camera lens is around.

A classic exposition of photography's pedagogical aspects is Erving Goffman's study of "gender advertisements." He introduced a multidisciplinary method for deftly combining nonverbal, symbolic, sociological, and biological analyses of images (Goffman 1979). His technique uses close observation of pervasive gender differences in advertising photographs in terms of posture, gesture, touching, and gaze. His central insight is that photographs serve as markers of identity by representing status and power.

Advertising confirms social stereotypes about gender roles and the relations of power in depictions of body posture and stereotypical posing conventions. For example, women in ads are consistently posed in deferential positions, lying down or physically below men. Goffman focuses our attention on standard advertising poses that signal women's vulnerability to men, magnified by disparities between the physical power of the sexes. Thus, men are portrayed as larger, more powerful, and dominant, whereas women are represented as smaller, weaker, and submissive. A conventional posture for a woman is reclining: on a bed, a couch, the floor, or the ground. This is a tremendously vulnerable pose: "a recumbent position is one from which physical defense of oneself can least well be initiated..." (Goffman 1979: 41). The woman is exposed and defenseless, serving only to advertise the product's and her own availability. Moreover, her identity is obscured and trivialized (see Schroeder and Borgerson 1998 for further applications of Goffman's approach to advertising images).

To read images is to call attention to their performative aspects. Advertising is often scripted by stereotypes about the way males and females behave, the way consumers interact with products and brands, and the role of the market in society. Advertising, then, is largely about performance – and identity is one of its main themes. Goffman's work points to the scripted nature of performing identity, showing how the visual conventions of pose, postures, and placement substantiate stereotyped gender relations. His analytic categories enable researchers to look critically at images with powerful, illuminating concepts. Advertisements are not just pictures, they are cultural texts informed by the social, political, and artistic worlds that produces them. One way to understand this is to view advertising imagery as spectacles – a type of market performance that invites consumer participation via exaggerated display, moral instructions, and focused attention (Peñaloza 1999).

Consuming the spectacle

Lisa Peñaloza's comprehensive study of Chicago's spectacular Nike Town relies on photographs for visual ethnographic data – a kind of photographic field note to complement written records. She took photographs of the site, its displays, lighting, and visual environment as well as consumers interacting within Nike Town, which is filled with gigantic photographs of celebrity endorsers like Michael Jordan, Gail Devers, and Monica Seles, *Sports Illustrated* magazine covers, huge shoes, display cases full of sports-entertainment memorabilia, and other spectacular stuff. Peñaloza distinguishes Nike Town from other market sites by pointing out several components of the spectacle. First, the memorabilia draws consumers –

like a museum, Nike Town promises unique, valuable, and treasured cultural artifacts. Second, Nike Town requires an audience actively consuming the spectacle. Third, spectacles are institutionally sponsored; this corporate patronage places a distinct stamp on the intentions, possibilities, and outcomes of Nike Town. They combine both market and nonmarket attributes in a way that blurs the lines between public and privatized space, entertainment and consumption, and cultural and commercial activities. Fourth, spectacles focus on a restricted set of meaning-making processes, by fostering focused collective attention, which can be contrasted to festivals, ceremonies, and fairs.

To understand such spectacularized consumption, Peñaloza employs photography, borrowing from the traditions of visual anthropology. After securing permission to photograph inside with surprising ease, she proceeded to shoot dozens of pictures of Nike Town visitors, many of whom were also photographing themselves amidst the dramatic displays. However, her use of photography is mostly relegated to content analysis of consumers, activities in the photographs, which included interacting with each other, looking at products, and looking at celebrity displays. She interpreted the photographic behavior of the Nike Town consumers as part of its participatory and communication consumption processes. However, the photographs rarely rise above illustrative examples of these processes, and little semiotic work is conducted to place the research apparatus within the space of consumers' own photographs, or the wider trajectories of photography and image consumption. Further, as I argue in the next chapter, photographing is not always a participative process. The camera lens often interferes with active engagement in the current scene – people sometimes take pictures to remember later, or to give them something to do in the meantime. Nevertheless, Peñaloza's study represents an important integration of consumer research, photography, and spectacular consumption. Her joining of looking and buying signals the lure of visual consumption, yet the logic of consumer spectacles such as Nike Town is typified by "sales associates guiding [visitors] back into the more customary subject position of a consumer" (Peñaloza 1999: 392).

Conclusion

Ironically, the leading image-producing technology – photography – remains under-studied within marketing and consumer research. Advertising photography, product package and label photography, documentary photography, pornography, journalism, corporate photography, domestic and family photography – all are critical photographic genres of image production. Photography usually is invoked to provide evidence or to illustrate research, rather than as a visual topic for investigation (Ball and Smith 1992). Photography as an information and communication technology as a subject is rarer still; most research on IT or the Internet focus on technical specifications, generic design issues, or strategic concerns.

Photography is an academic field of its own, and has developed disciplinary methods, theories, and journals. Most people who study photography learn production – how to take, develop, print, and perhaps digitally manipulate photographs. Despite photography's role in society, most of us have little training in apprehending and comprehending photographic images. I have presented a way of approaching photography from an interpretive, meaning-making perspective. The terms discussed, including the image, interpretation, categories, the gaze, and mere exposure are only a handful of useful concepts that photographic theory offers. Photography is much, much more than a peripheral cue or simple means of meaning transfer (cf. McQuarrie and Mick 1999). Photography is a way of life.

Photography clearly highlights representation as a central issue in understanding consumers' lives, and underscores problems in the attempt to represent "reality." Photographs show many realities and help construct narratives of existence. In this chapter, I have tried to blend personal and theoretical approaches to interpret photographs, describe identity construction, and discuss my own consumption of representation in order to sketch a theory of consuming representation. Moreover, I played the role of the tourist as I traveled to several areas far away from information processing consumer research. By interrogating our own roles as consumers, tourists, and researchers, we start on the path of recognizing the power of representation – a key process of experiencing the world.

Those of us who represent others through our research need to interrogate what it means to have that power. The gaze in its tourist and researcher guise is an important concept to address in consumer research, for it creates an awareness of the process of surveying, looking, and consuming the visual world (Hudson and Ozanne 1988). The metaphor is a useful reminder to consumer researchers on safari, out to collect useful trophies from other fields. The lesson is that we must avoid emphasizing the details of our gaze over the objects of the gaze lest we undermine the gaze's moral intention and interpretive power (e.g., Chow 1997; Gross 1988). A start might be to reconsider representing people solely as consumers, for our identities and life stories surely comprise more than consumption.

My focus on consuming representation underscores the political and ethical implications of this practice. Every representation of identity – man, woman, African, European, consumer – has the potential to construct the way society represents those categories. Representations are part of the lived experience; they construct reality. Whose representation? is a critical question framed by the use of photography in the dominant cultural discourse that consistently misrepresents as much as it represents (cf. Minh-Ha 1991; Rosler 1989; Goldberg 1996). Consumer research has come far in describing, predicting, and interpreting the ways that people consume and the influence of consumer culture worldwide. Representation remains a vital area for discussion, discourse, and disagreement.

Part 2
Consumption domains

4 Photography as a way of life

Photography introduced a new activity to perform and a new way for people to experience the world. Cameras directed attention to the visual landscape as a vast reservoir of potential pictures. Photography conveyed:

> An aptitude for discovering beauty in what everybody sees but neglects as too ordinary. Photographers were supposed to do more than just see the world as it is, including its already acclaimed marvels; they were to create new interest, by new visual decisions.
>
> (Sontag 1977: 89)

Photography quickly became a way of knowing things. In the words of photographer Henri Cartier-Bresson:

> As far as I am concerned, taking photographs is a means of understanding which cannot be separated from other means of visual expression. It is a way of shouting, of freeing oneself, not of proving or asserting one's originality. It is a way of life.
>
> (Cartier-Bresson 1999: 16)

One need not be a photographer to feel this way; contemporary life is infused with photographic images. Photography has become a way of life.

Photography shapes experience: it guides how people see, what they see, what they remember, what they consider worth seeing, how they imagine things look, how they think about their own identity and that of others, and how they think of their ancestors. Photography surrounds consumption: it informs, it shows, it communicates, it structures choice, it dazzles – and it offers a creative way of thinking about consumer experiences. Yet photography is relatively invisible – we take for granted that most of our information about the world is delivered to us via photography in the forms of still pictures, television, film, video, and Webpage design.

Despite photography's dominance of information technology and communication, there is little explicit training about photography in the educational process – especially management programs. Most photography courses focus on production – learning how to take pictures, process film, and produce photographic prints and slides. Photography just is, apparently; its transparency falsely lulls us into believing no special tools are needed to comprehend its communicative power. We have become so used to photographic representation that it seems inevitable, a natural record of what is there or what has happened. Further, advances in photographic technology – including cameras, lens, digital technology, film, and printing – push a realist vision that photography is becoming progressively more accurate, more realistic, and more able to capture almost any subject digitally or on film. Partially due to this invisibility "we pay little attention to this technology – to its workings and its effects on our lives – even as we ingest massive amounts of its outputs on a daily basis, produced for our consumption by ourselves and others" (Coleman 1998: 114). I consider photography to be a cornerstone of visual consumption.

In this chapter, I frame photography as an information technology – one that informs most of the media in use today. I turn to a wide variety of photographic writings – from photography theory to how-to manuals – to provide a context for theorizing how photography functions in consumer culture. I look at photography as a way of experiencing life – picturing reality, making things visible, bringing images into our homes and offices from around the world, designating certain sights relevant for our attention, and filling us with thousands of images each day. I begin with an introduction to theoretical issues in photography, then move to a articulation of photography as a way of experiencing the world, with particular attention to travel and popular photography. I then sketch some implications for consumer research that takes photography seriously as an information technology. Cosmopolitanism is invoked to produce a conceptual link between travel photography and larger discourses of social theory and consumer research issues. I introduce the concept of the "Web gaze" applying concepts of the gaze and the tourist gaze to the Internet, where every site is a potential picture, easily available by printing out the site. The Web is the ultimate camera, we can have a record of our Webvisits through the Web without a camera, film, or waiting for the pictures to come back.

Consumers are like tourists, touring the world for experiences, sights, and sensations. As social geographer Richard Sennett observed: "The spaces full of people in the modern city are either spaces limited to and carefully orchestrating consumption, like the shopping mall, or spaces limited to and carefully orchestrating the experience of tourism" (Sennett 1990: xii). Like André Malraux's conception of a museum without walls (1967), the Web promises the world – an incomprehensible range of visual material from all corners of the world – available from one's desk. Consumption is replete with images, visions, and encounters; managers are told to build relationships with customers, and to deliver experiences. Tourism is an apt metaphor for contemporary consumption, and will be discussed from the viewpoint of travel photography, for – like consumption

– the tourist experience encourages image gathering as a way of life (cf. MacCannell 1976; Nickel 1998). Lenses help us experience and make sense of the world. As an ad from the 1950s urges, "To be Sure of Getting Everything you see on the Trip Travel with a LEICA."

Life is a movie

The heading above is from a 1950s Kodak advertisement. *Life is a movie*, so you'll want to record every important scene with Kodak film and movie cameras. A travel photography guide echoes this thought: "life really is like a moving picture, one scene merging into another, so that we are left with a general impression, sometimes rather hazy, rather than a series of clear-cut pictures like the individual frames on a motion-picture film" (Nettis 1965). In this section I discuss some conceptual issues of photography and photographic practice, drawing on several theorists, personal narrative, and examples from the consumer world.

If life really were a movie, viewers might find it interminably boring. One summer my cousin videotaped a family dinner. My grandparents, parents, uncle and aunt, and cousins were there in Northern Michigan – we ate together rarely, as we lived spread out over the US. Watching the video, I was struck at how mundane and, well, boring it was. "Please pass the butter" and "it was a nice day" seemed to be the leading lines. Our faces looked washed out. My grandparents couldn't hear very well, so many things were repeated – a bit louder and slower. It wasn't that we were negatively affected by the filming, I think it was just that the dinner was not scripted for enduring interest, we were not made up to look good on film, and our family's norms about dinner conversations do not often produce eloquent and timeless dialog. We thought the video would be a nice record of our grandparents, now dead, but I have not seen it since; in its place I treasure beautiful, well-preserved black and white photographs of my grandparents taken when they were young.

A photographic way of life

In 1990, Japanese Photographer Nobuyoshi Araki's wife Yoko died of cancer. In an interview several years after her death, he remarked:

> I don't know how much I love Yoko but I was surprised at the amount of pictures I took of her. All the time: as she brushed her teeth in the morning, as we made love, as she waited for a train, as she ate. Seeing the amount of photographs I took of her, I feel I must have loved her very deeply.
>
> (Quoted in Bornoff 1997: 100)

Araki's comment reflects a way of thinking about photography as knowing. In social psychological terms, behavior has predicted attitude – the act of photographing his wife and looking at those photographs influences his loving attitude toward her. The photograph is often taken for evidence of emotional attachment; taking pictures of something signifies its importance. Susan Sontag sees this effect in negative terms: "needing to have reality confirmed and experience enhanced by photographs is an aesthetic consumerism to which everyone is now addicted. Industrial societies turn their citizens into image-junkies; it is the most irresistible form of mental pollution" (Sontag 1977: 24).

Sontag's book *On Photography* remains a key treatise on photography. She is provocatively insightful about the intersection of photographic practice and consumption; she shows how photographic consumption exerts a tremendous hold on our consumer culture:

> Photography is acquisition in several forms. In its simplest form, we have in a photograph surrogate possession of a cherished person or thing, a possession which gives photographs some of the character of unique objects. Through photographs, we also have a consumer's relation to events, both to events which are part of our experience and to those which are not – a distinction between types of experience that such habit-forming consumership blurs.
>
> (Sontag 1977: 155–6)

Furthermore, photography made possible a way of "capturing" experience – a way to concretize lived existence in pictures. Life is like a movie, having an experience is like taking a photograph of it: "through the camera people become customers or tourists of reality" (Sontag 1977: 110). The camera selects and highlights. Taking a picture of something gives it presence, at least in the photograph. Photographers can make anything look good, or aesthetically pleasing – the real work of photography is "*making things look,* deciding how a thing should appear in an image" (Coleman 1998: 57). Anything can be made interesting with a camera (Sontag 1977). We acknowledge a gap between life and photography, yet we desire Kodak moments.

Furthermore, photographs are the standard of beauty – actors, models, and celebrities dominate our perception of what is attractive. What is beautiful will appear beautiful on film. To be *photogenic* implies that not everyone appears attractive in photographs. Photographic appearance is an employable attribute in many industries. Beautiful scenery "would make a good photograph," sights "look like a postcard," and or are "picture-perfect." Photography influences how we record our lives, providing ubiquitous images of social comparison for social rituals such as births, graduations, and weddings.

I once attended a daytime wedding in rural New Jersey where the pull of photography seemed to intrude on lived experience. During the reception, the new bride and groom were given photographs to look at – from their wedding that had taken place only hours ago. A well-meaning guest had taken his film to a one-hour developing lab and he brought them to the reception in a triumphant burst of enthusiasm – why wait to see your wedding photos? The busy bride and groom gazed wide-eyed at the photos, in between talking to guests, sipping champagne and nibbling hors-d'oeuvres. They really couldn't concentrate on the freshly printed pictures – it seemed strange that the photographs existed at all so soon after the wedding. It struck me that things were a bit rushed – the couple had enough to do at the elaborate well-attended party without poring over wedding pictures. The wedding wasn't over yet. But the possibility of developing wedding pictures quickly inserted itself into the reception, superimposing one meaningful event onto another, collapsing time and space in strange ways, lending a surreal effect to the wedding. Looking at photographs as significant as these interfered with the couple's ability to be in the moment – at their marriage celebration. The ritual of looking over the wedding photographs collided with enjoying the reception. The very recent photographed past overwhelmed the lived present.

Picture-perfect Kodak moments

Cartier-Bresson made the phrase "the perfect moment" famous within photography, referring to the patient search for striking images to record, recollect, and recount. Photographers are encouraged to develop "a good eye" – one that sees interesting pictures where others merely see. Sontag calls this the "heroism of vision" which she considers an encompassing feature of photography. Taking pictures takes on quest-like forms – waiting for the perfect moment, discovering beauty in the commonplace, exalting objects via the lens. Photographers are charged to boldly go and seek out new sites to photograph, new visions to record. Photography offered a lower cost, less violent, and quieter safari to a growing market of camera consumers (Sontag 1977).

I wish I had a camera!

Photography, like all cultural forms, can be understood with the conceptual domain of function, form, and meaning. In my research on photography, I often ask people what cameras are for, that is, what functions do cameras fulfill? Engineers have a quick answer: cameras should take good pictures. Reliably, they add. When I ask photographers, they describe cameras as vehicles for artistic expression. A camera is only a tool, they insist. If I inquire about the kind of camera they use, they scoff, and emphatically state the camera doesn't matter: they can take good pictures with any camera. One insisted that asking a photographer about cameras is like asking a writer about word-processing software – both are merely technical aids. From a marketing point of view, cameras are status symbols, particularly small, expensive models with silver, platinum, or titanium cases, costing thousands of dollars. Nikon markets "cameras that fit your lifestyle." A camera functions to signal and distinguish consumers as sophisticated, cosmopolitan, and technologically cutting edge. Furthermore, photography engages consumers – anyone can take pictures, and photography is a recognized means of self-expression, social commentary, and family togetherness, to name a few of its many functions (see Belk 1998; Schroeder 1998; Zaltman and Coulter 1995).

On one occasion I was in the Louvre Museum in Paris. As I strolled toward the *Mona Lisa,* the usual tourist throng surrounded the small masterpiece, jockeying for viewing position – or should I say photographing position? Despite a large sign nearby the painting, stating in six languages "Do Not Photograph" – plus the universal slash through a camera – dozens of cameras clicked away, some held high above the crowd in an attempt to get a clear shot of Da Vinci's famous visage. I decided to seek out a few lesser-known paintings, and returned some time later. Now, the "Do Not Photograph" sign was placed directly in front of the *Mona Lisa*, almost completely obscuring it from view. Undeterred, the photographers inexplicably continued to snap away. I suppose they now have a unique version of the Louvre's landmark painting, definitively establishing they were there on the day a sign replaced the *Mona Lisa*. The ritual act of photography seemed paramount – one must take a picture when confronted with such an important sight. The camera acts as a proxy for seeing.

Picture taking can be interpreted in two ways: as a precise act of knowing, or as an intuitive, chance mode of encounter. Scientific photography promises faithful visual records of phenomena; artistic photography promotes perfect moments that evoke the human condition. Taking pictures infiltrated the worlds of both science and art:

> Photography introduced a mobile visual system whose realism met the demand for what was considered to be scientific objectivity and whose ability to fascinate produced visual objects of reverie, fantasy and idealisation, effects equally valued by the ruling the aesthetics and popular spirituality of the time.
>
> (Osborne 2000: 9)

Compare these theoretical thoughts to this straightforward description from *The Golden Guide to Photography*: "it is a universal language, equally effective whether its task is factual or fanciful, scientific, artistic, or recreational" (Zim and Burnett 1956: 2). What began as a sophisticated, scientific enterprise rapidly transformed into everyday consumer practice. Today, a camera-toting tourist has become a signifier of shallow experience, a trope of the harried leisure class, rushing from sight to sight, understanding little, appreciating less.

On holiday: travel and visual consumption

Travel suspends some of the rules and habits that govern behavior, and substitutes different norms and customs, in particular those that are appropriate to being in the company of strangers. Traveling can lead to new and exciting forms of sociability, play, inquisitiveness, extraversion, and gregariousness that is lacking at home. Travel is a performance (Urry 1995). There are rules and rituals for travel. Witness a Stockholm guidebook, written for "Visitors who want to see all the right places, make all the right moves, buy all the right things ..." (Björkman and Hägglund 2000: back cover). How do travelers know the right behavior? How do we organize and make sense of what we see? Urry outlines several aspects of "consuming places" that shed light on the complex interconnections between travel, photography, and consumption (1995).

First, places are reinvented as sites of consumption, providing an arena for shopping, hanging out, using goods, and photographing or videotaping friends and family. Second, places themselves are in a sense consumed visually. Third, places can be literally consumed; what people take to be significant about a place – industry, history, buildings, literature, environments – is over time depleted, devoured, or exhausted by use. Fourth, it is possible for localities to consume one's identity so that such places become almost literally all-consuming places (Urry 1995). Industries such as arts, tourism, and leisure are all important in the cultural transformations of places into consumption sites.

Consuming places represent a complex integration of consuming place and consuming goods and services. The travel industry combines with retailing to provide scripted sites for consumer. Disney is in the business of entertainment travel. Nike Towns spectacularize shopping, museum gift shops are as popular as the collections. Places are well integrated into marketing. Images of place are used to signify products and services – and lifestyles (Urry 1995). For example, advertising, television news, travel shows, and travel magazines recruit well-known images like the Eiffel Tower, Broadway, Red Square, Tuscan Hills, Pyramids, and so forth, to promote particular messages about culture and lifestyle. Travelers often seek out so-called authentic products, such as local wines from France, Russian caviar, Cuban rum, Greek cheese. Sights can also be ordered on an authenticity scale; there is a growing business in off-the-beaten-path tours for consumers in search of non-tourist sights, eco-travel, and adventure travel. There is even a guidebook for "dangerous travel" for globetrotters who are "adventurous, curious, intelligent and skeptical of the soundbite view" (Pelton 2000: vi).

What's worth seeing?

As soon as there was photography, there was travel photography. Photography brought visions of distant places home to millions of people who might never travel far from home, giving them a first glimpse of places – sights previously available only from engravings, drawings or paintings. The effects were enormous, yet photography's present ubiquity makes it difficult to imagine how early photographed functioned: "faced as we are today with familiar images of exotic places beamed across the world in seconds, it is easy to forget the intense curiosity photographs of faraway lands excited at the time" (Ford 1989: 54). Photography supplanted earlier forms of travel images that played critical roles in geographic, anthropological, and physical knowledge about the world. In the US, the nascent photographic enterprise supported the westward expansion: "photography went west with the railways, which hired photographers to depict their progress and assure the public it was safe and thrilling to tour this magnificent territory" (Goldberg 1996: 16). Travel and travel photography soon became prerequisites of modernity, a signal of affluence and a mark of the good life (Osborne 2000).

Holidays last longer in snapshots

Travel often involve rituals. Vacationers, for example, often return to the same place year after year. Family members participate in family rituals developed before they were born. Vacationers tell stories about their trips, highlighting amusing, amazing, or mundane experiences. The first day of school often involves producing a report on "what I did on my summer vacation." Theme parks, such as Denmark's Tivoli Gardens, Brooklyn's Coney Island of yesteryear, and of course, Disneyworld, give consumers a highly ritualized experience in a convenient package. Taking pictures overlays a structuring ritual – prescribing what to see, how to see it, and influencing how it will be remembered.

Taking pictures has become an important vacation ritual to the point that many vacationers experience much of their trip through the lens of a video camera. Photographs and videotapes seem to offer the traveler a ready means to preserve memories and make the vacation last. Yet photography has become a way of structuring our lives, especially travel and other special events like weddings. Pictures signify what we do, where we go, and how much we enjoy ourselves. Kodak's marketing is part of a concerted effort to join photography and tourism. As a Kodak ad from the fifties claims: "Holidays last longer in snapshots."

Orvar Löfgren has produced insightful scholarly work on vacations. His scholarship is a compelling blend of scholarly insight, historical research, and personal narrative. Löfgren combines his personal expertise and interests with a rigorous eye for detail to build a fascinating account of tourism as an industry as well as the personal experience of vacationing. He adroitly balances insights from his native land of Sweden, the United States, and the rest of Europe with his research on tourism as a global industry. His work covers tourism as well as travel, images, brand names, destination marketing and relates them to social movements, such as labor, leisure, and lifestyle. His work suggests that tourism – and how consumers experience vacations – is central to understanding the global economy (Löfgren 1999).

Academics often have a conflicted relationship with vacations. Summer is usually the time when we try to get that research report written up, revamp our courses, or travel to scholarly conferences. We consider a day or two tacked on before or after the conference to count as vacation – while our non-academic friends assume our entire summer is somehow vacation. Furthermore, vacations are a chance to learn, network, and stay connected with colleagues. As Löfgren points out:

> Vacationlands may appear like territories of freedom, freedom from work, worries, rules, and regulations. But behind this carefree façade there are many unwritten rules. The skills of vacationing have a long history, and into each new vacationscape we bring expectations and anticipations as well as stable routines and habits.
>
> (1999: 5)

This paradox – working at leisure – is at the heart of his analysis, both in terms of the vacationer and the tourist industry, for it takes a great deal of effort to enjoy a vacation.

Löfgren views vacationing as a kind of cultural laboratory "where people are able to experiment with new aspects of their identities, their social relations, or their interaction with nature …" (1999: 7). He contrasts the vacation with work to understand the wants and needs of the vacationer. Löfgren shows how the tourist phenomenon was created, and how tourists came to expect certain experiences. Thus, a "new mode of consumption was emerging, based on the idea of leaving home and work in search of new experiences, pleasures, and leisure" (Löfgren 1999: 5). With the rise of industrialization, tourism, too, became mass produced: "tourism often appears to be the ultimate form of globalization, an industry so standardized that any weekend resort basically would look the same elsewhere, as long as there are some palm trees and a stretch of sandy beach available" (Löfgren 1999: 8).

This standardization led to new niches in vacation travel, market segments, and the development of new resorts in exotic locales as well as obscure outposts. The typical tour brochure or vacation ad promised a lot – many island resorts, for example, were (and are) promoted as "paradise on earth" (see Wood 1999 for an interesting history of Hawaii as paradise). This points to an interesting and important problem that affects many marketing campaigns – promising too much to the consumer. If travelers truly expect paradise, then most vacation spots fall short. If marketing campaigns overpromote, they may lead to generalized consumer cynicism and disappointment. The tourist industry has done well by managing both consumer's expectations and experiences. However, as expectations escalate, consumer dissatisfaction may rise.

Within the tourism sector, experiences become commodities via marketing a more eventful life to tourists eager for change, diversion, escape, or relaxation. Tourists often go in search of "peak experiences" – those events or feelings that take them away from their daily life. Löfgren proposes that much like the great Swedish botanist Carl Linnaeus, who collected plant specimens in order to develop a comprehensive system of classification, tourists collect scenes that are evaluated, compared, and described. Moreover, tourism reflects a certain way of selecting, framing, and representing views. The rules of the modern vacation, scripted by the industry, "taught tourists not only where to look but also how to sense the landscape, experience it ..." (Löfgren 1999: 19). Often, vacationers are looking through a camera, more recently a video camera.

Travel research often revolves around issues of work vs. leisure, labor vs. rest, home vs. away, tourist vs. host. Löfgren proposes several useful dichotomous frameworks for understanding and researching the vacation experience. He suggests that leisure is a symbol of modernity, yet often vacations involve getting back to nature. He discusses the role of authenticity vs. camp; hedonism vs. togetherness; global vs. local; work vs. leisure. He returns to the question of motivation: Why do we need vacations? What is travel? He writes that a basic structure in the vacation mode of consumption is that "it deals with the organization of appetizing otherness" (Löfgren 1999: 281). Vacations usually involve trying new lifestyles or forms of consumption, displaying wealth and taste, interacting with different people. A current television campaign designed to entice people to visit Ireland ends with the tagline: "Ireland: Live a Different Life." Travel, at least in tourist discourse, seems to allow travelers a chance to become a new person, to interact with people in a novel way, and to see things afresh. Photography supports this change, affording the traveler a ready pretext for insightful, gregarious, novel behavior.

Don't forget your camera!

An interesting intersection of photography and travel occurs within advertising imagery. In William O'Barr's compelling study of advertising, he pores over advertising images from the middle of the twentieth century, with particular attention, those promoting the visual pleasures of travel and picture taking. He argues that we gain critical distance by looking at images from the past (O'Barr 1994). We learn to ask questions about contemporary images: Why did these particular conventions arise? How do codes develop and change over time? His central argument involves considering advertising as a model for living, one that supplies instructions for personal, social, and cultural behavior. His anthropological perspective on the social ideology of advertising emphasizes how these instructions are expressed in visual terms.

O'Barr shows that identity issues inform a century's worth of advertising – that ads invoked conceptions of the other repeatedly and systematically. Ads reflected a view of social relationships based on fundamental understandings of inequality and power; and that these relationships were generally depicted without comment or criticism. He acknowledges that there are many unintended and intended consequences of advertising imagery, but he contends that ads, like archeological artifacts, provide clues to broader concerns of cultural economics and visual representation of identity and difference. For example, images of "foreigners" in American and Japanese ads play on ontological assumptions about identity and essential being.

Ads helped create and reflect an image of American identity, wealth, and status. Americans were linked to the West – with a rich venerated culture and a recognizable history, achieving, masculine, independent, fast, dominant. Ads spoke to "us" – usually blond, blue-eyed, citizens. While we play, the other works – to serve us graciously, silently, gratefully. The servers in most ads are non-Western: "traditional," exotic, mysterious, primitive, feminine, childlike, lethargic, slow, or timeless, submissive, racialized, dependent natives. They smile, dance, and work for the us represented in the ads. They produce, "we" consume (O'Barr 1994).

O'Barr's themes interlock with Löfgren's travel dichotomies, but his analysis highlights the routine portrayal of inequality, the blatant use of stereotypes, and the pictorial selectivity of advertising representation. Traveling, in this thorough sample of advertisements, is about us vs. them, work vs. leisure, culture vs. nature, wealth vs. poverty, modern vs. primitive, developed vs. undeveloped – visual codes of cultural dominance that reflect philosophical assumptions about human existence. The visual consumption of travel and the production of tourist imagery act as a lens to analyze broader cultural issues; photography serves as a modern, technological badge, symbolically and behaviorally distinguishing tourist from host.

Viking visions

In 1998, I found myself on a guided tour through Scandinavia – a Viking Capital tour that took me from Stockholm to Oslo to Copenhagen in ten days. After a whirlwind tour of Stockholm, we boarded a train and headed for Norway. At the Sweden–Norway border we transferred to a bus and continued our journey through stunningly beautiful central Norway. Our bus was brand new; we rode high up in the coach and looked out through windows that curved gradually from our knees well into the roof. As we were driven through the mountain- and waterfall-filled countryside, I realized that this is what we had paid for – these views. The bus allowed us to "see" Norway.

While we wandered around the Norwegian countryside, some tour participants grew restless. They wondered aloud "when are we going to get there," eagerly anticipating shopping at the next town. Unfortunately for them, Norwegian shopping times are short compared to lengthy American hours, and stores were invariably closed when we arrived at our destination each evening. During the ride, many fellow tourists read. Not travel guides, nor Scandinavian history, however – romance novels seemed to be the favorite genre. They seemed bored with the spectacular scenery, not realizing that the view was the tour's core benefit. We paid for that view out the bus window; the entire tour was planned to drive us by an amazing assortment of sights – the Viking visual consumption tour.

Fortunately, our tour guide was excellent. He kept us informed of cultural, historical, and geographical aspects during the journey without lecturing at us, and his admonitions about smorgasbord etiquette have served me well during my extended stay in Sweden. He recounted a visitor from several summers ago who kept posing perplexing questions to him. During a ferry ride she asked him what a fjord was. "You're on one," he replied, and pointed to the astonishingly beautiful waterway they were traveling on. She said that she kept reading about fjords, but had not been able to find out what exactly they were, but now she knew, and could go back home and tell her sister. What I wonder is what was she experiencing before she knew she was on a fjord – those distinctive Norwegian waterways that form the basis of many Scandinavian tours. I suspect that the boat trip suddenly became much more meaningful for her, to be remembered and recounted years after the experience. Our expectations influence our experiences – expectations profoundly shaped by photography.

Plan your travel pictures

The first time I visited Paris, the Pompidou Center was on the top of my must-see list. I had seen a picture of the celebrated, unusual museum building in my junior high school French class, and it remained vivid in my memory over the years. The building did not disappoint me and the surrounding area was full of energy and life. I took one of my best travel pictures from the Pompidou roof – a typical Parisian scene made strange from my elevated vantage point. The extreme angle lent interest to the image, just as many travel photography guides promise. Inside, one gallery filled me with desire. There, in the middle of the room, were several Le Corbusier chairs – plush, leather-covered modern furniture icons. I had never seen one, so I promptly sat down, sinking slowly into the well-cushioned architecturally designed seat. I asked my traveling companion to take a picture with the camera she had given me. She balked, a bit embarrassed at my regal pose, perhaps momentarily unwilling to collaborate in a bit of self-presentation.

I think she thought I was being pretentious – posing there amongst the modern art masterpieces. Maybe it was my serious look – my mother always insists that I don't smile enough, especially in pictures – certainly I was affecting a rather pompous pose. She got over her momentary hesitation, and snapped a picture. Right at that moment, someone walked into the frame behind me, you can see her looking at me in the photograph, a faint recognition that she had stepped into my picture flickers across her face. The photo is one of my favorites. There I am in the Le Corbusier classic, within the Pompidou; my shoes white with dust from the morning's excursion to Versailles. This portrait acknowledges my intellectual pursuits – I am solitary, inside, sitting, surrounded by images. I have few pictures like this from my youth – my family emphasized brightly clothed outdoor activities for our voluminous picture making – it represents a major obsession. Just the idea of the picture is important to me – I don't look at it often – but it looms large in my preferred self-concept. Perhaps my memory fails, but I think that the other visitors in the gallery enjoyed the spectacle. After all, we were all doing a bit of performing that day.

Travel is often purely visual consumption – visiting museums, historic sites, or natural areas. Photographing travel, aside from structuring the journey, helps travelers resolve dissatisfying aspects of any trip. It is difficult to guarantee positive holiday experiences. Furthermore, there is an unclear relationship between goods purchased and an overall tourist experience (Urry 1995). Photographs offer evidence of a trip well spent. Photographs can help dispel cognitive dissonance – they can "prove" that you had a good time. One travel photography guide wryly suggests that "the fun of seeing it all again is often more enjoyable than the original experience, for the second viewing is without the tensions that complicate the trip" (Wooley 1965: 132).

Photographic norms usually proscribe taking pictures during times of stress – lost luggage, vanishing waiters, exorbitant ice creams; instead most focus on documenting the emotional and visual high points of travel. For example, back home in Michigan, I saw photographs that my parents took during their trip to Stockholm during the first year I lived there. The pictures looked very European, foreign, and exotic compared with my familiar Midwestern surroundings. The city looked magnificent – there I was living in a faraway land. None of the photographs showed the typical hassles of moving to a foreign place. No camera was ready to record loneliness, light deprivation, banking screw-ups, or those exasperating occurrences that I ruefully came to call "cultural learning experiences."

Photography lends behavioral and technological support to the tourist gaze (Urry 1990). Travel is infused with visual consumption: "central to the tourist experience then is to look individually or collectively upon aspects of landscape or townscape which are distinctive, which signify an experience which contrasts with everyday experience" (Urry 1995: 132). Visitors to Florence are often overtaken by "Uffizi syndrome," an exhaustion that comes from trying to see too much during a day. Moreover, taking pictures can set up a unifying structure for the trip: "photographs document sequences of consumption carried on outside the view of family, friends, neighbors" (Sontag 1977: 100). Taking pictures is frequently comforting. We will be able to check what we saw later, we have a visual record, in case we might have missed something when the sight was physically present.

Photography formalizes looking, making it both more noticeable and more acceptable. The camera stares when it is not polite to look. Once on a boat traveling across San Francisco Bay from San Francisco to Sausalito, we abruptly changed course. As the passengers – mostly tourists – looked to see what was going on, we saw a small sailboat circling in the distance. Soon we came close enough to see that there was someone in the water, clearly in danger. Although he was wearing a lifesaving ring, his face was submerged. The ferry crew was able to position a crane and lift him out of the water, his wet, limp, bluish body dangled in mid-air before being hoisted up and over the rail. During this dramatic rescue, a passenger next to me pointed her video camera at the hapless sailor, recording the unusual incident. Only as he was lifted from the water – obviously in serious trouble – did she avert her gaze from the viewfinder, turn to me and say, so I and the others close to her could hear: "maybe I should turn this off now." She didn't know what to do, and I think she felt terrible. An exciting diversion had turned into a traumatic event – shifting the photographic protocol, and changing her videotaping into ugly voyeurism. I don't know if the man survived. I watched the television that night to find out, but it wasn't on the news. I wonder what that woman felt as she watched her tape.

Life through the viewfinder

Travel can turn into "a search for the photogenic, ... a strategy for the accumulation of photographs" (Urry 1995: 176). Photography gives travelers something to do other than just look. Taking pictures asserts itself as a priority:

> A photograph is not just the result of an encounter between an event and a photographer; picture taking is an event in itself, and one with ever more preemptory rights – to interfere with, invade, or ignore whatever is going on.
>
> (Sontag 1977: 11)

People needed to be convinced that holiday making is not slothful, especially in Anglo-Saxon and Puritan cultures with strong work ethics. Taking pictures provided a solution – it gave people productive work to pursue on holiday. Men, particularly, often hide behind a camera or video camera – observing, filming, distancing themselves from the scene.

Tourist brochures are a major source of information about the world. They show how things can be visually represented and consuming. Brimming with lush photography, wonderful tales of adventure and reassuring images of relaxation, these brochures develop potent visions of a good life. *South Africa through your viewfinder*, an earnest example from the 1950s, put out by the South Africa Tourist Corporation, entices with its vision of a photographic safari through the Apartheid republic. The brochure's cover shows a boxlike medium format camera – a serious photographer's type that produces much larger negatives than a standard 35 millimeter model. These cameras' viewfinders are perpendicular to the lens, so this kind of camera is held at waist level while the photographer composes the subject. The cover camera model is photographed from the vantage point of a photographer looking straight down into the viewfinder – the camera thus reveals an image of South Africa. A pair of white hands cradle the camera – which is reproduced in black and white. The viewfinder shows a color photograph where the refracted image would appear – a large African elephant, shot photographically from about 10 yards away.

On the back cover photo a black South African woman holds a basket on her head. A target is graphically superimposed on her, bisecting her, as if she were in the crosshairs of a gun. We know it is a camera, however, due to the brochure's context. She is naked from the waist up. Below this image are the words "Facts for Photo Fans." Clearly she is not the photographic traveler for whom the brochure was created. Instead she is photographed subject – objectified colorful "native life." Inside, the *South Africa through your viewfinder* brochure reassures the photographer that "the maiden who displays her superb figure with such an innocent purity will have no objection to it being photographed …" This image is typical of photographic representation of "natives" by tourists, locals by globals, wherein "the people of the third and fourth worlds are portrayed as *exotic;* they are *idealized;* they are *naturalized* and taken out of all but a single historical narrative; and they are *sexualized*" (Lutz and Collins 1993: 89, emphasis in original). At the same time, it reifies distinctions between the worlds of Europe and Africa, the primitive and the modern, the tourist and the native. Part of photography's power lies in its ability to appear natural, as if this picture was taken as a record of what is there, without posing, searching, composing, and without any ideological stance or contrived position. Photographs have a "desirable 'neutral rhetoric' as they continue to be perceived by the casual reader as representing a non-interpreted reality" (Triggs 1995: 83).

The *South Africa through your viewfinder* brochure animates a spectacular site of deeply problematic representational practices and exemplifies how photography structures consumer experience in travel and tourist discourse. Photography is a surrogate memory: "only a camera can store the intensity of those first impressions, and reveal them to you again and again …" Travel is often organized around taking pictures, as this guide attests: "it will be a good idea to plan your itinerary along the lines of a 'shooting schedule,' for the things you most want to see are the things you most want to photograph." Shooting pictures implies an itinerary of interest: "the main thing is to get out in the sunshine with your camera, and discover just how colourful and varied these subjects can be." Photography can turn a trip into a scientific expedition of discovery. South Africa, in this case, offers new and unusual vistas to photograph. Photography leads to new understandings, new sights, and novel images: "we have all seen pictures of St. Paul's Cathedral, the Empire State Building, or the Eiffel Tower ..."

Furthermore, photography reinscribes interpersonal, cultural, and political relationships and status. No need to worry that the people won't understand photographic behavior codes: "even the most primitive native has seen a camera before and the sight of it immediately informs him of your desires." Visual connotations of interpersonal relations are so familiar that an entire range of race relations can be summoned with a single image of a South African bushman or woman (cf. Leiss *et al.* 1990). The brochure's chapters – Animal Life, Native Life, The Cape, and Mountains – equate native life with animal life. Animal life takes precedence – the elephant on the front cover visually dominates the brochure; the animal life chapter appears before the native life chapter.

Photography did not invent stereotypes: pernicious representations of Africans circulated widely in Western scientific, philosophical, and cultural discourses for centuries before the first European tourist posed an African in front of a lens. These stereotypes continue to populate advertising, magazines, film, and music videos, among other media forms. *South Africa through your viewfinder* is only one of the more spectacular examples I have seen, but the discourse of traveling with a camera is informed by regressive ontological assumptions. A large number of instructional guides for travel photography exist, and travel photography itself has become a scholarly subject (e.g., Osborne 2000). I turn to several guides from the mid twentieth century for insight into how photography and travel intersect to produce folk knowledge about how the camera affects and structures experience. I chose this period because this was when color photography, mass tourism, and internationalism collaborated to create a booming market for travel. Furthermore, the guides combine an enthusiastic, quixotic desire to conclusively demonstrate the camera's potential to open the photographer's eyes, break down cultural boundaries, and connect people, all the while providing a reason for taking a holiday.

"Photography: the ideal means of spending inactive hours pleasantly and profitably"

Travel Photography with the Miniature Camera was published in 1934 to capitalize on the popularity of recently introduced small cameras such as those made by Leica and Contax. This guide embodies many of the relations between travel, photography, and consumption that inform photography as a communication and information technology (Barleben 1934). According to the author, photography can be productive. For the traveler not content merely to travel, a camera provides a busy agenda, especially for those interested in venturing outside typical tourist sites. *Travel Photography with the Miniature Camera* sets up a long-standing opposition between tourist experience and authentic experience with statements such as: "The wise tourist cares nothing for the sight-seeing tours and special trips designed to show a group of travelers the sights. He goes by himself to the countryside where the natives are to be found in their natural habitat." Photographic selectivity signifies sophistication – by avoiding tourist sites, the photographer embodies rarified knowledge about other cultures, as well as expertise about how to encounter the true culture. The camera becomes a tool of distinction – not only as an expensive, sophisticated, enthusiast status good, but also as a way of experiencing the world (cf. Bourdieu 1990).

Photography commodifies memory. *Travel Photography with the Miniature Camera* connects this photographic function with modernity itself:

> Many psychologists and authorities on modern life have gone so far as to say that one of the most important factors in progress in the United States has been the ordinary snapshot, with its marked effect on the individual who makes it.
>
> (Barleben 1934: 55)

In the fast-moving modern world, pictures preserve our values, ideals, and relations. We recall and treasure what we photograph – pictures represent what was important, what is significant, and what will be remembered. This simple relationship, repeated in most travel photography guides, underscores a critical component of photography – one that has become difficult to isolate as one of photography's main effects

"Photography for the Traveler"

"Always Take Your Camera," orders this post-World War II guide from the publishing house Ziff-Davis (Nibbelink 1948). In *Photography for the Traveler*, travel becomes an excuse to photograph things; indeed "endless photographic opportunities open up to those who travel anywhere." The title might have been "Travel for the Photographer," for this guide is aimed at expanding the amateur photographer's pictorial realm: "Travel is fascinating and is an ideal supplement to a photographic hobby or profession." Moreover, the guide introduces photographic expression as a key guiding principle for travel and photographic experience. Photography doesn't merely record sights like a postcard: a camera is an expressive device. "People take pictures to tell others what they see and feel," *Photography for the Traveler* instructs, echoing debates about photography since its inception over whether it a scientific technology or an artistic medium. According to this guide, photography can be both – it can record memories and it can express inner visions.

In addition, *Photography for the Traveler* encourages the reader to consider travel "as sort of an investment, wherein you exchange time and money for pleasant experiences." How better can the thoughts, views, and experiences of a trip be preserved than through photography? Travel is expensive, you pay for memories: "photography will help you keep them forever." The prudent photographer is exhorted to take more pictures. Always take your camera to "record the beauty you see and the fun you have." Instructions include rules about prefocusing, prewinding, and thinking for the camera. Also, to plan. Picture planning comprises an entire chapter, an essential travel duty for producing good pictures.

The camera must be a constant companion, seeking out picturesque scenes worth recording, opening the traveler's eye to new visual experiences. Under the heading "Dealing with People," the guide lays out an etiquette for photographing human subjects on holiday. Acknowledging that some people – albeit extremely picturesque – have other things to do than pose for a picture, the guide gives advice for winning over reluctant subjects. "Part of your job lies in making the subject feel important," we read; so convince the Mexican fisherman that you are not "a gaping tourist merely trying to show the folks back home what these strange people look like." Create win-win situations: "the secret in obtaining pictures of interesting people is to make them want to have their pictures taken." Generally, however, the candid portrait photographer is in luck – "it is human nature for people to want to have photographs of themselves." An interesting element of human nature – one that remained latent until photography came around. This discourse – of photographer and photographed, camera and "game" – underlies photography in general and travel photography in particular.

"Traveling with your Camera"

Cameras seem to impart agency to the photographer. These sentiments resonate with many theories of postmodern perception and the hyperreal, but it is beneficial to document how these guides create consumer expectations, how they play a role in constructing the society of the spectacle (Debord 1994). A 1965 guide, *Traveling with your Camera: Creative 35mm Photography*, part of an extensive series from American Photographic Book Publishing, boldly announces that photographs "illustrate a revised frame of mind toward people and things" (Nettis 1965). With chapter titles such as "How to See" and "What to do When You Get There," this guide outlines the photographic orientation to visual consumption. The camera helps you see, notice, frame, and experience. Photography enhances the ordinary – taking pictures influences social perception and interpersonal interaction, and heightens perceptual experience. Photography transforms everyday life into ocular occasions – events that "can be better appreciated if our eyes are open to the action. And if we see the action, we can photograph it" (Wooley 1965: 9).

Photography serves as a proxemic device for interpersonal engagement; cameras are gregarious gadgets. Photography has been called a social lubricant – it supposedly breaks down interpersonal and cultural barriers (Heilemann 1997). Another guide titled simply *Traveling with your Camera* dispenses abundant advice about photographing people. Noting that the camera instigates interpersonal encounters, the guide observes that travelers "photograph strangers on a trip, but not back home due to lack of interest." What might seem commonplace or trivial back home is noteworthy on holiday. Cameras allow one to find that "different people are *you* with different languages and different customs" according to *Traveling with your Camera.*

Travel photography also includes behavioral and pictorial prescriptions. The guidebooks exhort their readers to shun clichéd, boring pictures. How? By becoming actively involved in scenes, vigilance, and creativity. To create captivating images, the photographer must reconsider how people should appear in photographs: "People are not grinning faces posed awkwardly in front of monuments and classic gardens." Acknowledging that consumers are visually jaded, the guides instruct travel photographers how to obtain more interesting, candid people shots. Dress, behavior, and attitude are key:

> You'll discover that the best method for shooting people you don't know is to simply relax and act natural, to look as if you belonged to the scene ... Dress casually. Shoot freely and openly as if it was the most normal thing imaginable. Don't be afraid to get near people.

The camera is an agreeable ambassador – "most of the people you photograph are delighted by your attention." By 1965 the guidebooks realized that all are not delighted by peeping photographers, however, and told shutterbugs that they must "decide if the risk of antagonizing the population is worth the photographs you want" (Wooley 1965: 72).

Photography's role cannot be contained by personal needs, it is informed by financial concerns, constructed as a consumer good. Several of these guides suggest selling photographs to magazines or stock photo agencies, further bolstering the productive appeal of taking travel pictures. Chapters such as "Making Travel Pictures that Pay for the Trip" detail how to contact agencies and describe what kind of travel picture is most marketable. So, in addition to the productive act of photography, traveling with a camera is transformed into a money-making proposition. The traveling photographer not only sees more, but is able to cash in on his experience, transforming the vacation into a revenue producing opportunity.

A camera you'll never outgrow

The guides take photography seriously, and impart useful rules for photographic technique and compositional style that seem lost in a snapshot culture of disposable cameras. Furthermore, they offer poignant pointers about seeing expressive potential on the journey, telling readers to consider "travel as a means of broadening one's creative scope." Each guide analyzed here emphasizes equipment. Travel photographers are urged to become familiar with the camera: "the secret of good photography is to know the camera." Rules about lens choice, film, focus, and exposure usually fill several chapters. The traveler is informed that, much to his amazement – these books are clearly written for male photographers – film is widely available around the world. Each remarks on how much progress has been made in photographic technology – smaller, easier to use cameras loaded with faster, more reliable film offer better hassle-free results with minimal effort. Reading these guides today, I am struck by the careful concern for equipment, and photographic knowledge assumed or recommended – filters, films, focus. These were the glory years of travel photography, before instant-focus automatic cameras, one-hour film processing, and a prevailing attitude that the camera will "do all the work."

Photography replaces cultural knowledge, photographs supercedes cultural history. Travel photographers need not worry about knowing too much about sites: "history you can not change, but different, unusual, and exciting pictures are yours to create" (Wooley 1965: 38). Historical locations become photographic opportunities (cf. Sontag 1977). Sight is subsumed to sites. The traveler can learn more with a camera; photography generates knowledge: "tours are usually conducted by very verbal guides who explain in detail the facts which you can usually read for yourself in a good encyclopedia" (Wooley 1965: 38). Thus, the visual act of photography triumphs over the verbal account of the guide. Rephrased in theoretical terms: "the signifier has been liberated and image takes precedence over narrative, the aesthetic is dominant, and the viewer is seduced by the free play of an excess of images" (Urry 1995: 216). Photography grants tourists auteur-ship; cameras frame travel, create original views, and generate an experiential travelogue. As *Traveling with your Camera* rather existentially declares: without film "pictures would be images recorded only in one's mind" (Wooley 1965: 23).

Cosmopolitans with a camera

Mobility and travel are central to what Urry calls "aesthetic cosmopolitanism" (Urry 1995; see also Hannerz 1990). Travel photography is an instance of a wider worldview that lionizes "travel as the key to self-enhancement and the attainment of a sophisticated, worldly outlook" (Thompson and Tambyah 1999: 217). Although the travel photography guides analyzed here were aimed at a mass market, each is implicated in a quest for self-improvement and self-expression via photographic practice, underscoring the philosophical and psychological links between consumption and identity.

These travel photography guides are documents of desire; they provide material evidence of the reach and everydayness of cosmopolitanism, technological progress and visual consumption discourses. Travel photography subsumes cosmopolitan motifs: curiosity, appreciation of cultural differences, novelty, and skill (see Thompson and Tambyah 1999). The camera is an icon of cosmopolitans, yet its presence is often ambiguous. Cosmopolitans cannot appear too shutter-happy. Photography occupies a secure place within the cosmopolitan lifestyle, carefully positioned to signal expertise, insider knowledge, and elite tastes. Furthermore, photography exemplifies the aesthetic frame of reference and an artistic sensibility that is crucial to cosmopolitan lifestyles (Thompson and Tambyah 1999). Cameras help reveal and concretize personalized meanings of travel and tourist encounters. Photography structures consumer experience within a tension between personal engagement and intellectual detachment. Taking pictures offers a strategic tool to avoid entrenched cultural barriers that block typical tourists' view of the local community.

Photographic practice distinguishes cosmopolitans from mere tourists (cf. Hannerz 1990). The travel photography guides discussed here advise how to avoid the tourist gaze trap – they often suggest photographers reject the expected, seek out different gazes, and celebrate the local, "authentic" culture via the camera lens. The travel photography guides all encourage wandering off the beaten path and closely observing the novel environment for its aesthetic pleasures. Moreover, they inject a modicum of reflexivity into photographic practice. They encourage travel photographers to reflect upon the photographic act, and to consciously plan the pursuit of good pictures, which in turn, reveal their sophisticated tastes and photographic prowess.

The photography industry caters to global-savvy consumers who desire simple, easy to operate, yet expensive looking cameras – portable badges of sophistication and taste. Small cameras eliminate the nerd factor of lugging around bulky equipment. New high-tech models incorporate telephoto lenses, powerful flashes, and sophisticated focusing systems, and are often housed in shiny, precious metal casings. All have prominent name brand markings. Cameras rival watches as *the* status symbol for men: both are highly portable jewelry-like technological gadgets, worn or held close to the body.

Mass media makes travel possible without movement and computers make photography possible without cameras. The World Wide Web is perhaps the ultimate tour package, encapsulating the world within a computer screen. Although influential tourism scholars Lash and Urry predicted the end of tourism, a breakdown of the distinctions between travel and home, work and holiday, tourism and everyday life, I would argue that instead a kind of hyper-tourism has developed, exemplified by Disneyland, shopping malls at the Louvre, New York's mega stores, and Las Vegas, which makes sure you can experience the temples of Luxor,

Paris, and New York within a couple of blocks. People experience "simulated mobility through the incredible fluidity of multiple signs and electronic images" (Urry 1995: 149). Furthermore, the Web provides easy picturing possibilities of every site visited.

I offer a further articulation of the gaze concept – the Web gaze. The Web gaze acknowledges the Internet as ultimate tourist machine. On the Web, one can quickly travel to foreign sites; the whole world is online, available with a click. Furthermore, on the Web, we can take pictures of each site we visit with a few keystrokes – by printing out Websites. The Web is filled with travel and navigation metaphors. We enter the Web through portals, we get on the Web, we travel in cyberspace, surf the Web, and get lost in the net. Photography helped pave the way for acceptance and comprehension of the Web; visual graphics helped transform the World Wide Web into a growing facet of business and everyday life.

Photography is one information technology that most people are extremely familiar with; unlike fiber optic cables, broadband, or satellite technology, photography is part of everyday life. Furthermore, most people have experienced the role of the producer; by taking pictures, they feel some control over the technology, with a camera, one can hold it the hand, something that broadband will have difficulty achieving (for a discussion of how broadband is visually represented in marketing communications, see Dobers and Schroeder 2001).

Conclusions

Photography is a crucial part of everyday life: it structures consumer experience, provides images of the good life, and informs our understanding of the world. Many genres of photography exist, this chapter focuses on travel and popular photography as an illustrative exemplar of the potential for photographically inspired consumer research. Travel remains fundamental to consumer processes of fashion, identity formation, and desire. As Zygmunt Bauman contends, "What is acclaimed today as 'globalization' is geared to the tourists' dreams and desires" (1998: 93). Photography has become a major consumer activity, one that exemplifies the quest for images in contemporary life. Walter Benjamin observed, "the amateur returning home with his mess of artistic photographs is more gratified than the hunter who comes back from encounters with masses of animals which are useful only to the trader" (1980: 211–12). Photography guides – as documents of consumer culture – play an unheralded role in shaping the culture of seeing. They make instructive examples of the domain and reach of visual consumption.

Paradoxically, one sight that is off limits to travel photographers is that of many shopping malls and retail stores – most companies are unwilling to allow their merchandise displays, pricing practices, and inventory to be photographed. Only as a backdrop for other, travel or leisure-related activities are store pictures acceptable. Photography is a powerful intelligence gathering method, and business is war.

Travel guides invariably mention that military installations are out of bounds for travel photographers. Photography overlaps with intelligence-gathering technology, too – the famous Hasselblad camera was developed for reconnaissance work from a German model found in a downed World War II plane. This metaphor lingers, infusing shooting pictures and aiming the camera with multiple meanings: "when a photographer tires of one area he can quickly invade a new land and conquer it with his camera" (Wooley 1965: 154). In the sign wars of the modern market, photography is a weapon of mass destruction.

The next chapters survey the landscape of advertising and World Wide Web photography, marking how photography empowers marketing communications in powerful, persuasive, yet often unnoticed ways. There is much work to be done to acknowledge photography as an information technology. People often ask me if digital techniques alter photographic production and reception. I usually respond by saying that we still have the same perceptual system, and the rules of photographic expression are similar for both analog and digital imagery. Furthermore, it is the cultural meaning of photography that makes it a critical, grounding force of visual consumption. Digital photography represents one more step in its evolution as the dominant information technology of our time.

5 E-commerce, architecture, and expression

I once gave a talk to the marketing department at a large Northeastern United States university during which I presented my work on architectural metaphors of the World Wide Web, using the banking industry as an illustrative example. I began to sketch some basic concepts of architectural expression, only to be interrupted with impatient questions. "Are you talking about buildings?" I was asked, to which I replied, well yes, but also what buildings mean. "But don't most people use ATM machines for their banking now?" Once again, I replied in the affirmative, but that the form of banks has been, and I believe still is, an important strategic tool for communicating certain values about financial institutions. "Do people really know about the way bank buildings look?" – another scholar interrupted me, as I was trying to establish my research assumptions. I realized then that I was going to have difficulty making my point: that architecture provides a visual language that has served commerce well, and that this language retains its communicative aspect even within the virtual, electronic world of the Internet. Thus, to study this language's roots is useful to understand how architecture – as a cultural reference system – provides a symbolic method of representing human, commercial, and spiritual values.

As I look back on that talk, I realize there were several things that hindered my ability to make myself clear. First, my audience was mostly American, who have less first-hand experience with symbolic architecture than many people from other cultures. The US does little to promote architectural literacy. Whereas most educated Europeans know their Gothic architecture from their Baroque, Americans have a shorter visual record of architectural history. I am thinking specifically of monumental architecture of royalty, the church, and the state. Of course, there are some magnificent churches and government buildings in the US, but in general state buildings are often ugly, functional warehouses, and the church's separation from the state has made its power less apparent. Further, the US's most celebrated structures are commercial buildings like the Empire State Building, the Sears Tower, and the now destroyed World Trade Center.

Second, a functionalist bias pervaded the comments aimed at my tale of symbolic meaning. Granted, I was talking to a bunch of marketing academics who leaned toward the modeling end of the field, but I was struck at their inability to recognize the expressive functions of things. A building is a building, apparently, and if I brought up symbols, well I was just reading into it – how many other people would see *that*? I might have pointed out that I was talking in a brand new, expensive, well-located building that housed the management school, the university's chief administrators, as well as an impressive art collection. The building's size, prominent central location, and cost all contribute to its symbolic affirmation of the management school's importance to the university. So many have been trained to focus on the practical nature of things, to pare experience down to a basic model that attempts to "capture" the variance of the phenomenon under scrutiny. Particularly in the financial arena, "architecture beyond the 'merely functional' ought to have no role, especially not in the modern global economy in which increasingly automated financial intermediation of all sorts appears to be approaching the ideals of pure competition and perfect efficiency" (McGoun 2000: 8, in a critique). And yet, those of us interested in marketing should realize that expressive, symbolic aspects are at the core of branding, marketing communications, and customer satisfaction.

Finally, architecture is not part of the marketing scholar's toolbox. Although we talk about building brands, constructing networks, and structural models, there is little architectural discourse within marketing scholarship. There is a movement toward studying "servicescapes," some studies about design, and more on retailing atmospherics, but few studies place architecture – bricks and mortar as well as symbol and expression – at the center. Furthermore, most experimental research takes place in bland university rooms, focus groups meet in anonymous conference rooms, and modeling rarely incorporates the built environment as a variable. Of course, there is a growing concern with on-site ethnographic research, spectacular sites such as Disney, Las Vegas, and Nike Town, and the shopping mall often serves as a convenient place to "intercept" research subjects (cf. Peñaloza 1999; Sherry 1998). However, architecture is more than the place that we shop, the building that we visit, or where we have our office – architecture expresses psychological, and cultural, and consumer values

Architecture and expression

In this chapter I look at the role architecture plays in visual consumption, using the banking industry as an illustrative example. Buildings are part of the story, but mostly I will concentrate on how architecture expresses meaning, and how financial institutions manage that meaning. I focus on the abstracted qualities of architecture – especially classical architecture – for that is often how marketing incorporates and consumers experience architectural form. This is not to downplay the architecture's physical dimensions as buildings, spaces, and places. Rather, I turn attention onto the communicative use of architectural elements via a historical overview of how form came to be associated with image.

This chapter presents four assumptions about the visual language of consumption:

1 Architecture is a language – a language of metaphor. It has also been called a rhetoric. That is, built form constitutes a system of representation and signifying practices. Buildings mean something. Architectural form refers to the general style of a building – a castle, a church, or a strip mall, for example. Architecture is a complex signifying system encompassing art, technology, industry, and investment that represents ideals, goals, and values (Taylor 1981).
2 Classicism is a particularly important architectural style. Classical architecture has its roots in antiquity, in the temple architecture of the Greeks and in the military and civil architecture of the Romans. These forms were used in a common architectural language from that day forward, so that a classical building is one whose decorative elements derive directly or indirectly from the architectural vocabulary of the ancient world (Summerson 1963).
3 Banks, particularly in the United States, adopted classical architectural form for strategic reasons. Classicism expresses stability, strength, and security and communicates timeless values. A bank expressed, "by means of its bulk, its bronze doors, and its barred windows, that your money was safe; it also said, since it had a façade of a Greek temple, that money was holy" (Barnet 1997: 54). A bank's appearance should convey an impression that reflects the institution's character by its air of stability, dignity, and security. Thus, the less tangible attributes of a bank – its image – can be communicated through architectural form.
4 This strategic fit between architecture and banking is under strain in the virtual world of an electronic, online, and Web-based banking age. However, although space and time are transfigured within the information-based electronic world of contemporary commerce, classical architecture remains a viable method for communicating certain consumer values. A look at contemporary marketing communications and Webpage design reveals the staying power of classicism for transmitting certain key values about banks and building brand images for global financial institutions.

After a brief introduction to what has been called the classical language of architecture, I will discuss the role that architectural form plays in the financial industry, drawing on examples from architectural history, banking history, and marketing communication. Has the classical visual form of the bank been abandoned? Does the bricks and mortar world of the built environment present an anachronism in the information age? We turn to several sources of data to find that the answer is no: (1) advertising images incorporate classical architectural symbols – columns, temple form, interior space. Here we see the representational properties of architectural form; (2) the World Wide Web is infused with architectural metaphors – home pages, firewalls, portals, pathways and so forth – and Webpage design often reflects the building as icon; (3) automated teller machines incorporate architectural symbols; (4) corporate communications such as annual reports also integrate the language of classical architecture. A basic analysis of these materials reveal several uses of architecture as expression in contemporary marketing communications.

I draw the conclusion that the classical form is too culturally embedded and visually powerful as a communicative mechanism for financial institutions to jettison. Marketing usually blends the new with the old to reassure consumers that change is not too radical. The built environment has provided expressive visual clues for a long time. Thus, financial institutions seem reluctant to give up classicism. Furthermore, one of the governing metaphors of the Web is architecturally based. I close with some thoughts on the capacity for marketing communications to abstract and appropriate cultural symbols – one of the foundations of visual consumption.

Pillars and principles: the basics of architectural expression

Architecture begins with function, structure, and beauty – needs, means, and aesthetics – as laid down by the Roman architect Vitruvius centuries ago (O'Gorman 1998). By their form, location, style, size, cost, and purpose architectural form communicates. Buildings include and exclude, enclose, influence and structure, and protect and dominate.

Architecture is a blend of science and art, function and form, tangible and intangible: "buildings not only have an existence in reality, they also have a metaphorical existence. They express meaning and give certain messages, just as the way we dress or furnish our homes gives people certain messages about us" (Conway and Roenisch 1994: 22). Of course, what buildings communicate is linked to how much we know about architecture, what vocabulary we have at our command, our cultural background, and how we think about buildings and the environment. Architecture is something all of us experience, an extraordinary functional art that confines space so we can live, work, or worship; it creates the framework for our lives (Rasmussen 1959). However, many have little training in architectural form, expression, or history – especially in the US. Architecture remains, for the most part, a specialized subject within art history or architecture schools. We learn to identify buildings by the name of the corporation that builds them, the patron who supports them, and the famous person they were named after.

Function

Architecture ordinarily encloses space, creating interior environments congruent with the purpose of the structure. Building plans specify what is required: offices, classrooms, halls, amphitheaters, sanctuaries, and so on, and often will attempt to articulate what the building should represent. The architect's job is to oversee the transformation of words into three-dimensional forms, arranging the form into usable as well as symbolic patterns. The plan of a building, dictated by client, architect, and community, places a building in time as well, linking the structure to the wider realm of culture.

In 1998, the Museum of Modern Art in Stockholm (Moderna Museet) opened in its new building on the small island of Skeppsholmen. Rafael Moneo, the winner of an international design competition, designed the building. The building's functions include exhibiting and storing the museum's well-regarded art collection, as well as housing a café, bookstore, screening room, lecture hall, classrooms, offices, bathrooms, and equipment. The museum is situated on an island in central Stockholm, long a site of military housing, navy drill halls, and rope manufacturing plants. Several other museums and galleries have converted the island's military buildings. Moneo's design resembles the surrounding drill halls, including one that houses the Architecture Museum that adjoins Moderna Museet. He chose to echo the historic function of the island rather than signify its new, emerging identity as a cultural center (see Hultin *et al.* 1998). The building expresses a link between the modern art within and the museum's historic site. The design is understated, almost minimal – the building blends into the long, narrow drill halls that dominate the island. Thus, it represents an acceptance of modern art – art that is no longer new or contemporary, but a part of history.

Right about the same time that Stockholm unveiled its new Museum of Modern Art, the Spanish port city Bilbao captured worldwide attention with American Frank Gehry's sensational Guggenheim Museum. Gehry's building – a flowing, shimmering, metallic, organic shape rarely seen in built form – put Bilbao on the international art map, drawing acclaim for its stunning shape and whimsical design. A branch of the New York landmark, with its building by Frank Lloyd Wright, the Bilbao museum makes a strong, loud statement via its futuristic design and flamboyant architectural vision. Bilbao's Guggenheim and Stockholm's Modern Museum ostensibly share the same function, to house and display art, but they represent very different solutions to that problem. The Swedish museum is understated and practical – it represents the reuse of the older drill hall form for a new purpose. The Spanish example is brash, seemingly impractical, and exotic. These characteristics map onto cultural stereotypes about Sweden and Spain, north and south, Nordic and Latin. Stockholm's museum is calm, cool, and inconspicuous; Bilbao's is exuberant, exciting, and emotionally compelling – perhaps it is not surprising that foreigners, who may consciously or unconsciously reinforce cultural stereotypes, designed both buildings.

Structure

Interdependent with function, a building's structure defines space as well as its look and shape. Materials, technology, utilities, economics, and geography play key roles within architectural form. Basic structural choices were laid down long ago, new materials and technology modify rather than transform building processes (Scully 1991). Often structural choices are made for communicative or aesthetic reasons. Lighter materials, use of cantilevers, glass, and color can lend an airiness to a building, making it appear light or floating. Older buildings, including classical temples, appear to rest firmly on the earth, symbolically attesting to their permanence. Gothic churches soared toward the heavens, providing a bridge between humans and God. Structure signifies.

The dome and the arch are two significant structural devices, associated with ancient Rome as well as Renaissance architecture. The dome has come to signify notable buildings, from Rome's Pantheon to the United States' Capitol building. The massive amount of interior space that can be enclosed in a dome – or a vaulted ceiling – impresses the occupant, and often leads to attributions of importance, awe, and veneration – a scripted emotional response that serves the building's expressive purpose. A building affects both body and mind; "it is an experience of the senses of sight and sound, of touch and heat and cold and muscular behavior, as well as of the resultant thoughts and strivings" (Arnheim 1977: 4). Thus, we see how the dome has come to play a principal role within bank architecture and marketing communications, for a large domed interior is associated with many of the great masterpieces of architecture, and the physical experience of this space contributes to an overall impression of power. I will take up the functions of classical columns in more detail later, but it is important to note that the structure, too, communicates and represents, perhaps in a more direct way than form or style.

Art

The aesthetic dimension of architecture emerges from function and form. Decisions made by the architect, the client, and choices influenced by building site, zoning laws, and expense contribute to aesthetic results. Architecture is both an art and a communication system, "able to convey the moral of its programs and to stimulate sentiments" (Kostof 1995: 563). Further, it is a social art, "exhibited" in public, and often long lasting. Buildings have inherent meanings which result from their spatial and visible forms and contextual meanings which have evolved out of historical traditions, aesthetic standards, and cultural practice (Ruskin 1961/1849). The set of design decisions that must be made for each building carry with them a cultural and social message that is embedded within the structure. Some of these messages work on a psychological level – visual symmetry seems to have a close connection with emotional harmony, for example – others work on cultural and aesthetic levels (Arnheim 1977).

The literal building blocks of architectural design include structural support, symmetry, or asymmetry, as well as scale, rhythm, proportion, shape, and color. Symmetrical plans usually lead to formal architecture, that is, buildings that spread out horizontally and perpendicularly as one approaches the site (O'Gorman 1998). Often, these buildings relate to the classical or neoclassical style, even if they do not strictly follow the rules of the classical form:

> for much of the history of Western architecture the vocabulary of building elements (such as columns and pediments) and the methods of their combination (proportion, ratio, "figures") have been codified by tradition and precedent – what Campbell calls "techniques in conformity with long established principles."
>
> (Boys 1996: 231)

Thus, a fundamental building style refers to the classical form due its basic structure, but also as a reflection of the aesthetic design decisions. Ornamental style goes in and out of fashion, but contributes to the effect of the building (Carley 1994). Windows, roof, cornices, and columns are a few ornamental expressions that distinguish classical buildings from other styles. Openings such as windows and doors are particularly important to the overall gestalt – they signify the relationship of the private inner space to the more public outside realm.

Doors are crucial ingredients in building design and communicative potency – many important artists and architects won renown via designing important doors and gates. Doors, portals, and gates – and the way they are framed – are critical markers of power, protection, status, and served to stratify towns and cities into those within the gates and those on the outside. Christian churches usually have three main doors, often echoed by three stained glass windows, visually representing the Holy Trinity. Banks and other monumental buildings often have huge, oversize doors that dwarf the entrant. The portal, of course, is one of the guiding metaphors of the Internet which will be discussed below.

Materials also constitute aesthetic choices. Materials represent quality, cost, and luxury, as well as practicality and function. A bank lobby replete with marble, wood, and slate can impress the customer as much as its size and scale. Material also controls light and transparency, which affect the mood and atmosphere of the interior space. Buildings can appear open and welcoming or closed and forbidding, depending on material, openings, and light.

For example, Kulterhuset (the House of Culture) in downtown Stockholm was built during the massive 1950s and 1960s urban renewal that transformed the Clara District of small, wooden structures into a concrete, urban development. Kulterhuset sits diagonally at the end of Sveavägen, a major thoroughfare, blocking that end of the street visually as well as to traffic. It is a seven-story glass building, in the international style of a glass curtain, that sits perpendicularly to the street. The building houses several theatrical stages, restaurants, stores, and it serves as a unique cultural center for the Stockholm area. When I first saw Kulturhuset, I thought it was unattractive, one more unfortunate example of the international glass box. The building seemed oddly sited, sitting as it did somewhat askew to the major street leading to it, Sveavägen – an unfortunate choice for such an significant structure. It was only when I lived in Stockholm through the winter that I came to appreciate an important design feature that completely changed how I experience the building. Kulterhuset's glass walls and broad exposure to the street provides a glittering, bright, energetic vision in the darkness – and Swedish winters are very dark. The lights draw the visitor in, the wall seems open and alive, and the building works as a center of life in the concrete downtown. In the bright summer, Stockholmers look to their wonderful archipelago and many nearby natural areas for recreation, and Kulterhuset's cultural role recedes along with the some of building's positive qualities. In the dark of winter, however, the light and glass afford a welcome sight, and show how architectural choices need to be experienced over time.

A genealogy of classical form

For over two thousand years the classical tradition in architecture has been an essential part of Western civilization, building up a repertoire of meanings and associations that has become part of the cultural fabric. Like language, classical form gained in power and vocabulary from its long past (Adam 1990). Summerson uses rhetoric to describe how buildings speak the classical language of architecture:

> with force and drama in order to overcome our resistance and persuade us into the truth about what they have to tell us – whether it is about the invincible glory of British arms, the paramount magnificence of Louis XIV, or the universal embrace of the Roman Church.
>
> (Summerson 1963: 33)

Classical buildings are perhaps the most visible and widely seen remnants of ancient Greek and Roman civilization, providing testimony of the past glories of the classical world.

Antiquity

The classical form begins in Ancient Greece, with roots in Egypt, Mesopotamia, Syria, and Asia Minor. The basic ingredients, components, or "grammar" of classicism include columns of five standard varieties – Doric, Ionic, Corinthian, Tuscan, and Composite – applied in traditional ways. These five classical orders formed a kind of grammar of architectural form, not merely decorative, but structural: "the classical orders – Doric, Ionic, and Corinthian – are systems shaped by subtle proportions and endowed with a pantheon of meanings, but they are fundamentally arrangements of posts and lintels" (O'Gorman 1998: 37). Each column is composed of three elements, pedestal, shaft, and entablature – a tripartite formula that applies to the entire structure. A row of columns – a colonnade – can resemble an orderly line of people, a flank of soldiers, or a symmetrical forest. Closely spaced columns serve to signal strength and protection, slender columns can signal grace and beauty, massive columns connote power and dominance. Other elements of classical form include doors, windows, gable ends, moldings, and porticoes – all constructed in a particular, prescribed manner. Two other architectural devices critical for articulating the classical form are the entablature and the pediment. The entablature refers to the horizontal part of the building that the columns support. A pediment is a low-pitched triangular-shaped gable surrounding the entablature. Temples usually consisted of a rectangular structure with colonnaded porticoes at each end. The number of columns in the portico varied, but classical form required an even number. Roman temples were based on Greek design, and usually included a podium reached by a flight of stairs at the front of the portico.

Columns are the foundation of the classical form. Columns can be associated with many basic models – the human body, a tree, soldiers. Each column style has also been associated with various ideas – male or female, plain or fancy, serious or celebratory. Columns also represented status, strength, grace. Strict classical form involves a careful balance of form, columns, proportion, harmony, and so forth. Much has been written about the classical orders and how they ought to be used, and what counts as a classical building. In general usage, classical architecture "refers to the style of building of the ancient Greek civilization and later of the Romans" (*Dictionary of Architecture* 1995: 63). For our purposes, and for the meaning production today, I utilize this broad classification: "a classical building is one whose decorative elements derive directly or indirectly from the architectural vocabulary of the ancient world – the 'classical' world as it is often called" (Summerson 1963: 7).

The ancient Greeks, "aware of their own needs, and understanding the desires, anxieties, and uncertainties of others ... used architecture to develop a shared knowledge and to influence ideas and actions. Columns carried culture" (Onians 1988: 330). For example, a Corinthian capital is adorned with stylized acanthus leaves. In ancient Greece, the acanthus plant was associated with life and death, and often appears on tomb vase paintings. Corinthian columns were used in war memorials, temples to the gods Apollo, the healer, and Dionysus, god of renewal. The Corinthian column developed into an elaborate, ornamental element that is now associated with formal, fancy buildings. Thus, we see the poetics of architectural form, and its evolution over time. What was once a clear referent to nature and the gods becomes, over time, repeated usage, and veneration, a referent to the classical world, high ideals, and tradition. Material becomes metaphor – "classical architectural compositions are ingenious essays in stone, intelligently argued dialectics and hermeneutics" (Tzonis and Lefaivre 1986: 275).

Temples are the buildings most closely associated with classical tradition. In contrast to Christian churches usually designed for a worshipful congregation, classical temples served to house the image of a deity. Temples were thus imbued with expressive vitality in a process akin to literature. Every architectural element was designed for expression – doors, windows, walls, parapets, ceilings, and floors diverge from their normal everyday use, transfigured by the symbolic form and purpose of the temple (Tzonis and Lefaivre 1986). This building style came to dominate monumental architecture, providing a basic template for temples, government buildings, and later, private residences and extravagant palaces. Over the centuries up to the Renaissance "these forms were striking features of the buildings in which people in Western Europe formulated and developed their relationships to the gods, to each other, to themselves; and it was often through their use that these relationships were articulated" (Onians 1988: 3).

The Renaissance

The architecture, art, and thought of the ancient Greeks and Romans, renewed during the Renaissance, gave rise to a new classical era. The term classical derives from the social order of the *classici*, the highest social rank in ancient Rome. The rebirth of classical forms became associated with

> the vicissitudes of the money economy in Europe, the emergence of new social formations and new institutions, the birth of court culture and the reopening of world market routes, the invention of credit institutions, and the need to educate a nascent elite in such new ideas as the worth of time and profit.
>
> (Tzonis and Lefaivre 1986: 1)

In Renaissance Italy, status, morality, and character were the values most closely associated with classical architecture (Onians 1988). Thus, the language of classical architecture changed to include a grammar to describe subtle cultural values, including the status of the patron, the morality of the church, and personal character. Classicism, originally a fairly austere style, thus represents power, wealth, and taste – and "visually reinforces the power structure in any period, today and yesterday" (Conway and Roenisch 1994: 16).

Classical buildings, no longer limited to isolated temples, became a tool in city planning, image building, and social control. Although the form itself is somewhat arbitrary, and can be articulated in many ways, the cultural significance of classical motifs was fairly clear: "to walk down a street complete with classical facades during the eighteenth century meant reading the pattern of social registry of the town or, even more, a discourse legitimizing the structure of status and power in that society" (Tzonis and Lefaivre 1986: 246). Patrons came to understand that the power of buildings to affect those who saw and used them could be brought under their control and employed for their benefit (see Schroeder and Borgerson 2001). They did this by first identifying the values with which the patrons wanted to associate themselves publicly and then establishing that architecture could be made to materialize and express them (Onians 1988). These

> attempts to inscribe architecture with social meanings built on, or played with existing vocabularies of elements and the rules for their combination precisely because these reinforced a patron's claim to supreme authority – that is an authority legitimized by religious faith and the Ancients.
>
> (Boys 1996: 231)

Thus, by building a classical temple-like villa, wealthy Renaissance clients gained access to the classical era's status, prestige, and values.

During the Renaissance, several emergent cultural institutions took to the classical form, including the state, universities, commercial enterprises, and banks. Each appropriated the forms as well as many of the symbolic associations of an architectural style that conveniently represented high ideals, long tradition, and harmonious appearance. For example, banks needed to make a statement that they were virtuous, solvent, and stable institutions, and

> as Greece and Rome had come to be seen as the cultural sources of virtue, a return to classical architectural rules of proportionality, regularity, harmony, and decorum in the form of a neoclassical style would express this virtue in the form of a building.
>
> (McGoun 2000: 13)

A building was the most visible, tangible symbol for important cultural institutions – it represented investment, stability, permanence, taste, and wealth.

Modern banking practice has its roots in the Renaissance. The word banking derives from the benches – *banchi* in Italian – and tables used by the banker. The famed Florentine Medicis created a far-flung network of bankers, and their palace in Milan has been called the first bank office. A style of banks was to emerge in the 1700s that was to have far-reaching influence on bank architecture up to the present day. Western banks were built to resemble classical temples, the severe Grecian style helped the often unstable institutions express security (Pevsner 1976). This form, exquisitely expressed by the tremendously influential Italian architect Palladio, usually included one or more porticoes (a roofed entrance supported by a classical colonnade), a vaulted banking hall, and magnificent classical columns. Notable examples include the Bank of England which "with the scale of its halls and the forbidding silence of its outer walls remained right into the twentieth century the noblest of all bank buildings" (Pevsner 1976: 202). The immense Bourse in Paris of the early nineteenth century also adopted classical form, this time with Corinthian columns surrounding the inner temple of commerce and finance of the day.

The New World

The United States has thousands of banks, savings and loans, credit unions, investment banks, and credit card issuers – far more in comparison to European nations' limited choice in banking establishments. This decentralization was a critical response to the kinds of banking institutions that had grown up in Europe, and was designed to reflect the democratic ideals of the US. Banking was localized for most of US history, allowing cities and towns to build their own schools, utilities, and infrastructure. Bankers were primarily boosters of their local communities, until quite recently. It was only during the 1980s that many forms of interstate banking were permitted, and more recently that banks were allowed to sell investment products, life insurance, and other financial services.

Information technology drove many changes in the banking industry – money and financial matters are no longer confined to pieces of paper that must be sorted and stored in ways that leave a ledger and an audit trail. Instead they are electronic entries, generated via computers, and disconnected from particular spaces or buildings (Mayer 1984). This transformation was instrumental in overhauling the banking system from a loose network of numerous small local banks interacting with the Federal Reserve system to the current deregulated arrangement of mega banks, online banking, and international markets. The small town bank of the past, where customers knew the tellers, and met personally with the loan officer to discuss their mortgage, is gone, replaced by ATM machines, computerized forms, and secondary markets for mortgages. More efficient, certainly, but possibly less human. Perhaps this points to the continuing significance of classical architecture – it alone remains to symbolize banking's connection with the past by tapping into classicism as a powerful referent system. Although the premises of banking have changed, the promises of the banking industry have not.

Early US banks were modeled after the Athenian Parthenon, transforming an ancient temple to a temple of finance (Upton 1998). One of the first important American banks was the Bank of the United States, set up in the 1790s to help the states with budgets and cash flow. The American bank also modeled both its operations and appearance on the Bank of England, whose Greek temple headquarters set the style for many bank buildings up until the 1950s (Mayer 1984). The Bank of the United States building stands near Philadelphia's Independence Hall, complete with enormous Corinthian columns, and two large Doric porticoes. It was an impressive structure in its day, and remains on the tourist path as a revolutionary monument. The Second Bank of the United States, also in Philadelphia, was an imitation of the Parthenon, paving the way for many federal buildings to embrace the classical style (Booker 1990). The New York Stock Exchange also emphatically reflects the tenets of classical style. Temple-like inside as well, American banks almost invariably contain a grand interior space, or banking room, that reflects the expectations of the exterior (cf. Allon 1998).

The foundation of the contemporary US banking system was laid with the creation of the Federal Reserve system in 1913 – that rather obscure hybrid entity that Alan Greenspan seems to run by himself at times. This system protected local banks, and upheld state laws concerning, among other things, branch locations. The look of banks began to diversify, but the federal banks generally retained a classical appearance. Even when built as a skyscraper, a bank's first floors typically displayed classical themes (Chambers 1985).

The classical form – somewhat abstracted and altered for use by the secular sphere – has been applied to a growing range of uses that departed from the ancient world's monumental temples, paving the way for further appropriation during the industrial revolution to come. Architectural historians Alexander Tzonis and Liane Lefaivre identity three uses of classical form outside the canon: (1) citations of classical motifs, or freewheeling classicism; (2) syncretism – using multiple architectural forms within one design; and (3) the use of classical fragments in architectural "metastatements." Citationism – including adoption of classical motifs and patterns in advertising and consumer goods – is severely criticized as antithetical to the classical goals of poesis. They argue that citation of classical form has the effect of overfamiliarization, placing the temple within the world of reality, and stripping it of its representational power. The form, they argue, needs completeness to speak in its intended manner (Tzonis and Lefaivre 1985). However, the language of classical architecture is no longer confined or embodied in the built form – as I will discuss below, it radiates throughout culture via mass-mediated images of classical buildings, forms, fragments, and citations.

Visualizing values with the classical tradition

An academic example

During its centennial year, the University of Rhode Island adopted a stylized version of Green Hall as the university logo. Green Hall is one of the oldest and nicest buildings on the rural campus, which was founded in 1892. It is a fairly small building, with a beautiful colonnade of trees leading up to the classical portico, an architectural gem within a stylistically diverse modern university campus. Green Hall has served various functions through the years: once it was the library, lately it housed administrative offices. Recently, it was renovated to serve as the university's admissions office and main visitors building, a focal point for recruiting efforts, thus bringing its visual prominence in university communications in line with its physical use. The building appears as a simplified graphic element on all university letterheads, the university Website, periodicals, and promotional materials, representing all that the university stands for.

Buildings are a fairly common logo for universities. For example, the University of California at Berkeley's Campanile, Columbia University's stately Low library, and Duke's monumental Chapel are icons of their respective campuses. Furthermore, the classical form was also drafted to represent knowledge and learning. Thus, the temple-like appearance of University of Rhode Island's Green Hall was a natural choice for a school logo. Almost anything might have served to symbolize University of Rhode Island. Green Hall replaced an anchor, the state symbol of Rhode Island, which calls itself "the ocean state" as it is surrounded by the Atlantic Ocean and Narragansett Bay. Furthermore, the university has several old and stately buildings to choose from, including a group of granite halls surrounding the quadrangle of a classic New England campus.

Green Hall's appearance was clarified, modified, and stylized in its transition to university icon. Indeed, students were often surprised when I told them it represented an actual campus building. Thus, the logo serves as a somewhat anonymous university icon – many schools use similar buildings on their letterheads as part of their campus communication plan. By adopting this logo, the University of Rhode Island deliberately chose to associate itself with the timeless values of classicism, rather than portray itself as a contemporary, cutting-edge institution. Part of the goal was to move away from a persistent party school image – the anchor formerly used may have had too many associations with the ocean, surfing, and beach life. In any case, the Green Hall logo places the University of Rhode Island within the classical canon of traditional learning, the experience of living on campus, and the representational realm of the built environment. The classical image serves to build the university's image by communicating values of classicism – values such as stability, timelessness, tradition, and ancient roots.

Stability, strength, and security

Architecture continues to play a key role in persuading consumers about the merits of banks:

> Created by private capital to serve a pragmatic function for its owners, bank architecture at the same time turns a public face to its community in a vigorous attempt to communicate, persuade, assure, impress, and convince ... Contemporary attitudes regarding money, respectability, security, and corporate aesthetics are reflected ... bank architecture thus communicates the importance of banks as institutions, assuring us of their stability, prosperity, and permanence and inviting us inside to do business.
>
> (Nisbet 1990: 8)

Architecture provides a strategic method for banks to communicate key attributes of stability, strength, and security. The classical form visually generates "a sense of longevity, stability, rectitude, even stable power" (O'Gorman 1998: 94). Customers entrust banks with their savings – this distinguishes banking from most other business concerns. Although most consumers are aware that banks don't delegate space to store their particular money – money is represented by computer databases now – the physical attributes of the bank have played an important role in projecting a proper image, including stability over time, financial and material strength, and financial and physical security. Classicism helped legitimize banking, a role it played for the nascent nation as a whole:

> Classicism, like language, is precise but flexible. It can suggest commercial probity, as we see in the classical architecture of bank buildings and above all, in the New York Stock Exchange. It can radiate culture, as in the neoclassical art museum in Philadelphia and many another city. In the early nineteenth century the Greek temple form pledged allegiance to the democratic principles that American traced back to ancient Athens.
>
> (O'Gorman 1998: 95)

These values can be mapped onto the three structural problems of building: effectively spanning space, efficiently supporting the spanning walls or columns, and suitably enclosing interior space – the three dimensions of space, namely width, length, and depth. Stability includes both the conceptual reassurance that the bank will be around awhile as well as the perceptual confidence that the building itself will remain standing. Building materials and style convey strength, many banks resemble an impenetrable massive block, protecting the valuable content within. Security, related to strength, can also translate into construction choices and styles – classical banks usually have little glass, thus protecting the inner contents from view, distinguishing the private nature of banking from public view. Moreover, bank interiors were normally divided into a public hall, a private interior, and a vault.

Each of these strategic banking values – stability, strength, and security – have a psychological dimension as well as a material solution. Stability, expressed in visual form by a sturdy structure, provides a metaphor for long-term endurance – "this is why the posts, pillars, and columns which have assured people in many cultures of the buildings' structural stability have been just as critical in resolving other uncertainties and anxieties" (Onians 1988: 3). Colossal columns, heavy materials, and symmetrical form contribute to a building's appearance of strength. Of course, bank customers also desire financial strength, and an ability to withstand economic cycles. Security, for so long largely dependent on specifically designed fortresses, walled cities, and massive structures, also relates to psychological anxiety about financial matters. The closed form of most banks was meant to signal protection – a secure institution to entrust one's future. Furthermore, the use of the temple form created a visual of a special building protecting its valuables, allowing only certain people access to the interior space, and promoting a ritual element of bank visit. Banks are not just depositories of money, they are repositories of hopes, dreams, and anxieties – a modern temple:

> Whether we approached a bank in order to deposit money or borrow it, we were made to feel humbly grateful – indeed, that we were allowed to cross the threshold of the arcanum at all was in itself a reason for congratulation. Passing between majestic stone pillars and then through mighty gilded bronze portals, we would find ourselves at last inside a lofty chamber, vaulted and domed, floored and wainscoted in marble, and ringed round with tiny altars, each of which was set within a cage of slender, protective bars and presided over by a resident priest, usually male and wearing a habit of dark blue serge.
>
> (Gill 1990: 4)

Speed

A fourth banking attribute emerged along with the electronic revolution – *speed.* Now banks need to communicate the four S's: Stability, Strength, Security, and Speed, as customers expect quick and efficient transactions supported by computerized operations. However, the other values remain, and basic relationships between the consumer and the bank continue to require symbolic association. Indeed, speed may be the most characteristic attribute of finance in the virtual economy (e.g., Zwick 2001). In the rest of this chapter, I will explore the role that classical form plays today.

Current concerns

Certainly, banks are no longer primarily physical places – they are name brands that occupy space in the consumer's mind. I am not concerned here with recently built banks, or general architectural trends. Rather, I am interested in how the classical form resides in contemporary marketing communication – advertising, corporate reports, Websites, and the ephemera of electronic banking – for these are the crux of brand building and meaning making.

In the world of Internet banking, electronic communication, and computerized accounts, what is the role that architecture plays today? Has the classical tradition been abandoned, replaced with a newer, sleeker model? It might seem like associations to the past would be counterproductive for organizations wishing to project a contemporary, technologically sophisticated image.

Furthermore, some customers may also associate classicism with colonialism and domination. For example, when the World Bank designed its Washington DC building, they specifically rejected classical style – "the World Bank is in the business of assisting third-world countries and the whole language of classicism is very much associated with colonialism" (Sharoff 1997: 43).

Much has been written on how the computer revolution has transformed time and space, collapsing these dimensions via instant communication and information technology. The three dimensions of architecture – height, length and depth – coexist within photographic representation in marketing communication. Three-dimensional objects have a temporal dimension – one walks through or around them in time – the way two-dimensional images do not. Thus, the symbols of time – longevity, tradition, and history – become interwoven with symbols of space – stability and strength – within two-dimensional representation, thereby superimposing two powerful systems within a single image. Thus, electronic representations of buildings are able to carry a complex signifying framework to the viewer.

Furthermore, the building is no longer the primary banking site. Online banking, banking by mail, and automated teller machines have largely supplanted the ritual trip inside the bank building. Consumers no longer need be at the bank to access account information and perform financial transactions. Speed and ease of transaction are now important components of customer focus. Convenience rules. In a virtual banking world of the World Wide Web, one might assume that price, due to its ready availability and ease of comparison-shopping, might drive the consumer more than brand image. However, the 2000 downturn of the dot.coms demonstrated that brand power is still critical for marketing success – and this is true for the financial sector as well. To investigate the role that the classical tradition plays in current bank marketing practice, I turn to three sources of corporate communication: advertisements, ATM machines, and Internet sites.

Abstracted architecture in contemporary campaigns

Cut-up classicism in bank communications

Merrill-Lynch, one of the world's largest investment banking firms, created one of the most visually striking examples of the uses of classicism in contemporary bank advertising. One version of their late 1990s corporate image-building campaign features four Ionic columns in the background of a stylized Grecian amphitheater ruin. A circular, futuristic-looking podium sits at the center of the amphitheater, echoing its rounded form. Each architectural element appears as a separate photograph, morphed together to create a pastiche of classicism, resembling an ancient site that has been restored by Disney, or assembled for a film set. The golden columns are not supporting anything – they appear to float in the frame, hovering above the marble amphitheater's circular steps. Strict classical form demanded an even number of columns – so even these detached, decontextualized columns nod to tradition. On the left side of the two-page spread, there is a quote from Merrill-Lynch's CEO stressing that "we believe a more vibrant marketplace of ideas will make a difference in addressing the critical challenges of the day." This somewhat ambiguous statement refers to that decade's deregulation of the finance industry, opening up new markets for banking firms.

The classical elements, abstracted and stylized, appear almost as if they have been cut and pasted from a graphics program, in what Tzonis and Lefaivre castigate as "citationism" (1985). The image vaguely resembles an ancient site, but the Ionic columns show no signs of age, nor do the amphitheater steps – they have been taken out of context and harnessed for Merrill-Lynch's communication needs. The podium clashes with the columns, its sleek form jars the image into the twentieth century. Of course, debate flows from the podium, thus the speaker is assumed to be from the current epoch, discussing ideas in a time-honored tradition, within the classical forum of the amphitheater. However, the podium also signifies a special position from which to speak, quite different than the open marketplace. In ancient Greece, the amphitheater was the site of rhetorical competitions – thus the image obliquely connects competition of ideas, strategy, and rhetoric across the centuries.

Merrill-Lynch's quote refers to the classical marketplace – the agora – as an ideal for discussing ideas. However, the image shows an amphitheater – the domain of actors – and only certain people spoke in plays. Merrill-Lynch portrays itself within the foundation of free society, equating open markets with open dialog, freedom with financial freedom, and democracy with capitalism, but a close analysis of this ad reveals misplaced agency, confusing the scripted world of the theater with the agora. Furthermore, the classical motifs assist Merrill-Lynch in projecting a stable, strong, and secure image, but an image that is flexible, adaptive to new environments, and able to accommodate new forms, as the contemporary podium attests.

The Merrill-Lynch ad says a lot about contemporary redefinitions of public space and civil dialog, the power of the past to animate current ideas, and global reshaping of the financial industry, to name a few trajectories. Via reference to classical forms, the Greek ideal, the marketplace of ideas, and the roots of Western democracy, using the shorthand of architecture language, the company achieved a complex ad, simply realized. Their business, then, is not limited to financial matters, they deal in ideas, which require testing via dialog and debate. Architecture, then, functions as a heuristic for consumers in a cluttered marketplace of images. It is not necessary for viewers to identify columns as "Ionic" or "Doric," or know much about the history of classicism, for this ad to work as a reference to tradition, dialog and debate, and the classical past. By juxtaposing old and new styles, Merrill-Lynch sets up an implicit contrast as well as an allusion to time. Yet the ad shows no present day – no modern Athens, Rome, or New York infringes upon the pristine image of classical forms. This scene exists in a realm "that instantly encompasses everywhere, yet has no spatial coordinates in the social, political, or economic world" (Goldman and Papson 1996: 269). Classical motifs serve as signs of an ideal past, where ideas were debated in the agora. Of course, not everyone could speak in ancient Greek society, then, as now, wealth, power, and agency went hand in hand. Furthermore, Merrill-Lynch's campaign does little to support a marketplace of ideas or promote public debate.

A mid-1990s Boston's BayBank ad shows a woman surrounded by a classical gabled door frame, unattached to a house or building. The door, clearly from an affluent house or apartment, resembles a studio prop. She fills up less than half of the door, sits with her legs crossed on the top step of the door's short stairway as she leans forward toward the viewer. I read this ad as a way to communicate three messages. First, your home can function as the site of your banking via online transactions. Second, you need not give up the security of a strong bank – the classical door frame reflects the bank's resources transplanted to your home. Third, the classical door's association with wealth, status, and accomplishment serves to target this ad to an affluent – or striving – segment of consumers. Like the Merrill-Lynch image, the architectural motifs are not connected to a physical building – they serve as props within a stylized tableau.

The most blatant use of classic I've seen is found in a 1996 Chase Bank newspaper ad. A man literally grasps a chest-high Ionic column that displays a bundle of $50 notes. There are several columns in the ad's background, here a Doric column, there a Corinthian, each a singular element within a cluster of classicism. The ad is titled "Me and My Good Fortune" and seems to promote both the bank and a contest to win the bundle of $50s. Dressed in a suit and tie, the man holds the Ionic column almost as if it were his son or daughter, his arm wraps around it, his hand embraces its fluted surface. "I eliminated fees, got better rates, a $50 bonus and a chance to win a bundle," he appears to say. The column has been shrunk down to human size – he dominates it, and pulls it close to his body in an intimate, familiar gesture. Columns were common props in nineteenth-century photography studios, lending a classical touch to thousands of family portraits (Crary 1990). This straightforward use of classicism blends the old and the new – the bank is contemporary, with low service fees, competitive interest rates, yet classical, timeless. Although consumers desire conveniences and deals, they also need to be reassured of the bank's traditions.

Another abstracted column appears in an ad for a Croatian financial service institution, Zavod Za Platni Promet (ZAP). ZAP uses an elaborate composite column as a graphic element in a recent ad "You can lean on us." The main image, which appears on the top half of the ad, shows six dominoes about to topple a seventh. The column, much smaller than the dominoes, floats in the bottom left corner. The bank thus combines two main signifiers of classical columns: strength and Western civilization. Zavod is aggressively seeking Western business. Given the tragic recent history of Croatia, much needs to be done to reassure potential customers about Croatian financial and governmental stability. A column provides a quick way to communicate that customers can lean on the bank, which touts its experience and forty-year tradition.

The classical form is not limited to banking contexts, of course – it is recruited for many product marketing campaigns, including high-tech products. For example, MCI communications uses Corinthian capitals as pedestals to display various styles of telephones, from mid-century to mobile. Thus, products change, but the columns remain constant, an allusion to the classical tradition that I've been discussing. Other uses include a long-running Remy Martin cognac ad that places the product heroically on top of a Doric column, a Givenchy "Organza" perfume ad whose bottle resembles a fluted classical column, and a Mazda ad that compares a car to classical columns "designed by sculptors." In these ads the classical motif provides a link to the classical past, a claim that the product has stood the test of time, and a sense of aesthetics for many different product classes. Significantly, these products have nothing to do with architecture as built form – references to the classical tradition are strictly metaphorical.

Architectural aspects of automated teller machines

My ATM card from the Rhode Island State Employees Credit Union is gray with a graphic depiction of the Rhode Island State capital's classical dome. The credit union's main branch sits across the street from the capitol building in Providence, but its appearance is far from the majestic State House, designed by the architectural firm McKim, Mead, and White in the style of the US Capitol. The credit union's buildings are nondescript, devoid of much style or ornamentation, thus they borrowed a nearby architectural icon with its associations of classicism to grace its ATM cards, as well as their newsletters, customer statements, and logo. Many of the credit union's customers work in the public state capital, still the appropriation of the classical dome is a significant rhetorical move that reflects the architectural style of American banking.

My current bank solves the architectural dilemma another way. Sweden is a highly computerized society, with a high share of Internet banking. Through shrewd pricing policies, a restricted portfolio of services, and redesigning bank lobbies, SEB, one of Sweden's largest banks, has aggressively promoted Internet and automated tellers for the bulk of routine customer transactions. Most of the banks in Sweden share the same ATM network, and ATM cards can be used in most other bank machines without a separate fee. The SEB card shows no building, its design features a stylized fingerprint to signal security. However, during ATM transactions, the user interface screen presents a graphic of an ATM machine – or bankomat – sending signals to a distant bank building. The image shows wires connecting the ATM to the bank – which is labeled "Bank" – and a few childlike renderings of flying birds complete the scene. Seemingly, even Internet savvy Swedes need to be assured that their bank exists in material, architectural form (see Carlell 2001).

Internet

The Internet has emerged as a major force in the financial industry, offering online banking and investing, networked venture capital incubators, and a powerful communications forum for banking firms. Many online-only banks exist, and most viable banks have made some effort to offer online services, and provide online customer and investor communication. The Internet enables firms to place a large amount of information in customers' hands – including basic information about services, fees, the organization, financial information, marketing campaigns, and annual reports, which are often available to download via pdf files. The Internet itself is full of architectural metaphors – superhighway, portals, home pages, and so forth, and the classical language lives on in cyberspace.

Whereas the Internet might have heralded a new economic landscape in which consumers pursued perfect information, comparison shopped, and adopted "efficient" agents to obtain goods and services cheaply, it appears that brand names, trust, and familiarity are still important. Banking is an especially trust-centered business, so let's see how banks communicate on the Web. A basic content analysis of the top ten US banks reveals over half

Table 5.1 Architectural language on the World Wide Web

Name of bank	*Image of headquarters shown on Website*	*Architectural images used in Website*
Bank of America	Yes	No
Citibank	Yes	No
Chase Manhattan Bank	No	Historical pictures of classical Chase building in archive section of Website
First Union Bank	No	1998 annual report shows headquarters on cover, used throughout report
Wells Fargo Bank	Yes	No
HSBC Bank	Yes	Buildings are used extensively throughout 1999 annual report, including classical headquarters
BankBoston	Yes	"Building on Strength" motif uses architectural images throughout Website
Bank of New York	No	Classical building shown on home page; used as graphic element throughout site; clients shown ascending steps amid classical columns
Bank One	No	No
US Bank	Yes	No

Source: Bank information from bankinfo.com, a Thompson Financial Marketplace website, data derived from FDIC (Federal Deposit Insurance Corporation) directory.

Note: Ten largest US banks at 1999 year end.

use some form of architectural image on their Websites, including Chase Manhattan Bank, First Union Bank, HSBC, BankBoston, and the Bank of New York (see Table 5.1). Furthermore, several of these rely heavily on buildings, headquarters, and the classical motif for Web-based imagery. In the table, the architectural elements are briefly described; for example, some sites show the headquarters, others utilize architectural themes throughout the site. These images represent strategic choices. Although photographs of corporate headquarters may appear to be just "there" – a logical choice for a company's Website, most businesses do not show their headquarters on the Web.

The Bank of New York Website provides a clear articulation of the argument. Its home page shows a small image of a classical temple-like building – not the Bank's own building, but the United States Treasury building in Washington DC. Corinthian columns, a rusticated entablature, and a classical frieze are just visible on the Website, peering out from the lower right corner of the page, which appears in several places throughout the site. The bank points to its two hundred years of experience and achievement in words and images, adopting the classical language to the latest electronic forum. Alluding to both its tradition of providing the first loan to the fledgling US government, and banking's use of the federal government's embrace of classicism, the Website provides evidence of the enduring and flexible power of the classical form.

HSBC has become one of the largest banks in the world, thanks to mergers, the rise of the Pacific Rim, where it has many holdings, and global expansion. Its Webpage shows many pictures of its buildings and its 1999 Annual Report is full of architectural images, lending visual support to a brand-building campaign. The report's "illustrative theme," building the brand, is represented via color photographs of replacing old signs with the new corporate logo on various HSBC buildings around the world. For example, the cover shows a worker installing new signage on the HSBC Main Building in Hong Kong. Global branding was one of their strategic goals that year, their new logo a pillar in the campaign. Most of the report's images show the new logo on HSBC properties – including the classical headquarters in New York City, shown emblazoned with a huge HSBC sign stretched across the colonnade.

Although classical architecture is not the dominant visual element of most of these Websites, buildings and classical form maintain a strong presence in contemporary banking communications. Of the top ten banks' Websites, 60 percent include an image of the bank's headquarter building. Often, this image is found in corporate reports, but several show buildings on the corporate home page. Other architectural images of any kind appear in 50 percent of the top ten banks' Websites. These uses include historical pictures, graphical elements like those of the Bank of New York discussed previously, and buildings as themes, such as HSBC, First Union Bank, and BankBoston. BankBoston's Website employs the strategic slogan "Building on Strength" throughout the entire site, which features domestic architecture to depict consumers at home as well as home mortgage products, small firms such as retail outlets and manufacturing plants to portray small business customers, and skyscrapers to represent commercial accounts.

Immaterial matters

Traditionally, consumers have valued three qualities in a bank: stability, strength, and security. Banks adopted classical architectural form to communicate these to the public. In the electronic age, architecture no longer confines banking, nor do most consumer banking transactions take place within a bank's headquarters. Therefore, a change might be expected in communicative tools, classical motifs might seem outmoded or old-fashioned for the information society. However, banks have shifted the symbolic domain from the building to the marketing message, adopting architectural symbols for use in digitized images that carry on the communicative tradition of classical forms. Advertising, Internet sites, and ATM banking still incorporate abstracted architectural symbols, and buildings continue to provide many metaphors for the banking industry.

Conclusions

George Simmel proposed that money signified modernity. He suggested that money – especially abstracted paper currency – provides pleasure due to its exchange capacity (Simmel 1978). An abstract, distant relationship with money replaced more concrete conceptions, "it is now mere contemplation that is the source of enjoyable satisfaction; we leave the object untouched" (Simmel 1978: 73). Money is often an end, not merely a means; electronic banking has further distanced us from money. Information technology signals modern banking methods. Banks, then, enjoy an aura of modernity inherent in money. Classicism provides a necessary counterpoint to modernity, creating a novel entity – a modern ancient temple.

In 1997 the Rhode Island State Employees' Credit Union unveiled plans to remodel their Providence branch. A local columnist wrote positively about the credit union's proposed metamorphosis into a classical structure from "that awful box ... that rectangular pile of concrete blocks painted white and 'decorated' with a few vertical strip windows and a flat roof" (Brussat 1997: B7). He affirmed the drawings that turned a nondescript glass entrance into a imposing columnar portico, added columns to the building's plain front, and sheathed the concrete structure in the requisite temple form suitable for a bank. During a design review committee hearing, however, a professor of architecture from the nearly Rhode Island School of Design rose to contribute his staunch objections – "You've missed an opportunity to create a contemporary building with twentieth century design," he railed against the plan, as he complained that the design "wallows in nostalgia, mimicking the State House ... classical architecture is dead" (quoted in Brussat 1997: B7). The mimicked State House is the previously mentioned Rhode Island icon that embellishes the credit union's ATM cards. And classical architecture, of course, isn't dead, even the Association for Consumer Research's Website uses stylized Ionic columns to post its messages.

One study of contemporary bank architecture concluded that "we are left with the controversial notion that even in these financially sophisticated times, symbols matter, and the message communicated by these symbols is one which can not be conveyed any other way" (McGoun 2000: 50). Architecture provides symbols that are familiar and powerful. When the European Monetary Union's Euro notes finally commence circulation in 2002, the public will be spending bills featuring famous architectural icons. Far from dead, the language of classicism lives on in marketing campaigns, bank Websites, and corporate reports, lending rhetorical authority and visual presence to the business of image management.

Banks today are in the business of building brands as much as physical structures. Heilbrunn argues that brands are transformative devices that allow contradictory principles to coincide, such as nature and culture, the real and the imaginary, the past and the present, and the very distant and the here and now (Heilbrunn 1999). Classicism reinforces this notion, linking an ancient past to the present via rhetorical devices perfected during a classical era. Of course, these rhetorical tools are augmented via marketing information technology, selling the past to the future (Berger 1972).

Classicism remains a central cultural referent structure. Architecture provides spatial, historical, and psychological images easily appropriated by visual media. Furthermore, architecture is a basic metaphorical structure for perception and cognition – indeed it "presents embodiments of thought when it invents and builds shapes" (Arnheim 1977: 274). These shapes, translated into two dimensions, abstracted and isolated, are the building blocks of meaning making. By tracing visual genealogies such as classicism, we gain an appreciation of the complex composition of current marketing imagery, a topic for the next two chapters.

The eminent Bank of England has entered the electronic age via a comprehensive Website. Bank of England's homepage shows a photograph of its iconic building in the background – its classical form visually, psychologically, and historically hovers behind current ventures into electronic commerce. The faint vision of the Bank building's immense classical façade appears on *each* Webpage, under descriptions of secure online transactions, fiscal strength, and a long, glorious history. This type of image is called a "ghost" – it is not fully saturated with color, thus page designers can place ghosted images behind text without obscuring readability. Like a ghost, the classical spirit haunts our understanding of security, stability, and strength.

6 Marketing identity, consuming difference

Although advertising is largely a visual medium, consumer research, for the most part, has not adopted a visual perspective (for exceptions see McQuarrie and Mick 1999; Meamber 1998; Scott 1994a; Stern and Schroeder 1994; Schroeder and Borgerson 1998). Recently, however, advertising imagery has been analyzed by several art historians to investigate its use of photography (Johnston 1997), the connections between advertising and art (Bogart 1995), and the artist's role in producing advertising (Lears 1994). Greater awareness of the associations between the traditions and conventions of art history and the production and consumption of images leads to enhanced ability to understand how advertising works as a visual representational system.

In the following two chapters, I treat advertising imagery much the way an art historian treats pictures as I proceed to analyze illustrative examples through the classic art historical techniques of formal analysis, compare and contrast, and interpretation – all framed within representation understood as a cultural practice (Summers 1996). By drawing on art historical research, particularly an approach to criticizing photographs, I aim to produce close readings of popular and successful contemporary advertising campaigns. I show how art historical conventions inform consumer imagery, thus infusing it with visual, historical, and rhetorical presence and power.

My overarching framework views meaning, in advertising as well as art, as the result of social practices that are constantly changing. Thus, it is necessary to focus on how images work, that is, the social and cultural antecedents for contemporary visual culture and the ways that each contribute to understanding (cf. McQuarrie and Mick 1999). Images are not merely "nonverbal" information that convey more or less the same message that text might impart (Scott 1994b). Rather, images constitute a system of representations – a visual language that is both engaging and deceptive. Advertising imagery, as a subset within this system, interacts with it, borrowing from and influencing the larger world of visual culture. Art historical approaches generate distinctive ways of understanding consumer imagery. By uncovering an advertisement's art historical antecedents, art-centered tools open up possibilities for researching contemporary advertising: "[t]here is a literary and historical precedent for most types of ads now used, and analysis of past examples ... helps illuminate the present consumer context" (Stern 1989: 330).

A key concern in my analysis is identity, and how it functions within visual consumption. In discussing issues of gender, race, and sexual orientation, I open up considerations of how advertising functions as representation within the social contexts of cultural difference – including race, sexual orientation, and gender (Schroeder and Borgerson 2002). Specifically, how does advertising represent multicultural identities? By focusing on one well-known advertisement as an exemplar of these issues, we gain understanding and insight into its power as an image, icon, and cultural artifact.

In this chapter I introduce a visual method for advertising research. The analysis presented here starts with a brief description of art criticism as a tool for examining visual materials, drawing on several basic interpretive guides (Barnet 1997; Barrett 1996; Roskill 1989). Criticism – describing, interpreting, evaluating, and theorizing – provides a framework for interpretive advertising research. I first offer a short tutorial on the basic issues of criticism, and then apply these to a well-known CK One advertisement that introduced a visual style into 1990s advertising imagery. The chapter then presents an interpretive framework via the work of contemporary cultural critics to draw out multicultural implications. The concept of *consuming difference* is introduced to theorize how difference is represented in contemporary advertisements such as CK One. Moreover, the consuming difference concept implies that CK One's alternative-looking images merely reflect mainstream attitudes about multicultural differences. I argue that these insights emerge uniquely from considering the ad as a visual image and subjecting it to a variety of comparisons to other works, photographers, and art historical genres. Finally, the use of art criticism as a method for understanding advertising and visual consumption is discussed.

A visual approach to advertising imagery

Interpretive analysis combines detailed visual description with interpretation and cultural criticism, informed by a growing body of knowledge within "visual culture" studies. Visual culture is the term (not without controversy) used to characterize a growing interest – in and outside academia – in the importance of the visual image and representation (Mirzoeff 1999). As leading visual culture theorist Johanna Drucker states:

> Insofar as the visual forms of graphic design inscribe ideological values and cultural attitudes in the very specific modes of their consumption, finish, treatment, and other features of visual rhetoric, they are potent indices of the social conditions in which they are produced.
>
> (Drucker 1999: 42)

Literary scholar Robert Scholes suggests that interpretive reading is a process that we use not only to make sense of the world, but also to construct our life narratives. He underscores the influence of life experience and cultural context in understanding cultural works, and emphasizes critical comparison in seeing as interpretation:

> This "seeing" is a reading, a decoding, in which we begin with interpretive gestures so apparently simple and natural that we think of them as "seeing" but we end by becoming more aware of our own share in constructing this visual text, as we bring more and more information from our other reading, from our experience of art, from our lives, to bear upon the process.
>
> (Scholes 1989: 2)

Scholes's approach to reading is useful to conceptualize the role that interpretation can play in understanding advertising images and placing visual consumption within a broader frame of the interpreted life.

In the next section, art historical tools are described as techniques to analyze advertising. First, I discuss advertising as a cultural representational practice that produces meaning through signification. Next, I present important theoretical tools – representation, criticism, and photography. Then, I outline a method for incorporating art criticism into consumer research which is applied in the following section.

Art-centered methods for consumer research

Advertising is rarely discussed within an art historical paradigm, for it is usually considered a commercial form of low art beneath the purview of art historians. However, this is changing as visual studies expands to incorporate more forms of visual expression. Richard Leppert's art history textbook focuses extensively on the visual language of advertising:

> It is lost on no one that a significant portion of our conscious and unconscious understandings of ourselves and our immediate world is framed by the imagery of advertising, both in the medium of print and on television. This imagery urges what sort of bodies to have and to desire – or to build; it influences our sense of self, our belief systems, our individuality, and our status as social beings; it encourages what clothes to wear or car to drive, which political party to vote for, and so forth.
>
> (Leppert 1997: 3)

An art historical approach enables consumer researchers to look outside of the image or text to ground their analysis in social and cultural contexts. Art historical concepts and methods provide an historical and visual background to contextualize contemporary advertising imagery and complement more traditional social science derived research. The interpretive process is complex, "and there is no one way critics use to arrive at their understandings of images" (Barrett 1996: 106). In this section, I outline a basic approach to analyzing advertisements within the frame of art criticism.

There are many ways to begin an analysis of a work of art, a photograph, or an advertisement, but most critics agree that description is the starting point for interpretation. Basic descriptive work requires articulation of form, subject matter, genre, medium, color, light, line, and size – the building blocks of images. Some art historical knowledge is helpful for identifying form and genre and making art historical comparisons. For example, I approach the CK One image as a photograph. When working with photographs, relevant issues include production qualities, the photographer's vantage point, focus, and depth of field (Barrett 1996). The relationship between description and interpretation is intricate, but ideally, interpretations emerge from descriptive details.

Interpretive tools include information both internal and external to the object, such as context, comparisons, denotation, and connotation. In Table 6.1, an overview of basic interpretive techniques is presented, emphasizing the following art historical elements: subject matter, form, medium, style, genre and contextual issues. Internal sources of information include analysis of descriptive elements listed above, as well as photography-specific issues of tone, paper quality, and type of camera and lens used to generate the image. Contextual issues concern matters such as the picture's purpose – for the photographer, subject, owner, or client – and how it is presented, for example, in a museum, magazine, gallery, or family photo album. That is, contextual issues encompass concerns external to the photograph or advertisement.

Comparison is a key contextualizing interpretive process (Barnet 1997). Comparisons can be made to other photographers' work, other work by the same photographer, other images that seem connected, as well as cultural products such as other advertisements, novels or films. Comparison, in particular, demands a visual vocabulary of images, poses, and conventions. In addition, the cultural context of the photograph informs its analysis. For example, one reviewer of photographer Richard Avedon's work drew comparisons to his previous work, other photographer's work, writers, and plays. The exhibit "In the American West" comprised large black and white portraits of people who lived in the Western United States. Criticism of this exhibit made comparative references to many famous "storytellers" to support the argument that Avedon's photographs told stories (Barrett 1996).

In the following sections, an iconic 1990s CK One ad will serve as an promising example of an interpretation of a contemporary advertisement grounded in art history. The ad is first contextualized with information about its purpose and producer, then described. Following the detailed

Table 6.1 Comparative visual analysis of the 1994 CK One advertisement

Art historical element	*Description*	*Comparison*
Subject Matter	Group; Kate Moss; Different-looking models	Warhol's Factory Gang; "A Chorus Line" Icons
Form	Fold-out ad	Polyptych; Renaissance altarpiece
Medium	Several black & white photographs	Cut-up photographs
Style	Realistic, harsh	Richard Avedon; Robert Mapplethorpe
Genre	Group portrait	Dutch art; Cornelius Ketel
Contextual Issues	Difference; Multiculturalism	Cultural criticism: Erving Goffman on gender Susan Bordo on the body bell hooks on race, sex Henry Giroux on cultural history

description that draws from several sources, an interpretation is presented that makes several comparisons to the CK One ad – from the world of art history, cultural studies, and advertising research. The objective is to discuss how advertising imagery produce meaning through an art-centered reading of a provocative and popular advertising campaign. A further goal is to produce knowledge about visual consumption via a close reading of an important case study.

Analytic categories for visual analysis

This section presents basic descriptive categories in drawing out connections and comparisons to the CK One ad. I then move on to interpretation, and discuss the work of cultural theorists Susan Bordo, Henry Giroux, Erving Goffman, and bell hooks to contextualize the analysis of the CK One ad. I advance my argument that the CK One ad's implicit intention is to allow viewers to "consume difference" – that is, experience the feeling of doing something different and defying conventions. By difference, I mean lifestyle, looks, gender identity or racial identity that differs from the mainstream, especially in the relatively homogeneous world of advertising, which, up until recently, represented a very small portion of people as consumers.

The analysis will advance through four stages: description, interpretation, evaluation, and theorization. This detailed reading of an advertisement – informed by a theoretical framework of consuming difference – is intended to demonstrate the possibilities of an art-centered approach to visual consumer research. Although the method and interpretive stance may be separated, in this analysis they are intertwined.

Description

The first step in a visual analysis is to describe the image. This is accomplished by pointing out features contained within it, such as formal properties of composition, color, tone, contrast. This level of analysis will be most uniform among observers, varying mostly in terms of art historical knowledge, language, and jargon. A basic method of describing is to place the image within a genre, or type, in which the crucial variables are subject and medium. These categories are not wholly separate, and frankly, it is often impossible to prevent interpretation from seeping into description (Roskill 1989).

The CK One campaign

Background information: Calvin Klein's advertising campaigns have sparked controversy and comment for over twenty years (e.g., Lippert 1996; Miller 1992; Seo 1998). Sex appeal is usually invoked by Klein's ads and provides much of the equity in his products which cover the gamut from blue jeans to evening wear (see Schroeder 2001). Introduced by Calvin Klein in 1994, CK One is a fragrance marketed to both sexes. "*For a man or a woman*," reads the ad copy – noteworthy in today's targeted environment, especially in a product category that is closely linked with gender identity and sexual allure. CK One is marketed through unusual channels, as well. For example, it is sold in Tower Records music stores, and its packaging resembles an aluminum military-type water bottle (Sloan 1994). The fragrance is successful and the ad is well known among teenagers and twenty-somethings. Calvin Klein has introduced a second gender-neutral fragrance campaign, CK Be (Sloan 1996). The multi-million dollar CK One campaign, photographed by Steven Meisel, was the first to garner the Fragrance Foundation's top awards in both men and women's fragrance categories (Campbell 1995).

As an advertising exemplar, CK One provides a compelling image to subject to visual analysis. The CK One images seem to play and subvert gender norms, and they have generated much attention and controversy (e.g., Elliot 1994; Sullivan 1995). They were an icon of visual culture in the 1990s, and have been cited, referenced, and parodied by many other campaigns. The CK One ad has caught the attention of many, and has greatly influenced the world of advertising photography (e.g., Seo 1998).

Images from the campaign were displayed in the Whitney Museum of American Art in New York as part of the art exhibition "The Warhol Look" (Francis and King 1997).

Like so many image-based ads, the CK One ads make no mention of the product's physical attributes, but instead promote a highly abstract connection between the photographer's models and the brand (Stern and Schroeder 1994). We are asked to transfer meaning from the look of the people in the ad – their image, lifestyle, physical appearance – onto the product (Goldman 1992; Williamson 1978). Therefore, it is critical to understand how meaning is visually constructed in this ad. An important contributor to meaning is art historical referents that inform and influence the creation and reception of the ad. This not to imply that all viewers see the art historical antecedents in images such as the CK One ad, or that all viewers would make the same connections. However, the traditions of art history inform how we relate to the visual world, profoundly affect advertising imagery, and most advertising photographers have been exposed to the history of art and photography.

Subject matter: A useful starting point for descriptive analysis is to "identify and typify persons, objects, places, or events in a photograph" (Barrett 1996: 20). The CK One ad under scrutiny appeared across six pages in the September 1994 issue of *Glamour* magazine. There are many versions of the basic ad, all consist of a stark black and white image of several people standing, most facing the camera. In certain CK One images, several separate photographs seem to be joined together, resulting in a jarring, disjointed look that resembles a collage.

One focal subject of the ad is Kate Moss, the famous British supermodel, who dominates the scene through her fame. Moss got her start toward supermodel stardom in 1990 after appearing on the cover of *The Face* magazine. She gives the viewer a hook into the ad and guides its interpretation (Berger 1972). Kate Moss "hails" us, the viewer, by her fame, her roles in other Calvin Klein ads, and her image as a white, heterosexual woman informed by her well-publicized romantic liaisons with male stars. Moss's status overwhelms the other figures in the ad, rendering them supporting players in the icon-driven world of celebrity.

What characterizes this ad is the look of the people in it – they appear different, multicultural, and not often seen (at the time) in major ad campaigns. In the version of the ad analyzed here, the image is a fold-out. Closed, the two pages are covered by a picture of Kate Moss and another white women facing each other, turned profile to the camera, gazing into each other's eyes. In the first image, Moss, hands in her back pocket, head thrown back, dressed in a black bra and black cutoff shorts, is grasped at the beltloops by the other women's fingers. This opens out to reveal four pages of photographs depicting a small group of people standing together against a plain white background. Several of the figures appear in two of the images. They are dressed casually, the men in jeans and T-shirts or bare chests, the women in jeans or shorts, T-shirts, and high-heeled shoes or sandals. Upon unfolding this image, Moss is no longer interacting with the woman – indeed it is unclear if she is in the group image at all (I will return to this puzzle later). The models appear to be posed together, not really displaying characteristics of friends or a familiar group. Some are engaged in animated conversation, others are looking out at the camera. A few seem to be just standing in place.

The fold-out version of the ad consists of four separate photographs pieced together, with sixteen young people depicted in total. Most look at the camera. A few engage in conversation, or at least interchange. All are thin. At first glance, the models seem grungy, unkempt. All except one woman is wearing jeans, CK's undoubtedly, five of the men are bare-chested, two revealing their (Calvin Klein?) underwear. Excluding Kate Moss, the women are not particularly feminine in the traditional sense of being made-up, petite, and well-groomed. One black woman, in particular, has an angry expression on her face, and a group of two white men and a white woman seem to be engaged in a heated argument.

Form: Form refers to how the subject matter is presented. The CK One ad features stark black and white photographs of people who seemed – at the time – out of place in the advertising pantheon. Skinheads mingle incongruously with tough-looking black women. Feminine men are posed next to Moss. Long-haired men pose next to a short-haired women with large tattoos on her arm. In the first image of the two women looking at each other, there is clearly a sexual element. One analysis described the ad's formal treatment of its subject matter within sexual orientation terms:

> In Calvin Klein's latest ad campaign for his unisex fragrance CK One, he attempts to cross gender boundaries with an "androgynous" presentation. In this image, Klein has set up a "butch/femme" scenario in which the two women are about to kiss. The scenario is a perfect example of how the mainstream media suggests queerness; even though it is two women, it still suggests heterosexual role playing. The "butch" is wearing a masculine undershirt, jeans and has her hair slicked back into a pony tail. The "femme" is wearing a bra, short shorts and has long flowing "feminine" hair. Their facial texture is gendered through the "butch's" weathered, muscular look. The "femme" has a smooth, shiny, silky face. Furthermore, in order to allure the "butch," the "femme" exhibits culturally defined feminine, seductive body language.
>
> (Pinkel *et al.* 1995)

The CK One image plays to several audiences, and seems to subvert visual advertising conventions while simultaneously reinforcing stereotypical concepts of identity, sexuality, and difference.

An additional formal element is the fold-out nature of this ad; it swings open to reveal four photographs spread out over four magazine pages. This form is similar to a polyptych, a work of art composed of four or more panels, often hinged together (West 1996). Altarpieces are frequently polyptychs, and commonly open up to reveal hidden images of their sacred subjects. Renaissance altarpieces traditionally showed four saints, one for each panel of a polyptych. The panels open up to reveal an image of Christ, or the Madonna enthroned, and the Saint associated with the church or parish. This aspect gives the ad additional art historical resonance, and may contribute to the "worship" of the CK One icons.

An altarpiece's images fit the context of the church for which they were produced. For example, the St Anthony Altarpiece by Renaissance painter Piero della Francesca depicts the Saint himself along with figures related to the regional order of nuns who commissioned the altarpiece (Cole 1991). Thus, the images helped represent the local church as well as the Catholic faith. In much the same manner, advertisements create images to fit the advertised product's concept. Specific icons are often selected for their particular resonance and meaning for the brand's image. Ad agencies rise and fall on their ability to select and represent the correct images for their clients' products. This comparison is not meant to be a comment on religious iconographic practices, it is merely to show a connection between similar representational processes of meaning construction.

Medium: This term refers to the material form of object or image – canvas, wood, paper, bronze, and so forth. The medium of the CK One ad is a black and white photograph, specifically an advertising photograph that appears as a glossy woman's magazine reproduction. The use of black and white film helps to make this image somewhat gritty in contrast to many of the cosmetics advertisements of the era. The medium also signals fine art status – most art photographs are black and white. Black and white signifies a step toward signness, that is, it makes the photograph look more like a photograph than a brilliant color image. Black and white advertising photographs need something else to activate their rhetorical power – graphic devices, graphic signs, or words (Triggs 1995). The ad's copy – CK One in small type – are all that is necessary to remind viewers that this image is an ad for Calvin Klein cologne.

Photography is both a critical part of the visual world and an important process of representing identity. Historically, photography provided millions with portraits (Tagg 1989). Photographic portraits, in particular, are perhaps the most straightforward representations of identity. Yet the very artificiality of most portraits – smiling, touched up, well lit, posed – demonstrates a gap between image and lived experience. Much of the difficulty in apprehending and interpreting photography lies in the medium's surface realism. It is useful to remind ourselves that the models in the CK One ad are posed, paid, and pampered – despite its appearance, it does not capture a group of friends hanging out.

To interpret a photograph is to acknowledge its representational power both as artifact and as bearer of meaning, reflecting broad societal, cultural, and ideological codes (Schroeder 1998). Photography, like advertising, has deep ties to fine art:

> Much of the formal iconography and symbolic structuring has its roots in painting, but photography substitutes for the painting's presence a veracity and immediacy which, in going beyond questions of aesthetics, involves us in what has been called "the entwined problematic of representation and sexuality".
>
> (Clarke 1997: 123)

As discussed below, photographs of the body – like paintings of the figure – imply a larger politics of power and representation.

Style "indicates a resemblance among diverse art objects from an artist, movement, time period, or geographic location and is recognized by a characteristic handling of subject matter and formal elements" (Barrett 1996: 31–2). The CK One ads were photographed by Steven Meisel in the style of Richard Avedon, arguably the world's most influential modern fashion photographer. Meisel, known for singular, artistic portraits routinely "samples" other photographers' work (Daly and Wice 1995). Avedon is known for his stark, icon-making black and white portraits of the famous and not-so-famous as well as his technique of breaking away from still fashion poses to favor more naturalistic shots of people moving about, gesticulating, talking, and generally not appearing posed (Solomon 1994). Avedon also photographed one of Calvin Klein's most enduring images, Brooke Shields proclaiming that nothing comes between her and her Calvins (Schroeder 2001).

Avedon, known equally for his work in advertising and fine art photography, developed an influential style known for un-retouched, straight-on portraits (Rosenblum 1997). These photographs push our conception of what portraits are and should be, as many of his seem harsh and unflattering (Clarke 1997). Although his portraits often look jumbled and unposed, his style depends on strategically posed elements, and often "make art-historical allusions, even in photographs that are largely the result of studio improvisation" (James 1994: 107). The overall look of the CK One image is reminiscent of Avedon's work, and it echoes his use of multiple shots of the same group.

Specifically, the CK One ad closely resembles Avedon's 1969 photograph of the Andy Warhol's factory crowd (Francis and King 1997). This photograph of Warhol and various friends and assistants comprises four separate images placed together, and is strikingly similar to the CK One ad. Men and women in various states of dress and undress pose for Avedon's camera, staring blankly forward. The background is white, the black and white contrast is harsh, and the subjects look a bit unkempt and tough.

Warhol was well known for his entourage of "downtown" models, artists, and hangers-on, and the Factory came to represent a way of life outside the mainstream uptown world of established art galleries and museums. By photographing the CK One ad in the style of Avedon's Warhol gang photograph, Meisel superimposed one icon – Andy Warhol – onto another, CK One (see Schroeder 1997a).

Like many of Avedon's photographs, Meisel's CK One image is photographed against a plain white background that serves to de-center the subjects, de-contextualize them, and help to undefine the portrait. That is, it is unclear where this group is or where they might come together. As one critique of the Avedon style commented "the blank surround is puritanical; the unframed white represses any interest in the sitter's relation to the outside" (Sennett 1990: 217). Kate Moss's presence serves to ground us, and her vacant bored expression serves as a signifier – instructing us how to make sense of the image.

Genre refers to a type or category of art. A key genre reference to the CK One ad is the group portrait. Group portraits were an established genre type in the Golden Age painting of Holland. Dutch painters moved beyond pure description to idealize their subjects and to portray a glimpse of their personalities. Group portraiture of guild members was a particularly Dutch forte (Stokstad 1995). A well-known example is the "Dutch Masters" portrait that appears in packages and advertisements for a popular brand of cigars. The Dutch group portrait genre usually represented commissions by private guilds who wished to celebrate solidarity and good fortune. The basic pose in group portraiture

> was to organize a number of portraits of equal individual distinction into a coherent whole. One solution was to portray the group in one single row, unevenly spaced and further differentiated by agitated gesticulation and a variety of different and occasionally *rather weird poses.*
>
> (Fuchs 1978: 95, my emphasis)

The poses in the CK One ad are also oddly spaced. The group is lined up in a row; several pictures are placed together, the result is an odd montage of bodies. One visual theorist offers a clue by arguing that the elements in an ad need to signal something different than a mere photograph – "the disposition of each sign-value on the page must not be normal, rather, the positions must be other than ordinary, and be such that an interaction of their visual and conceptual aspect occurs" (Triggs 1995: 86). Thus the CK One ad's rather weird poses directly contribute to the conceptual meaning.

Group portraits, for all their seeming spontaneity, reflected and inscribed a strict social hierarchy. Dutch art is art of the here and now, anchored in daily actives of the middle class, preserving and recording the manners and mores of an entire society (Schama 1988). For our purposes, a particularly relevant example of Dutch group portraiture is Cornelius Ketel's dramatic group composition *The Militia Company of Captain Dirck Jacobsz,*

Roosecrans ca. 1588, which hangs in Amsterdam's Rijksmuseum. In a grouping comparable to the CK One ad, we see a jumble of people posing for a picture, arrayed in apparent random order, presenting a mixed social tableaux. The men, in this case, are posed at odd angles, lacking uniformity, and bring a dynamic composition to what is largely a static image. Each man has an assigned place within the portrait, based on rank, favor, and, often, payment to the artist (Schama 1988). What unites the subjects is their guild membership, they represent a group linked by a common activity. As in most portraits, what is revealed upon closer inspection is a mannered series of poses, calculated and scripted for a particular effect.

Another more subtle connection to Dutch art resides more in the cultural milieu of the Golden Age, where religious freedom flourished, and class systems were being broken down. As English Ambassador William Temple contemporaneously observed about seventeenth-century Holland, "men live together like Citizens of the World, associated by the common ties of Humanity, and by the bonds of Peace, Under the impartial protection of indifferent laws" (quoted in Herbert 1991: 19–20). One of the implicit messages of the CK One ad is that different-looking people can live together, and that to be different is acceptable, a message further underscored in the CK Be campaign. This message has visual antecedents within Dutch art.

I find these two images to be strikingly similar, disparate as they are in time, place, and purpose. Each represents group identity through visual conventions. In the Dutch example, production constitutes membership – the guild produces something in common. In the CK One ad, consumption implies membership – we assume that the group shares use of the promoted fragrance. This is not to suggest that Calvin Klein consciously or unconsciously set out to imitate Ketel's painting, although CRK, their in-house ad agency, is certainly aware of Dutch art. Rather, I point to a resonance that one can build between the images, and identify an important visual antecedent of the CK One image.

I claim that this is one of the reasons that ads like CK One are so meaningful – they build on the visual past, remind us of the tradition of artistic expression, and re-present images that are celebrated and valued. For, in the Holland of the past, like today, "the visual culture was central to the life of society. One might say that the eye was a central means of self-representation and visual experience a central mode of self-consciousness" (Alpers 1984: xxv). Art historical traditions influence contemporary images directly and indirectly: directly through their impact on pictorial conventions, artistic and photographic training, and cultural capital of specific images. Furthermore, art history indirectly influences the current visual scene through its power as a cultural process, that, over time, produces a mode of representing and seeing the world.

Comparison: The rationale for comparison "is to call attention to the unique features of something by holding it up against something similar but significantly different" (Barnet 1997: 92). Several comparisons to the CK One ad will be made in the following section. Here I will discuss another photographer whose work is both important and relevant to the analysis. Robert Mapplethorpe, whose pictures included portraits of his friends and lovers informed by domination, leather, and sadomasochistic themes, is one of the most famous – and notorious – photographers of the twentieth century. Mapplethorpe's images, perhaps more than any other photographer, have come to represent a subculture's – the gay underground – way of life. His photographs explored the contexts of race, gender, unconventional sexuality, and the conventions of portraiture and often rejected the codes "through which identity, private as much as public, is assumed, determined, and declared (Clarke 1997: 117). The CK One ad shares a blank background, brightly lit subjects, and a way of representing the Other with Mapplethorpe's infamous X portfolio, which thrust Mapplethorpe into the political arena when its images of S & M and gay lifestyles were attacked as pornographic and obscene.

In this section, a thick description was presented to lay out art historical categories of analysis. In the following section, these descriptive insights will be used to develop a rich contextual interpretation of the CK One ad's many meanings to demonstrate its representational power – its poetics. Consuming difference provides an interpretive and evaluative framework for understanding the representational politics of ads like CK One.

Interpretation and evaluation

Race, class, and gender have emerged as three crucial contextual issues for interpretive work (e.g., Heller 1997). Although class is certainly invoked in these status-symbol ads, I focus mostly on gender and race, acknowledging that these facets interact within identity and culture (see Schroeder and Borgerson 2002). To formulate interpretive conclusions about the CK One ad's meanings, I draw on several cultural critics who write about identity and images. First, I briefly describe Goffman's brilliant work on gender advertisements. I utilize philosopher Susan Bordo's analyses of cultural images to complicate our thinking about issues of the body, gender, and race in advertising. Finally, I draw on the writings of Henry Giroux and bell hooks, two contemporary cultural critics who analyze race, gender, class, and sexuality in popular culture. Calling upon other critical interpretive work helps contextualize images within a cultural system of visual representation (Hall 1997). I conclude by placing CK One within a frame of consuming difference.

Gender

Gender refers to a "social concept referring to psychologically, sociologically, or culturally rooted traits, attitudes, beliefs, and behavioral tendencies.

Because gender is a pervasive filter through which individuals experience their social world, consumption activities are fundamentally gendered" (Bristor and Fischer 1993: 519). Gender is also a critical issue in art history and art criticism (e.g., Davis 1996). Goffman turned to advertising to demonstrate how gender roles are inscribed in what appear to be natural expressions, situations, and poses (Goffman 1979; Lemert and Branaman 1997). Several advertising studies have employed Goffman's work to investigate gender in ads (e.g., Kolbe and Albanese 1996; Schroeder and Borgerson 1998).

Like painted portraits, ads are carefully constructed for rhetorical effects. Goffman pointed out that ads are part of the real world and a powerful influence on our self-concepts, how we view right and wrong, and how we conceive of living a good life. Most importantly for this analysis, ads influence how we think about sex roles, male and female, what is sexy, and what will be seen as sexy and be desired by others. Goffman was interested in how gender is displayed – how male and female identities are represented in social interaction as well as visual images. However, a closer look provides insight into how advertisements represent and construct gender (see Schroeder 1998).

Gender is a critical marker of difference:

> Gender ... means knowledge about sexual difference. I use knowledge, following Foucault, to mean the understanding produced by cultures and societies of human relationships, in the case of those between men and women. Such knowledge is not absolute or true, but always relative.
>
> (Scott 1988: 2)

Goffman, in analyzing advertisements as well as social interaction, showed that "every physical surround, every box for social gatherings, necessarily provides materials than can be used in the display of gender and the affirmation of gender identity" (Goffman, in Lemert and Branaman 1997: 207).

What makes gender such an important issue in the CK One context is the clear gender identity of most American colognes. That is, colognes are marketed as an integral part of gender identity and sexual attraction – most fragrances are for a man *or* for a woman (cf. Stern and Schroeder 1994). Gender plays an important part in how consumers relate to products, advertising, and consumption. In the marketplace, scent is a critical marker for gender. One noticeable feature of the CK One campaign is that it seemed to deconstruct this connection – it's for a man or a woman, after all. However, Calvin Klein's other well-known scents, such as Obsession, are still marketed to specific genders – although a percentage of each is used by the non-targeted gender – and certainly not discontinued. CK One remains well within the target marketed realm – it is only one more market segment, that arguably does little to disrupt or question entrenched gender roles and gender segmentation.

Susan Bordo adds an important contextual issue to the interpretation. Bordo briefly discusses the CK One ad under consideration here as an example of a false diversity. She claims that it "seems to be making the visual point that whether you are male or female, young or old, gay or straight, black or white, you are required to have the same toned, adolescent-looking body" (Bordo 1997: 5). She argues that ideals of beauty reinforced by advertising and popular culture are damaging, particularly to women, a claim marketing scholars echo:

> Beauty not only divides women from men but also women from other women. While a man's looks embellish his worldly successes, a woman's defines her. Cosmetics do not merely state, "I am an attractive woman." Instead, they make women want to be attractive to men.
>
> (Joy and Venkatesh 1994: 351)

This stands in sharp contrast to the calculated indifference that models project with statements like: "I've never even thought about my body, never weighed myself" (Kate Moss in White 1994: 95). Bordo's approach moves away from a strict focus on the ad alone toward a culturally connected analysis informed by feminist scholarship and philosophical analysis:

> Once we recognize that we never respond only to particular body parts or their configuration but always to the meanings they carry for us, the old feminist charge of "objectification" seems inadequate to describe what is going on when women's bodies are depicted in sexualized or aestheticized ways. The notion of women-as-objects suggests the reduction of women to "mere" bodies, when actually what's going on is often far more disturbing than that, involving the depiction of regressive ideals of feminine behavior and attitude that go much deeper than appearance.
>
> (Bordo 1997: 124)

Race

An important contextual issue concerns how racial identity has been depicted in the history of art as well as advertising. CK One appears to break down racial barriers via its multicultural milieu. A relevant comparison is Benetton's ads, which also have captured the attention of critics and consumers alike through their use of provocative imagery. One commentator claims that within the trend of shock advertising, the positioning of CK One is similar to Benetton's graphic images of violence and social injustice (Teather 1995).

Social historian and prolific cultural critic Henry Giroux analyzed the Italian multinational Benetton's long-running "United Colors of Benetton" campaign and scrutinized how culturally loaded images of race, class, and gender work in a commercial context. In one Benetton ad, a black female torso, breasts exposed, is shown holding a naked white baby, nursing on the woman's breast. The woman is wearing only a cardigan, which is unbuttoned and pulled back, thus displaying her breasts for the baby as well as the viewer.

Giroux brings to bear a cultural analytic technique to underscore the racist, colonialist meanings pulsing through this image (Giroux 1994). Benetton claims to be promoting racial harmony and world peace, but if so, why would they choose this loaded image? Perhaps the CK One images are not quite so alarming as the Benetton campaigns, but I believe that by including images of marginalized segments of society some of the same stereotyping processes are at work (Schroeder and Borgerson 1999; Ramamurthy 1997).

A critical essay about other work by CK One photographer Meisel provides a contextual comparison to discuss racial and sexual stereotyping. bell hooks discusses the pop superstar Madonna's provocative book *Sex* which features photographs by Meisel (1994). The photographs that accompanied writing about various sexual scenarios – ostensibly directly from Madonna's imagination – share several features in common with CK One images. In many of the scenes, Madonna is shown interacting with black men and women in images reminiscent of the CK One ad – although far more sexually explicit. The photographs are reproduced in crisp black and white, and many have a plain background. Comparison to Meisel's other work provides more context for the CK One images, and hooks' analysis of how his images work in the *Sex* book show how consideration of matters beyond what is shown in the photograph contributes to an interpretive stance. hooks' discussion of the sexual and racial context of Meisel's photographs contribute to a reading of the CK One image that shares several features with the *Sex* photographs.

Class

Madonna – white, affluent, "beautiful" – experiences various sexual encounters, emerging unchanged, still Madonna. hooks writes:

> increasingly, Madonna occupies the space of the white cultural imperialist, talking on the mantle of the white colonial adventurer moving into the wilderness of black culture (gay and straight), of white gay subculture. Within these new and different realms of experience she never divests herself of white privilege. She maintains both the purity of her representation and her dominance.
>
> (1994: 20)

Thus, she serves as a kind of tour guide through a Disneyland of difference, assuring us that our own gender identities are not at risk. I believe Kate Moss serves the same tour guide function in the CK One series. Madonna consumes race in her *Sex* pictures – she experiences black lovers, uses them, but remains unaffected by the experience, contends hooks. She does not become black, or lose white status, rather, she serves as a guide for us, the viewer, to experience the stereotyped exotic erotic pleasures of a ethnic culture. Madonna's pictures exploit many clichés about blacks – oversexed, sexual experts, animal-like – and do nothing to assess, counter, or interrogate these notions. After reading – or at least looking at Madonna's book – the average consumer will only have stereotypes confirmed, not liberated. These images work to reproduce cultural differences:

> Though *Sex* appears to be culturally diverse, people of color are strategically located, always and only in a subordinate position. Our images and culture appear always in a context that mirrors racist hierarchies. We are always present to white desire.
>
> (hooks 1994: 21)

Thus, the rich, white pop star Madonna consumes race and alternative sexuality, according to hooks.

Theoretical issues: consuming difference

In the CK One ad, Kate Moss serves as a visual anchor. She is well known, non-threatening (especially when compared to others in the ad), her image is that of a famous supermodel. In other words, she represents the world of cosmetics, fashion, and glamour. As Calvin Klein said of his famous model: "there's an air of reality about Kate that sets her apart. She represents the generation that is now coming along, and she appeals to them – her attitude, her look and her style is very easy, natural and unaffected" (quoted in White 1994: 90). She can fit in anywhere. She has entered this world of difference for a mainstream audience, and is able to maintain her identity in the midst of difference. Thus, those normally outside the "different" segment are unchanged by the experience of this ad. They do not risk actually becoming different, racially or sexually. It is unclear why white skinheads – who are associated with intolerance in popular discourse – are lumped in with others, especially black women. What are they were doing in this group, and why are they so angry? The lesbian image from the fold-out disappears, along with the promise (threat) of homosexual activity, much as gays, lesbians, and bisexuals have historically disappeared. In the mainstream world of major brand advertising, gay and lesbian consumers are largely absent, reflecting a culture of homophobia and hetereosexism (Frye 1983).

CK One ads give mainstream viewers an opportunity to consume difference without risk to their own identity. Goffman and Bordo's analytic perspectives help frame broader cultural issues derived from Giroux and hooks. By representing these "different" characters in one ad, I believe Calvin Klein is lumping them together, equating stereotypes of difference – black, lesbian, tattooed, androgynous – and playing them off the image of Moss. This lumping, or designating as "different" or "other" deprives the group represented of individual expression (Gordon 1995). That is, difference – multiculturalism – is represented as a commodity that superficially corresponds to differences in lived experience. As Goldman argues, advertising "continuously reproduces the appearance of difference" within the fashion system (1992: 152).

In comparison to most advertisements the world of CK One appears to be an unhappy place, populated by dissatisfied, angry people. In the words of one of my students "it looks like a freak show, as if the only thing these people have in common is that they look strange." This echoes an art historian's claim about representations of difference in fine art:

> The rhetorical traditions of Western painting have long traded in the coin of social class and racial difference as a means of marking human value. Thus there is a radical distinction between portraits ... and scenes from everyday life, especially those involving the lower social orders, representing not individuals, but types – simply "people" defined en masse.
>
> (Leppert 1997: 173)

The CK One imagery signaled a shift in advertising representation toward grungy looking models – a short-lived trend, but one that paved the way for shock advertising.

The CK One ad is like a casting call – it visually rounds up different-looking people, removes them from any context (except the ad) and presents them for consumption. The popular musical "A Chorus Line" comes to mind, with its drama about performance, casting, and playing parts. The drama metaphor is an important one in advertising (cf. Stern 1994; Stern and Schroeder 1994), and seems apt for an ad that plays with gender. Contemporary gender theorists have described gender as performative, focusing on the social construction of gender as an embodied identity (Butler 1990). Gender is also called a role, as in gender roles. In one sense, we might view this ad as what happened when Calvin Klein put out a request for different-looking models. Kate Moss was hired to play Kate Moss. She stands alone – enacting a persona that has helped elevate her to superstardom (White 1994). Someone else showed up to portray an angry black woman. Another aspiring model practiced being fashionable, yet aloof.

Kate Moss's expression indicates that she does not belong in this world of difference, she seems bored and unaffected by the others in the ad. She is with them but not of them, she emerges as a voyeur, she looks and asks that we look at her looking (hooks 1994). She is present in an image that encourages consuming the exotic other (Borgerson and Schroeder 1997; Lalvani 1995). She is merely more well paid than most painters' models ever were. In this analysis, I do not mean to imply that Kate Moss herself is somehow responsible for the ad's effects, the ad scenario, or the cosmetics industry's practices. Men, largely, still retain control of the image-producing industries (Ohmann 1996). However, as a spokesperson and icon of fashion, her image contributes to much of the meaning construction.

In the CK One ad, homosexuality is also sublimated to heterosexual pleasure, and becomes merely an exploration for Moss's (heterosexual) experience. Her image usurps the others through her fame, her sexual identity – inscribed by her presence in Calvin Klein's more heterosexual-appearing advertisements – and her feminine demeanor, diminutive, thin, and submissive. The image teases with a potential lesbian encounter, then retreats, leaving us unsatisfied, discontent. Moss's control over her body – demonstrated here in her aloof pose – is of paramount importance to her fame and success. Her statements about her body and eating, such as the one quoted above, are standard model fare, calculated to create an aura of naturalness for their valuable image; these calculated claims are not particularly surprising nor illuminating about her lived experience.

CK One is not marketed as a specifically gay, lesbian, or bisexual scent (although a substantial percentage of CK One consumers certainly represent these groups) – perhaps that might be too small or risky a target market for a national advertising campaign. Moss's image in the media – the only way most of us will ever know her – is fueled by her appearances in fashion shows, other advertisements, and magazine covers. All of these point to her heterosexuality, her whiteness, and her thinness – an identity of a desired female. Her flirtation with a lesbian encounter notwithstanding, she remains Kate Moss – aloof, white, "normal." Drawing upon their thick description of the ad's visual elements, Pinkel and her colleagues conclude that its presentation of gender images does nothing more than perpetuate and reinforce gender stereotypes (Pinkel *et al.* 1995).

By using stereotyped models, CK One draws on codes of appearance influenced by social relations, the media, and prejudice (cf. Jhally 1987). In one variation of the CK One ad, we see a big, burly white guy with a shaved head – coded "skinhead" – talking to a black woman. Given no other information to contradict cultural representations, we may assume that they are not having a lively conversation about a mutual friend. Within the media, skinhead is a codeword for racist, neo-Nazi, and intolerance – iconographic functions rooted in representational practice. This is not to say that all white men with shaved heads are in fact racist, only that the overpowering image of skinhead is associated with violent fanaticism. In the absence of disrupting information within the ad, the reading of this image is overdetermined (Goldman 1992). In addition, until recently, advertising showed very few individuals who looked like this. This fact accentuates his difference – he is pitted against traditional male models that populate fragrance ads. In showing these two figures engaged in what appears to be a heated discussion, the ad further draws on stereotyped conventions of race and gender. Imagine these two as lovers, smiling, arms draped around one another. Or perhaps both laughing together, bodies engaged in mutual pleasure. These images *might* serve to disrupt stereotypical notions of gender, race, and ideology. But this is not what is represented. Instead, we see a white man arguing with a black women, physically engaging with her space, using his mass to make his point. They are portrayed as natural antagonists, playing into cultural stereotypes of racial and gender relations (see Davis 1981). Given the skinhead's large size, and aggressive in-your-face gesture grounded to the social reality of the historical and current oppression of black women, it is not difficult to interpret this image as racial oppression. Given the history of white men's exploitation of black women, for slave labor, for sex, for wet nurse, for nannies, the meaning of this image – contextualized within a racist world – must be read as reflecting, not challenging, the *status quo* (cf. Gordon 1997).

In the CK One campaign difference is presented as a consumable entity. The CK One image includes stereotypes of difference – the angry black woman, exotic black men, brawny skinheads, emaciated model – that stand in contrast to the usual representations of white, heterosexual consumers that have dominated advertising imagery (see Bristor *et al.* 1995; Pinkel *et al.* 1995). Goldman refers to this phenomenon as "commodity difference" in describing how advertising "continuously reproduces the appearance of difference" (1992). Furthermore, close visual attention to the models in the image reveals that several are repeated within the ad. It seems as if the group depicted is indeed a small one – they had to use several members twice to fill out their numbers. In any case, this ad seems to reinforce the notion that representing difference is a viable advertising strategy. Might these types of ads make multicultural identities more visible via mass media representation? I cannot resolve this important question here, but I can point to the majority of Calvin Klein's imagery that in no way disrupts sex, race, and gender stereotypes.

Consuming difference through images, cologne, clothing, is not equivalent to standing up for difference. To consume CK One and its advertising imagery does nothing to challenge heterosexism and homophobia, racism, and sexism. It is unclear what position Calvin Klein, man and company, takes on these highly charged issues – what is clear is Calvin Klein's consistent success in generating media attention via what I call the *strategic use of scandal* (Schroeder 2001). For all its multicultural appearance, the CK One ads portrays difference in contrast to the idealized imagery of advertising. CK One voyeuristically presents those people that society does accept. By taking those stereotypes out of context, the ad trivializes their true or at least possible difference. Lumping them together, the ad makes it seem as if they belong to one category – other. The CK One image works much like Western art's representation of racial and cultural difference that until recently provided "no hint of paradox, problem, or criticism. Indeed, it celebrates a system that operates to keep the racist linkages intact ..." (Leppert 1997: 209).

Methodological synthesis

Techniques drawn from art history, particularly photographic criticism, were applied to an exemplar to demonstrate a rich analytic framework to analyze advertising. Connections were made from the CK One ad to art historical traditions of group portraiture, altarpieces, iconography, and fine art photography. Further comparisons were made to discuss identity and representation through the work of contemporary cultural theorists. This approach assumes four things about advertising images. First, ads can be considered as aesthetic objects. This is not to claim that advertisements are necessarily art, nor that they are not primarily marketing tools. Rather, it acknowledges the creativity and thought that goes into the production of most national advertising campaigns. Second, I situate advertising within a system of visual representation that creates meaning – often beyond what may be intended by the photographer and advertising agency. Third, a visual analysis informed by art history does not compete for authority with other approaches. Rather it represents an useful, distinct level of analysis, particularly suited to sort out meaning construction in visual images. Interpretive work *requires* personal engagement, quirks, biases, and most of all, passionate interest. Fourth, ads not only are aesthetic objects, they can also be considered socio-political artifacts. These categories – aesthetic and political – are often constituted as mutually exclusive (Solomon-Godeau 1991). My analysis attempts to locate advertisements within a complex signifying system.

In this chapter, I tried to demonstrate some basic building blocks for a method of apprehending visual imagery. These include description, interpretation, evaluation, and theorization. Description requires sustained attention to the visual image to capture what it depicts. Interpretation is more subjective, but ought to emerge from descriptive details. For example, the careful description of Kate Moss's appearance led Pinkel *et al.* (1995) to interpret the image in sexually coded terms. Evaluation often focuses on issues of value and quality. In this analysis, I have instead stressed an evaluation of the ad's social psychological meanings. Theory construction may develop from the previous three activities. In this analysis, I presented a theory about how the CK One ad contributes to a discourse about consuming difference which guided the interpretation.

Many insights emerge from this analysis that would be difficult to generate with other approaches. The link to the Dutch art tradition serves to remind us that advertisements have a visual and historical genealogy. For example, the CK One ad can be understood within the art genre of the portrait, particularly guild portraits associated with the "Dutch masters" – largely a male tradition. The form of the ad is, of course, situated within the world of fashion, specifically fashion photography, that is largely a feminine realm, that is, women's fashion dominates the fashion scene. I propose that the juxtaposition of these gendered genres contribute to the representation – and commingling – of gender within the CK One ad. Quoting or mimicking an art historical tradition helps ground it for the viewer, drawing associations to the visual tradition. Furthermore, although advertisements often strive to present a new fashion, they still must establish some link to the past, some sense of familiarity between the consumer and the product (Lears 1994). By linking a new image to an old tradition, CK One establishes itself through visual representations that transcend the here and now.

The fold-out format of the CK One ad is used often in fashion magazines. An interesting comparison can be made to the form of a religious altarpiece, which also opens to reveal other images within. Once again, I am not claiming that all CK One viewers exclaimed "a polyptych!" upon first seeing the ad, but I do find the connections useful in understanding the formal context of the ad. Furthermore, Kate Moss and other fashion models are certainly worshipped in our culture where fame is highly valued and rewarded. We see some of the same meaning-production processes at work in the formal properties of the CK One ad and a Renaissance altarpiece – covering, revealing, and isolating individual figures. We also see similar social processes of image construction, worship, and icon making (for a more detailed analysis of connections between Renaissance art and contemporary images, see Schroeder and Borgerson 2001).

Is CK One a resistant image?

My students consistently see Calvin Klein as taboo breaking, encouraging gender experimentation, and norm questioning; the press generally labeled the CK One campaign transgressive. Is it? Can advertising really afford to subvert gender roles by creating gender-neutral products and campaigns? Does it help things to have images of difference within the mainstream media? Can Calvin Klein be a force for change? Some would contend that any portrayal that is not explicitly stereotyped helps break down negative cultural assumptions about marginalized groups. Certainly, it makes for more interesting and provocative advertisements. However, the cosmetics industry, which flourishes on sexual stereotypes, sexual dualism, and insecurity about appearance seems unsuited to break down stereotypes about gender roles, racial identity, and sexual orientation.

Consumer resistance is another critical matter for interpreting advertisements and consumer culture within the consuming difference concept. In one recent study, students claimed to resist and often reject the "meanings" of particular fashions and brand names. Overall, however, the authors claim that "consumers appropriate fashion discourses in ways that 'reinscribe the culturally conventional meanings of garments, styles, and fashionable brands' within gender stereotypes, but leave room for individual resistance" (Thompson and Haytko 1997: 16). At issue here is how purchasing and using CK One may or may not lead to "resistance" – of gender roles, of media influence, of corporate control of consumer desire (cf. Thompson and Hirschman 1995). At the level of the individual, resistance is difficult to quibble with, but at a broader social level, campaigns such as CK One co-opt consumer resistance and turn it back on itself. In this way "corporations cleverly use the images and words, style and look of rebellion to market their products through buying mass-produced goods that somehow symbolize nonconformity" (Frank 1997: 19).

Paradoxically, consumers visually proclaim their difference by wearing mass-produced scents, shoes, and global brand names. Consumption is a major process of constructing a self-concept, and cologne is closely linked to sexual identity, self-image, and gender roles (Schroeder 1998). Like a novel or movie, advertisements let us feel as if we are participating or at least experiencing a different reality – it is much easier to buy cologne than it is to change one's appearance or lifestyle. Furthermore, these images work against political values, constructing, reflecting, and reinforcing a consumer lifestyle-based world in which "social change is replaced by a change in images. The freedom to consumer a plurality of images and goods is equated with freedom itself" (Sontag 1977: 179).

Consumer goods also serve as a stabilizing object-code, disarming innovations and diminishing their potential for change (McCracken 1988). When marginalized groups, such as lesbians, gays, bikers, or skateboarders, use consumer goods to declare their difference, they use a representational system that is easily recognizable by society (cf. Ritson and Elliot 1999). Thus:

> The act of protest is finally an act of participation in a set of shared symbols and meanings. Embraced by culture and its media of communication, the "act" of protest becomes an act of rhetorical conformity. The use of the object-code by radical social groups has the unintended effect of finding them a place in the larger cultural system.
>
> (McCracken 1988: 133–4)

Consuming brand names to differentiate oneself – one of CK One's messages – is an interesting paradox of consumer culture.

Consumers *are* active in the meaning constructive process, creating meanings that are sensible to them in particular life circumstances (Scott 1994b). Many people are unaware of the history and iconology of images, and often interpret advertising for their own uses: "the media – particularly the new media – are accessible to and used frequently by less powerful members of society – children, ethnic minorities, and marginal members of society – to create realities that more satisfactorily fulfill their needs" (Edelstein 1997: 3). Thus, it may be that CK One is a positive force in representing people and images that have been absent from advertising imagery. My reading does not precludes images like CK One to serve identity-affirming functions for individual consumers, and I do not mean to suggest that CK One has not shaken up the iconography of contemporary advertising.

This analysis is centered around Anglo-American culture. Calvin Klein is a United States company with virtual worldwide recognition; Kate Moss is British. The image, with its absence of text, cultural scenarios, or country-specific markers, is readily transportable within the global marketplace. Further analysis is required to situate this reading for other cultures, particularly in light of the rise of global capitalism, which makes it important to study how identity and aesthetics are transported cross-culturally (Joy and Venkatesh 1994).

Gender identity remains central to the world of advertising. It is difficult to conceive of most products without male and female target markets. Furthermore, many consumers do respond negatively to the way specific groups are portrayed in advertisements (e.g., Beatty 1995). Many consumers resist gender stereotypes, and gender roles themselves may be changing:

> However, we do not yet live in a post-gender age. Avant-garde magazines may offer images that unsettle and challenge ideas about masculinity and femininity and that ultimately may alter them. But most of us live in social contexts that exact stiff penalties for resisting or failing to conform to existing conventions, and that offer significant social and material rewards (in jobs, sexual desirability, and the like) for those who successfully obey them.
>
> (Bordo 1997: 150)

An important issue to consider is how the art historical antecedents and connections discussed affect consumers' perceptions. Most consumers are not necessarily visually literate, and art historical references and conventions may not consciously inform their viewing of an ad. However, even if the target market for CK One has no experience of Dutch group portraiture, for example, the art directors and photographers responsible for producing the ad certainly were aware of art historical referents discussed here. The CK One ad is one example of a spectacular combination of old and new representational systems, or what has been called "complicated contemporaneity" (Polan 1986). I believe that interdisciplinary readings are critical for explicating particular advertising campaigns.

But that is not enough. In addition, two other analytic processes are necessary for the study of the culture of visual representation (Polan 1986). We need to understand the cultural and visual context of ads such as this within the flow of mass culture. We also must realize the role advertising plays in both the political economy and in the constitution of consuming subjects.

Philosopher Margaret Urban Walker developed the concept of "stereo-graphy" to refer to the interrelationship of representation to ethical issues. Stereo-graphy refers to ways of representing groups of people in particular ways that "school us in perceiving certain patterns of human expression and comportment in particular ways or not at all" (Walker 1998: 313). Walker discusses how images of those in minority groups by majority groups are often governed by "practices of representing certain people in certain ways, where these ways are consistently different from the ways *other* people are represented" (ibid.: 309). She takes pains not to suggest that these representational practices "are the sole or even primary causes of moral mis-recognition or mis-treatments [and] might be symptomatic or expressive of prejudices propagated and sustained by other means" (ibid.: 313). Walker's theory is an important component of an interpretive project that takes the signifying power of images seriously.

Visual representation of cultural groups is fraught with difficult issues. Many argue that by making marginalized groups visible, ad campaigns like CK One help create awareness and respect for cultural differences. Others point out that often representation leads to stereotyping and offensive images, particularly when those images are used to sell products. Advertising is a powerful player in these debates. Firms and ad agencies have gained an increased awareness of the politics of representation, and the world that advertising portrays is changing. Art historical studies such as this can help place these issues in a broader cultural and historical context – for the history of art is replete with examples of exclusion and mis-representation. Acknowledging the visual past of advertising is one path to greater understanding about advertising as a representational and communicative system.

Embedded in this analysis is my contention that CK One offers viewers a chance to consume difference. This concept was utilized to point to insights that each element of the visual approach can reveal, and to argue that CK One does not disrupt categories of difference. In other words, the CK One ad presents a multicultural world from a dominant cultural point of view. The representation of gender, race, and identity in the campaign is an emblem of consuming difference. Given the iconic form of the CK One ad, the way it functions as an altarpiece, and the way that the models are portrayed in a group portrait; and given the connections drawn to Avedon, Mapplethorpe, and the cultural identity issues discussed – it is clear the CK One ad's meanings as a visual representation are powerful and multi-layered.

Visual consumption, identity, and interpretation

The CK One image struck a responsive chord among consumers. The ad appears in posters, postcards, and is now referred to obliquely in current ad campaigns (e.g., Kinosian 1997). To fully understand why ads like this leave such a mark, it is crucial to bring diverse tools to bear on the problem. In particular, art historical theories of identity construction and representation seem particularly relevant for understanding how brands and products fit into consumer identity.

Art-centered visual approaches to consumer research offer a means of developing unique insights into advertising imagery's prominence within visual culture. Art historical techniques help articulate a grammar of visual representation that producers and consumers use to decode consumer messages. Regardless of intention, ads often invoke art historical themes, settings, and references that contribute to their meaning – as an advertisement for a particular product as well as a cultural artifact. As discussed here, meaning in ads is not wholly contained within the image itself. Furthermore, advertising's success has depended on a way of seeing ads as connected to the larger worlds of art museums, movies, and lived experience (Lears 1994). Increased sensitivity to visual elements and their social, historical, and cultural contexts is critical to appreciating the power of advertising imagery.

This analysis provides a look at the possibilities of a visual approach to consumer research. The CK One ads appeared on television, but this analysis did not consider these images. Film was not discussed here, nor television and video as art forms. Film theory shares a concern for visual representation with art history and photographic criticism. Furthermore, film has often been excluded from fine art canons and considerations, much like advertising. Although photography is the most pervasive form of communication in the world, most of us have had little formal training in the historical background of photography, the processes of photographic production, or the function of pictorial conventions. Advertising, like photography, seems to present a world that just is, even though photographic images are cropped, selected, and edited for consumption. A fully developed art-centered research program will include issues of film theory and criticism, graphic design, prints, and artistic production, to name a few.

7 The fetish in contemporary visual culture

Advertising ripples through the culture, widely circulating information about the social world, largely through photographic representation – a key concern for reflections on visual issues in contemporary society. Furthermore, advertising has become a complex part of visual culture, blending seamlessly into the visual landscape, invoking a range of issues formerly reserved for the political sphere, and implicating itself in almost all information transfer. The debate of the last decade over whether advertising should be allowed on the Internet seems quaint, as the Internet has emerged as *the* marketing tool of the twenty-first century, seemingly. Ads themselves are displayed in galleries and museums, blurring distinctions between fine and applied art. Recently, advertisements have become collectibles, and one particular campaign stands above the rest in this regard – Absolut Vodka.

This chapter takes a look at an icônic element of consumption and introduces a conceptual framework for understanding the fetish in contemporary visual culture. Fetishism is a useful concept for analyzing visual consumption; representations of fetish objects occupy a substantial place in the contemporary visual landscape, and images are imbued with fetish-like attributes in art, advertising, and film. Moreover, the image constitutes a major presence in the modern market – goods are sold via images, and consumers buy products as much for their symbolic qualities as for their utilitarian aspect. This analysis conceptualizes advertising as the engine of consumption. I do not mean to equate visual culture with advertising, nor do I underestimate advertising's power outside the purely visual realm. I suggest that advertising – the face of capitalism – is the dominant communication force today, and as such it deserves close scrutiny from visual culture scholars. Rather than a secondary offshoot of fine art, or merely a management tool for selling things, advertising represents the epitome of visual power. Furthermore, visual trends and conceptual themes often emanate from the advertising realm, rather than (always) trickling down from the rarified world of high art. Within the world of advertising imagery, photography, fetishism, and cultural values intermingle. The fetish represents a critical concept for understanding visual culture.

The fetish object often symbolizes control and release, power and helplessness, sexuality and infantilism. In clinical terms, a fetish may be a dysfunctional response to sexuality, eventually replacing human contact for arousal. Fetishism is associated with displacement and disavowal – sexual energy becomes directed toward something other than the genitals – a substitute that is charged with sexual power and attraction (Hall 1997). Examples, of course, abound, but a mainstay of the visual culture of fetish is tight-fitting clothing, particularly made from materials such as leather and rubber. In popular terms, fetishism often refers to a psychological relationship or an intra-individual practice, but it can fruitfully be considered a kind of cultural discourse (Apter and Pietz 1993).

I will use two compelling print advertisements as a point of departure to theorize the fetish in visual consumption. I am interested in how photography reifies objects in a fetish-like manner, as well as how advertising capitalizes on cultural stereotypes about fetishism to both communicate certain messages, and create novel associations in viewers. I do not adhere to a strict paradigmatic view of the fetish; rather I draw on basic conceptions of fetish objects from psychoanalytic and anthropological approaches to fetishism as a cultural issue. I am most interested in how the fetish functions in contemporary visual culture, and how advertisers create powerful and positive images for their products via fetishistic themes. My examples are meant to be both illustrative and knowledge building, I do not include them merely to point out exemplars of fetishism in visual culture, for I believe that a case study approach produces cultural knowledge about visual phenomena. Previous work in this vein includes literary and art historical analyses of a famous Paco Rabanne cologne ad (Stern and Schroeder 1994), Victoria's Secret catalog imagery (Schroeder and Borgerson 1998) and the tourist images of Hawaii (Schroeder and Borgerson 1999).

The chapter introduces two images from the Absolut Vodka print ad campaign for Absolut Au Kurant. I chose these ads because Absolut is a popular, widely heralded, long-running, and iconic ad campaign that demonstrates the triumph of image over product function. Absolut ads images are readily available on the Internet, and several books have been written about the brand (i.e., Lewis 1996; Hamilton 2000). Furthermore, the two ads under consideration feature a black leather corset and a black garter belt – fetish staples – photographed in a way that clearly makes a fetish association of the images. I then turn to a consideration of fetish clothing, and I present a theoretical framework of fetishism in visual culture.

Fetishism generally revolves around particular items of clothing. I argue that fetish clothing often is inscribed with three significant qualities. First, it is liminal. Fetishized clothing straddles the divide between nature and culture. For example, leather is a natural material; it comes from animals. To convert an animal skin into a wearable garment, however, requires a cultural and technological process that transforms leather into a liminal object. Fetish clothing is often tight, or worn close to the skin, which express its liminal qualities. Shininess also visually underscores the liminal quality of fetish apparel. Shininess signifies a manufactured characteristic that contrasts with the material's natural essence. Second, fetish clothing is most often dyed or colored black – black leather is the most common color available. Black, of course, is a racial signifier, one that works to emphasize the erotic, sexualized connotation of blackness in semiotic terms. Blackness contributes to the fetishization of clothing in part due to the exoticization of black skin by the Western world. Third, photographic techniques such as close cropping, lighting, and depth of field imbue photographed fetish objects – or those made so via photography – with an additional layer of fetish qualities. I discuss my approach in relation to Abigail Solomon-Godeau's conception of the fetish as a confluence of factors, including photographic practice and reception (1993). This discussion is followed by broader considerations of the fetish's role in visual culture, with specific emphasis on the fetish as a conceptual tool to understand visual rhetoric and the contemporary market. The chapter concludes with a discussion of the role of photography in visual culture, and makes suggestions for further inquiry.

Illustrative example: Absolut Vodka

Absolut Vodka has produced one of the most successful and celebrated ad campaigns of the past twenty years. The campaign, which included a new bottle design, transformed an obscure Swedish snaps into one of the leading global brands in any product category (see Hamilton 2000). Absolut brannvin was the former name of Absolut Vodka; in Swedish, it meant pure and unflavored vodka. The Absolut brand has several line extensions, such as Absolut Citron – a lemon-infused vodka – as well as Absolut Kurant, which is flavored with red currants.

The liquid product has not changed, but its image has been catapulted into the heights of brand ecstasy by a consistent, long-running marketing strategy that centered around an ongoing ad series that featured the Absolut bottle in a wide variety of characters and guises (Lewis 1996). Many artists have been commissioned to produce an Absolut ad; perhaps the most famous example is Absolut Warhol, introduced in 1985. Absolut ads are collected and displayed by an enthusiastic group of admirers, and ads are offered for sale on many Internet sites devoted to the Absolut ads (e.g., http://www.absolutcollectors.com). Absolut has been aggressive in supporting the arts community and the gay community in a promotional effort to link its brand with hip trends. An Internet search revealed an Absolut Fetish ad in the form of a black rubber insert imprinted with the Absolut bottle in the British gay magazine *Attitude* (see http://www.absolutad.com/davezzz98.htm).

Absolut Au Kurant, a version of the popular and critically acclaimed Absolut campaign, will serve as an in-depth case study. The positioning of the Absolut Kurant brand has evolved into a cutting-edge image; ads often feature cool nightclubs or sexual references. Websites featuring Absolut often feature racy recipes for Absolut Kurant flavored drinks such as Swedish Pinkie, Absolut Sex, and Purple Stealth. Absolut Kurant also holds an "Absolut Visions" art competition each year, offering cash grants and a group exhibition to winners, selected from art schools such as the Art Institute of Chicago and the Rhode Island School of Design.

The images

Two Absolut Au Kurant ads will constitute the main target of my analysis. One depicts a tight, shiny black leather corset, with lavender laces forming the shape of an Absolut bottle as they crisscross and tightly bind the model, and the other shows a leg dressed in a black stocking and garter belt, with a tiny purple Absolut bottle-shaped garter clip holding up the stocking. Both of these ads appeared in the *New York Times Magazine* in 1997. These provocative, erotically charged images reinforce the Absolut Kurant brand as representing cutting-edge sexuality through the use of familiar tropes of bodily representation and photographic techniques of cropping and highlighting. Furthermore, an undercurrent of S & M and fetishism is present in the images. One visual message is that opening the Absolut bottle by unlacing or unfastening its representation in the ads leads to sexual activity, or at least an undressed model.

The corset ad

The first ad is a color photograph of a human torso dressed in a black leather corset with lavender lacing, tightly cropped to show only a small patch of bare white skin, perhaps an inch at the top and two inches at the bottom of the image. The words "Absolut Au Kurant" run along the bottom of the ad, in lavender capital letters that match the corset's lacing. The ad is brightly lit. A subtle lavender filter gives the corset a purplish cast. The corset's lacing hooks are arranged so that the lavender laces form the shape of a bottle – the Absolut Vodka bottle – with a bow tied at the bottom of the corset. Thus, the laces represent the bottle in the ad.

The laces criss-cross the figure, tightly binding the model, pulling in the stomach and pushing up the chest. These laces signify the effort that goes into being corseted; usually two people are required to restrict the waist as tightly as shown. The laces are laced perfectly flat through a series of shiny metal rings, or eyes, which are riveted to the leather. Their bottle-like simulation is familiar from Absolut's ubiquitous and long-running marketing campaign. Thus the laces echo the containing properties of the glass bottle – they hold the "contents" only to release when undone. The laces also suggest striptease or foreplay. Dressed like this, it will take a while to undo the laces. This sense of slow undressing serves well as a visual signifier of desire and temptation. An invitation is issued: open the bottle in the ad by undoing the laces; the bow that secures them looks awfully insubstantial. Thus, the viewer participates in sexual ritual.

In a fairly simple and straightforward image, Absolut links itself to leather corsets, fetishism, alternative sexuality, and sexual allure. The message of the ad centers on the resonance between opening an Absolut bottle and consuming the product and opening the black corset and consummating a relationship. The lace-bottle opens up the person within, undressing for potential intimate activity. The Absolut bottle serves as the key prop for sexual readiness. The magic properties of the Absolut bottle are hinted at by these elements, a common theme in liquor advertisements (Williamson 1978).

The stocking ad

The basic layout of the Au Kurant ad with stockings is similar to the corset ad. Both ads highlight body parts and each tightly crops the image so that no facial identity shows. Both have a similar color scheme of black and lavender. Each shows a glimpse of skin, in this case a stretch of the thigh not covered by black stockings and a short, black skirt. The clip that hold up the black stocking resembles a tiny lavender Absolut bottle. The bottle-clip holds the stocking that contains the leg. Opening the garter fastener frees the leg from the confinement of the stocking – a basic move scripted in many music videos, films, and pornography.

These ads say "alcohol provides access." Absolut is the key to undressing. Opening the bottle – in this case the garter clip bottle – paves the way for sex. Both corset and garter exemplify old-fashioned garments – designed in an age before the women's movement, before spandex, and before aerobics. The corset, for example, became a symbol of oppression, molding women to an ideal as confining as the garment. However, there are other ways to read this image.

Queering the image

Lavender is the adopted color of the gay rights movement. In the corset ad, we see only the back of the model, most corsets lace in the rear. Therefore, it is difficult to tell – visually – whether the model is a man or a woman. True, the upper body reveals a feminine shape, complete with small waist, but this could be the corset restricting a male body or the camera angle. Unquestionably, most viewers would see a woman, for corsets are a feminine item, linked to female identity. However, men wear corsets too. Most corset manufacturers feature several models designed for men. Some corset-wearing men are looking to hold in a growing gut or perhaps help a chronically sore back, but many are participating in a bit of gender-bending by donning a fetishistic item, usually off limits for male attire.

Corsets change the body's shape when worn tightly laced. They whittle the waist and exaggerate the hips and breast to achieve an "hourglass" figure – an archetype of desirable female form. Likewise, a corset is a convenient way for men to acquire a "female" form; corsets can reduce men's waists, too. A corset will also push a man's breast up and out, a start on obtaining a womanly bosom. Corsets were originally made from cotton or linen, and were usually white or off-white. A leather corset is clearly not an old fashioned type. It is meant for today's sexual libertine. Furthermore, the black corset is an icon of leather-influenced sex. By casting a black leather corset in the Absolut Au Kurant ad, the ad director signified transgressive hipness rather than merely waist reduction. The corset depicted is fetishized as an object unto itself, made expressly for sexual display, rather than concealment or restriction.

Hence, the ad's figure can be read as a man in a corset. Is he gay? Not necessarily. One scenario would be a female lover – or perhaps a dominatrix – has laced him into the corset. Perhaps he is wearing it for his pleasure, for the feeling of being firmly held in by tight leather. Absolut ads, of course, can be read as "gay" ads. The corseted figure could be lesbian or bisexual. It is clear that viewers are able to project a range of visions onto this image and in the absence of clearly identifiable body features it could easily be seen as a male, opening up a range of possible interpretations and responses.

In the stocking ad as well there is no specific reference to the model's sex, other than the highly feminine clothing. Of course, men once wore hosiery – as any viewer of a film set in the Elizabethan era can plainly see – but now full-length hosiery is mostly reserved for women. Stockings and garter belts – or stockings and suspenders – are staple props of pinup photography, "R" rated films, music videos, and pornography. A shot of a gartered leg glimpsed through a slit skirt has become an overused trope to titillate (mostly) male desire. However, stockings and garters are also a mainstay of male efforts to appear female, from drag shows to Hallowe'en costumes. Nothing prevents the viewer from identifying this model as a male masquerading as a female or perhaps experimenting with sexy, feminized – and taboo – clothing. Photographed differently, the ad would not be as open to such interpretations. Like the corset image, the tight cropping produces a malleable picture of interpretive possibilities, including a knowing nod to male cross-dressing or gay fashion. Clearly, Absolut Kurant has created compelling imagery that works differently for different target markets (cf. Lewis 1996). Given Absolut's presence in the gay market, this is not surprising. These fetishistic images are infused with alternative sexual energy, which is a cornerstone of the Absolut brand strategy.

The fetish

The fetish is a useful concept for analyzing visual consumption. It illuminates important aspects of consumers' relationships with products, as well as how marketers create objects of desire. In the magical realm of advertising goods are often infused with fetish qualities Products are worshipped for their ability to complete the self, to help the user gain satisfaction – or even ecstasy – and revered for their capacity to project an image. In this way, goods function similarly (in a psychoanalytic sense) to the fetish object, which promises gratification but ultimately is unable to deliver, forever displaced within a fetish relationship. Further, a fetishized relationship, in some cases, interferes with the ability to have more "human" relations. Fetish items are typically linked to sexuality. Fetishized articles are usually contextually isolated; the shoe that by itself arouses, the disembodied body part, the black stocking disconnected from any recognizable body.

I am not proposing a theory of fetishism *per se*, rather I am interested in how the fetish is visually represented, particularly in contemporary advertising, as well as how fetishism interacts with photography and the circuit of visual culture. Photography has also been called a fetish. In the words of one writer, commenting on the work of Barthes: "Like a fetish [...] the shoe or dress of the person depicted – expresses and stands for the viewer's desire and, metonymically, for his or her experience of the photograph itself" (Weissberg 1997: 109). Photography further abstract objects, compounded by their fetish potential.

Two factors underlie the visual power of fetish: associations made through repeated usage of stock items in fashion, photography, and pornography and what I call the *liminal* element of fetish clothing. The word liminal reflects a gap, a space between, or an edge. Liminal zones are often spaces of uncertainly, creativity, danger, and passion. The space between – a space to be entered or crossed – can be exciting and unnerving simultaneously. Many fetish objects – particularly items of clothing – represent a powerful liminal zone. Shoes, boots, corsets, stockings are typical fetish items – usually colored black or bright red. In popular discourse fetish clothing is usually desired by men on women.

Stockings are liminal items. Extremely close fitting, a stocking accentuates and conceals the leg, both revealing and covering the wearer. Further, the space at the top of the thigh that is left uncovered – save for the taut garter straps that hold up the stocking – represents another between zone. This seems to be a key in the fetishization of garters and stockings, that a small patch of skin remains bare, unclothed. Stockings were once made of silk, a natural product transformed by manufacturing into a wide range of textiles and garments. Today most stockings are made of nylon; furthermore most hosiery worn are pantyhose without the need for a garter belt to keep them up on the wearer's leg. A myriad of things can be fetishized – perhaps anything – but I will concentrate on fetish clothing's iconic implications of the fetish in visual consumption.

Fetishism in visual culture

The visual vocabulary of fetish has become a staple of the culture industries, television, fashion, film, music video, comic books, and advertising, that draw on the cultural stereotype of the fetishist, a male whose sexual identity is linked with the fetish object (see Heller 2000). For fetishism "is not really a *human* perversion at all but a uniquely male one" (Grosz 1991: 39). This projection – of lust, of desire, and of want – onto a fetish object seems the simplest way to present such imagery, which is usually recruited to lend an edgy sexuality to the advertised product. Ads for anything from cologne to telecommunications networks feature fetish themes of high-heeled shoes, stockings, tight leather, S & M, and bondage (cf. Cortese 1999). Often these motifs are invoked with a wink to the knowing audience, a hip sign that the viewer understands – and appreciates – what is implied by the image of a handcuff, an extremely high heel, or a leather corset.

These ads draw on motifs developed by such photographers as Helmut Newton, Horst, and Jean-Loup Sieff, who featured women in corsets, leather, and high heels in their photographic work for mainstream fashion magazines. In the 1970s this trend accelerated, pushed by the art world, a growing awareness of "underground" sexual practices, and a market hungry for extreme imagery. By the 1980s fetish and dominatrix imagery had established a firm place in the visual pantheon of fashion, music video, and film, and was adopted by such celebrities as Grace Jones, Madonna, and Annie Lennox, and via the photography of Robert Mapplethorpe. Today, fashion designers such as Thierry Mugler, Versace, Jean-Paul Gaultier and Sisley regularly include fetish-themed clothing in their clothing lines and ad campaigns. A current hit movie, *Charlie's Angels*, portrays actress Lucy Liu in fetish form (an apparent reprise of her role in the Mel Gibson vehicle *Payback*), complete with crop, leather ensemble and high-heeled black leather boots.

Typical manifestations of this type include the dominatrix, appearing lately in Altoids mint print ads, Johnnie Walker Red whiskey, and Breil watches, to name a few. The dominatrix has become a visual culture icon. The image of a woman, usually dressed in black leather, high-heeled black boots, carrying a whip or riding crop, who desires to inflict both pain and the promise of pleasure on her (usually) male victim seems appropriate to sell most any product. One charming example: an Internet connection company's ad depicts a leather-clad woman, complete with whip slung over her shoulders – a whip that has computer cables and connection plugs morphed onto the leather handle. Something about connectivity .... Dominatrix-like women appear regularly on the tremendously popular

World Wrestling Federation telecasts. Furthermore, the dominatrix image populates singles ads in freely distributed newspapers in the US such as the *Chicago Reader*, the *Boston Phoenix*, and the *San Francisco Bay Guardian*, which feature prominent relationships and "variations" personals advertising pages usually found in the back of the papers. Often, a stylized dominatrix graphic marks the alternative lifestyle portion of these advertising sections. Dominatrix iconography is closely linked to stereotyped notions of fetishism, although there are important distinctions between the two concepts. In this analysis, I investigate how fetishism works in contemporary visual culture – the dominatrix is one icon that deserves further investigation. Others include the vampire, the cowboy, and the cyborg; each populates the visual pantheon, contributing to the visual consumption of identity.

The dominatrix is imbued with a certain power. However, the dominatrix's power revolves around sexual power, a kind of power under oppression. It remains unclear if power in the bedroom translates in a meaningful way to power in the living room, dining room, or boardroom. Furthermore, the dominatrix tends to exist to fulfill male fantasies of passive participation in sexual activity. The fetishized fantasy works best if she performs scripted scenarios of seduction and sadomasochism fueled by male desire. The man gets to endure and enjoy. The dominatrix embodies many of the forces of fetishism, a fiercely dressed female who exists to serve sexually. Most of popular dominatrix imagery revolves around extreme stereotypes of sexual interaction involving fetish objects, leather, or other accoutrements of "deviant" sexuality (Schroeder and Borgerson 2002). Some may argue that representations of alternative sexuality are useful to question entrenched norms and push limits of acceptable behavior between consenting adults, but, in general, these images are used to titillate, tease, and move products off the shelves, not to disrupt notions of cultural behavior. Furthermore, the dominant image of the dominatrix hardly expresses the variability inherent in alternative sexuality, rather it serves to reinforce stereotypical understandings of the role that power and leather play in real relationships.

Visual representation and fetishism work together to create fantasy images of desire and inaccessibility. Fetishism has been discussed from many perspectives, including psychology, anthropology, and Marxism. Representation draws on each of these, creating objects of desire through visual techniques and symbols. Psychoanalytic theory holds that a true fetish is based on paradoxical repulsion and attraction that charges fetish objects with power as it simultaneously represents attraction and taboo. (Shoes are seemingly an essential fetishistic item, and they probably need a much longer treatment than given here.) Visual representations of fetish objects – made possible by photographic reproduction, mass media, and photographic techniques – add another dimension to the fetish concept. Solomon-Godeau has theorized the fetish in nineteenth-century photography as a

> confluence of three fetishisms … : the psychic fetishism of patriarchy, grounded in capitalism, shrouded in what Marx calls the "veil of reification" and grounded in the means of production and the social relations they engender, and the fetishizing properties of the photograph, a commemorative trace of an absent object, the still picture of a frozen look, a screen for the projective play of the spectator's consciousness.
>
> (Solomon-Godeau 1993: 269)

The fetish emerged as an important tool of advertising, via direct representations of fetish objects and the fetish-like worship and power of consumer goods inherent in contemporary advertising.

Longing and liminality

Fetish clothing, usually of leather, rubber, or other tight-fitting materials, stretches over an important cultural and psychological liminal zone between nature and culture (see Ortner 1996). Leather and rubber are natural materials, in the sense that they have roots in the natural world – leather as animal skin, and rubber as a botanical extract. However, when made into clothing, each is culturally transformed into a manufactured product (cf. MacKendrick 1998). Each has a distinct genealogy yet functions in a similar liminal way. Fur has a history as a fetish material as well, made famous by the Victorian novel *Venus in Furs*, but here we will concentrate mostly on leather and rubber.

Leather

Humans have a long relationship with leather. Only recently has leather been associated with sex, fetishism, or being an outlaw. The leather jacket, for example, has undergone a significant transformation in the past fifty years from rebel badge to everyday fashion accessory. Leather pants, formerly reserved mainly for motorcyclists or rock stars, have become a staple of department store clothing lines. Leather jackets have been closely associated with the police, punk rockers, rock 'n' rollers, fighter pilots, and motorcyclists. Further, part of the iconography of leather clothing comes from the Nazis and the SS which most people know mainly via film, television shows, and photographs. Thus, the repertoire of cultural associations for leather accommodate countervailing images of control and resistance.

Leather is also associated with the gay community. Leather often obliquely refers to sexual preference, as in "are you into leather?" or "he's a leatherman." Thus, leather in this sense refers to leather as fetish. Although leather clothing has gone mainstream, certain kinds of leather goods such as collars, leather bras, leather jocks, and tight leather shirts for men remain within the underground domain. Certainly, these are worn and used by people of all sexual preferences, yet many leather items signify homosexual practice, and a leather "lifestyle" is more often linked to gay men than to straights. There is a huge market for leather fetish clothing, aimed at both straights and gays, served by catalogs, a growing number of specialty stores, and the Internet. Moreover, a leather community is often referred to, particularly during public spectacles such as gay pride parades. Leather gains an alternative sexuality image from these associations.

Many of the symbols of leather clothing are male stereotypes, yet women are the ones most often depicted in leather, and form a more specific image than men. Where do their images come from? Emma Peel, from the British television show *The Avengers*, often wore leather top to toe; Catwoman from the *Batman* movie series sewed her own shiny tight-fitting catsuit; Xena the warrior princess wears stylized leather armor; and a generic female biker – although she was often the biker's girlfriend – requires a leather ensemble. (My spellchecker just suggested "Cattleman" for "Catwoman," another reminder of the iconic dominance of male types.) This is not a huge reservoir of images, and yet the woman in leather plays a powerful role in contemporary visual culture. One recent source for these images is MTV, which provides a playground of fetishized women twenty-four hours a day. One formula was set by ZZ Top, whose early 1980s videos featured women with "legs," who know "how to use them," often wearing a tight, black leather skirt, high heels, and stockings. The video scenario invariably centered around a young man, minding his business, who would ultimately benefit from this "knowledge" and be ushered into the world of sexuality and adulthood by the leather-clad woman. In the absence of compelling icons such as cop or rock star, women are relegated to sexual stereotype. Associating visualized leather with sex may diminish somewhat as leather clothing for women becomes more widely available in many styles. Of course, it varies by culture, too. In Northern Europe, for example, leather pants are commonly worn by women without too much sexual association, but in the US, leather pants remain "hot."

Both men and women wear leather clothing, but leather is readily available in many more forms for women. Gloves are necessary for Swedish winters, and Stockholm has many stores that sell gloves exclusively. When I went to buy leather dress gloves in Stockholm, I found two or three choices, brown or black, whereas the shop was filled with women's gloves in many colors and styles. There is one basic men's style. Men's gloves are cut fuller, less shaped to the hand, with three or four ridges or seams along the back – they rarely have a smooth surface. Women's dress gloves, tight-fitting, cut close to the fingers, are more difficult to take off. They are often made of smooth leather, and are available in many lengths, from wrist to elbow length. The gloves I bought, nice as they are, were big and boxy, with raised seams on the back and oversize fingers that somehow signify male gloves. I have not found a single pair of men's gloves in a regular store that have a smooth finish. The threat of feminization seems too large, or perhaps the stereotyped practices of the clothing industry are too entrenched to feature unisex leather gloves, at least at mainstream stores.

Leather is a sensual fabric when processed in certain ways. Variable associations to types of leather are based on their place within the liminal system of nature vs. culture. Leather is considered a skin, a natural product of the animal it came from. Most leather sold today is cowhide, but many other animals' hides are made into leather goods – goat, pig, lamb, deer, and so forth. The process of turning a hide into a garment is a cultural one; leather is skinned, tanned, dyed, cut, sewn, and finished before it winds up as a jacket or pair of gloves. Thus, leather – especially leather clothing, worn near the skin – is liminal, between the zones of nature and culture, or what anthropologist Claude Lévi-Strauss called the raw and the cooked (1983).

The more leather accentuates this liminal factor, the more it can be fetishized. Leather can be worn tight or loose. Tight leather, of course, is more associated with sexuality and fetishism – particularly in visual representations – due to its capacity to mimic human skin, form a second skin, stretch across to suggest a superskin. Skin is natural. Tight-fitting leather is often achieved with zippers or laces, a subtle reminder of its cultural status.

Smooth, shiny leather is most often associated with fetishism. Few gloves or corsets are shown in contemporary visual culture made of rough suede, or bulky "unfinished" hides. Suede certainly can be sexy, yet it is also "safer" than leather, easier to integrate into a conservative wardrobe, less "suggestive." Suede often appears more like rawhide. Fuzzier and less shiny than leather, suede shows more of the dull nap of the skin. Shininess is an indicator of human handling; leather has to be highly processed to achieve a high sheen. Patent leather, which is perhaps the pinnacle of fetishized leather, undergoes even more finishing to achieve a stiff, almost plastic look that is highly prized by the fetishistic boot licker – at least in representations of the foot fetishist. Patent leather is a hybrid material, originating from a natural source but treated to such an extent that it begins to resemble plastic – that icon of manufactured substance.

Rubber

Rubber remains outside mainstream fashion – for particular kinds of clothes. Non-fashion garments such as rain jackets, boots, hats are often made of rubberized materials. Rubber gloves are used routinely used for medical or cleaning use. Diving gear, once made of natural rubber, is now primarily made from neoprene, a synthetic material that closely resembles rubber. Rubber fishing waders are often made of nylon and Gore-Tex. Thus, most rubber clothing is associated with special uses. In general, however, rubber clothing is considered fetishistic; rubber has not achieved leather's ubiquity in the modern marketplace. Tight rubber pants, shirts, or gloves usually occupy the realm of the fetish. Every few years designers try to incorporate rubber into their clothing lines, but rubber has yet to appear as a department store staple. Rubber clothing, also called latex, is found in shops featuring club wear, leather stores, specialized boutiques and catalogs, and on the Web. Recent representations of rubber appear to challenge Absolut's domination of the hip Vodka segment. In a reference to the pop artist Allen Jones, Svensk vodka, another Swedish export, features a woman's legs forming a cocktail table clad in bright green rubber tights. Other popular images include the pop group Destiny's Child, whose members often appear in leather and rubber, and mainstream magazine covers such as *Spin*, *Elle*, and *Esquire*. Black rubber seemed to be the preferred clothing for the lead female character in the recent movie *The Matrix*. There is also a rubber community, served by a myriad of magazines, Websites, and social events (see Mitchell 2000).

Rubber, particularly the thin, shiny rubber depicted in contemporary visual culture, is perhaps the ultimate liminal clothing. Rubber is a natural product – it comes from plants – yet it renders the wearer alien-like, with a smooth, sleek skin. The use of rubber in condoms fuels a sexual association. Rubber can be manufactured in many thicknesses and textures and could also be made to drape loosely on the body, yet most rubber garments are shown worn skin tight, thin, and shiny. Once again, black is the preferred color of rubber garments. Rubber – even more than leather – is a sexual, liminal substance.

Photography contributes to this meaning construction via the use of flash, which accentuates the shininess of rubber. Kobena Mercer, commenting on Mapplethorpe's infamous photographs of black men, argues that the photographed black skin signifies transgressive fantasy: "the glossy, shining, fetishized sheen of black skin thus serves and services the white man's desire to look and to enjoy the fantasy of mastery precisely through the scopic intensity that the pictures solicit" (Mercer 1997: 293). Thus, the combination of artificial lighting, photography, and shininess associated with certain skin and special rubber garments each contributes to a fetishization process – photography plays an important role by highlighting and objectifying rubber.

Liminal implicatons of fetish gear

Leather and rubber were originally meant for protection during outdoor use. Wearing these materials inside signals a transgression of a liminal zone between inside and outside, home and away, stranger and exotic. Visual representations of leather and rubber draw on these distinctions – the fetish world is usually indoors. Other fetish icons including shoes, gloves, and masks exemplify protection from the elements. These items serve as bestial body extensions. Donning leather may represent an animal-like quality;

rubber pushes this transference into an amphibian or almost reptilian world. Leather is a tough material, and this quality signifies tough work – manly outdoor tasks. Visually, wearing leather indoors – in the bedroom – appears as a breach of the important zone between inside and outside, private and public, perhaps work and pleasure. Dominatrix imagery calls on these associations to build up power and mastery connotations.

PVC or vinyl, also shiny and stretchy, occupies a smaller place in the visual fetish pantheon. Vinyl is cheaper, more durable, and easier to take care of than leather or rubber yet it has not attained similar status as an alternative clothing symbol – although it has its fans. Vinyl does not exude sensuality like leather and rubber does, nor does it mold to the body quite so well. Furthermore, PVC is a wholly manufactured product – it's polyvinylchloride, after all. Hence it doesn't push the wearer into the liminal zone between nature and culture, animal and human, inside and outside as effectively as leather and rubber do.

Fetishism and the body

Many things are liminal in the way they fall between nature and culture – it is not this quality alone that accounts for fetishized materials. Visual associations are important and contribute meaning in conjunction with prevailing cultural codes. Furthermore, a critical factor in fetish clothing is the way it conforms to and transforms the body. The tighter the clothing, the stronger the fetish potential. Tight clothing accentuates the human form, often isolates certain body parts like the pelvis or the breasts, and reveals the body's shape. Tight clingy clothing, for the most part, is a recent development, owing to changes in cultural norms, mores, and manufacturing technology. Many tight clothes are made of nylon, stretch cotton, spandex, which is part rubber. Leather and rubber clothing can be made to fit loosely, but usually the tight kind populates the cultural imagination. This tightness is achieved through careful manufacture: sewing, zipping, buttoning, lacing, and binding. The icon is the *tight* black leather skirt, after all. Of the three adjectives – tight, black, leather – so far I have discussed two.

Black is the preferred color of fetish iconography. Tight black leather and rubber resemble what gets referred to as black skin. Black, as a semiotic category, functions as the antithesis of white – the good (Gordon 1995, 1997). Blackness is associated with primitivism, savagery, animal, nature – non-human, in other words. Black has become exoticized via cultural stereotyping processes. Moreover, blackness has ontological status:

> Blackness and whiteness take on certain meanings that apply to certain groups of people in such a way that makes it difficult not to think of those people without certain affectivity charged associations. Their blackness and their whiteness become regarded, by people who take

> their associations too seriously, as their essential features – as, in fact, material features of their being.
>
> (Gordon 1995: 95)

Thus, blackness refers to racial identity in a semiotically charged way.

Tight black clothing, such as stockings and tights, long evening gloves, and corsets, represents a second skin. Indeed, skin color has been called "the most visible of the fetishes" (Bhabha 1983). For whites – and most of the models in the images discussed here are white – this representation is another foray into a liminal area, this time of racial categories. The point is not that people in black clothes look black, or somehow experience blackness. However, visually their skin is altered toward blackness – it appears "black." This phenomenon led one writer to conclude "such fashion-fetishism suggests a desire to simulate or imitate black skin" (Mercer 1997: 289). Blackness is associated with fetishism – a deviant sexuality – via representations of white people wearing black skins. That the categories of sexual, animal, and savage characterize semiotic coding of blackness helps explain why most fetish clothing is black.

Black is semiotically linked to nature, white to culture. Black fetish clothing is able to signify a sophisticated sexuality via its liminal status and its associations built from elements of visual culture, by means of what Suren Lalvani called "consuming the exotic" (1995). Black and white photography emphasizes black tones, and implicitly contrasts black with white. Of course, black and white pictures do not contain only black and white tones, but millions of varying tones between black and white. The language of photography, however, reinforces a dichotomous conception of black/white, inscribing racial categories with technological markers, in a process of racial fetishism (Mercer 1997).

Fetish clothing interacts with visual representation in intricate ways, ways that are furthered within contemporary advertising photographic practice. Photography supports a fetish relationship with things by representing items devoid of context, reifying objects, and visually emphasizing tactile qualities like shininess. Photography enhances the shine of fetish garments with flash, studio lighting, and image tone. Although nylon hosiery doesn't possess the natural origin of leather or rubber the way silk does, its shiny quality is often enhanced via photographic techniques in advertising. Images of hosiery-clad legs are routinely secured to sell many products unrelated to clothing. The fetish object is also emphasized by the use of composition, cropping and color. In the Absolut Au Kurant ads, the fetishized bottle is given a contrasting lavender detail color to accentuate and isolate it as a graphic element. Similarly, fetish photographers such as Trevor Watson, John Carey, and Doris Kloster all highlight abstracted and reified clothing as the subject of their work, supporting the fetish relationship by visually focusing on garments over bodies, things rather than humans (see Schroeder and Borgerson 2002).

Fetishism, fashion, and advertising

Absolut Kurant continues to promote a cutting-edge image via its advertising campaign, and the two images discussed here have been replaced by many others in the three years since they first appeared. The ads can be bought on the Internet, although they don't seem to command an especially high price. They ranged from $2.00 to $12.00 in November 2000. Many current ad campaigns draw on fetish imagery. A quick look through a representative stack of fashion and lifestyle magazines reveals Gucci loafer worship, Prada fetishism, Gap black leather jeans, Sisley pornography, a Flexform furniture ad featuring usually high-heeled black patent shoes, a Costume National ad featuring more high-heel worship (a man grasping a woman's pump-clad leg). Although most consumers do not exhibit classic fetishism – foot worship, for example – the relationship promoted between consumer and goods has many fetish-like tendencies.

One image that strikes the eye is an ad for Nokia mobile phones stating "Orange is the new black." The Nokia model 8210e, photographed in color against a black fabric background, looks strangely similar to the Absolut Au Kurant stocking ad. Popping out of the close focus ad, with a short depth of field, the phone is brightly lit, so that its silvery buttons shine, and it reflects the bright studio lighting. The phone is a "hero" in advertising vernacular, a lone figure that dominates the image.

The copy refers to the owner's ability to change color "as often as you change your image." The ad invokes the fashion industry's yearly announcement of some other color as the "new" black invokes the cultural theme "black clothing as staple." Orange in this case refers to Nokia's customer service plan, and is marked by a small orange square with the word orange on the bottom of the phone. The phone featured has a blue cover, and presumably there is a wide variety of covers available – one of Nokia's design triumphs. Clearly mobile phones are a fashion accessory, and most people in the highly "mobilized" Nordic countries would agree that owners have a close relationship with their "mobiles." Furthermore, the logic that guides mobile phone marketing certainly is touched by beliefs about the power of objects to positively influence one's life.

The Absolut Au Kurant stocking ad and the Nokia ad share several visual features. Both borrow from portraiture to illuminate product personality, and both employ Rembrandt-like "light from darkness" lighting to great effect. Both present their products on a black background, shot in with a narrow depth of field, and centered within the frame. Each places the subject of the ad on a diagonal, bisecting the image. The black material in the background of the Nokia ad resembles the black skirt in the Absolut stocking ad. The look of the Nokia ad, and its uncanny resemblance to the Absolut Au Kurant image, reinforces the arguments about the fetish in visual culture. The Nokia phone is represented as a precious object, a fashion item for one's image. Moreover, Nokia's reference to black is provocative, underscoring associations of black with fashion, with coolness, and to blackness as a racial, political, cultural, and semiotic phenomenon.

The fetish relationship – object worship, delusional belief in the power of the fetish, and substitution of human relations with fetish relations – are also invoked in the broader dimensions of consumer culture and its aggressive object worship. Advertising is able to appropriate and harness the power of fetishism to sell goods. Moreover, advertising is able to create meaning with photographic techniques, injecting new associations into the circuit of culture. Whereas many campaigns rely on cultural stereotypes (of fetishism, for example) advertising has reached a stage where it produces novel meaning. Advertising is a significant and powerful player in visual culture. Researchers attempting to understand its meaning-making capabilities miss a great deal by relying solely on rhetorical forms from other cultural arenas, such as fine art and film for themes and insights. Advertising is intertextual – it often refers to itself – it creates its own heroes and characters, and the logic of advertising underscores all aspects of visual consumption.

Fetish themes may attract the eye to products or services in an economy fueled by obtaining consumer attention. Fetish themes may also serve to perpetuate sexual stereotypes and gender stereotypes – women are most often the object of the fetishistic attention, or women are portrayed as slaves to fashion (see Schroeder and Borgerson 1998). Although there might be some transgression of sexual stereotypes, these are mainly in the service of entrenched visions of human relationships – woman as object, black as exotic, out-of-the-ordinary sex as deviant. Whether or not companies like Absolut benefit from their appropriation of these themes and sell more vodka is another question. These print ads are only one component of a sophisticated marketing campaign to build the brand identity of Absolut Kurant as cutting edge, sexy, and hip.

Conclusions

Many alcohol manufacturers visually reinforce cultural stereotypes that alcohol makes women accessible. Advertising fetishizes goods by offering them as substitutes for human relationships. By drawing on powerful imagery, Absolut and other advertisers harness the power of visual representation to create a global communication force. Advertising is not merely a vehicle to move goods, it is a central feature of visual culture, which it supports through its relationship with mass media. Furthermore, advertising imagery functions at several levels simultaneously – unlike the art world, all advertising has a clear, shared purpose to make positive associations between product and image.

The Absolut Au Kurant ad campaign invokes many issues central to visual culture: advertising and allure, representation and ethics, identity and difference. These two ads invite the viewer to participate in the sexual realm, a common theme in contemporary ad culture. The Absolut bottle is graphically represented by corset lacing and garter belt clip, two objects closely linked to fetishism and sexuality. Absolut Vodka may also be positioned as a way to enter the liminal zone between everyday life and fantasy, between sobriety and inebriation, between mainstream and alternative. The visual and photographic facets of the ad point to a link between Absolut Kurant and its iconic bottle shape and sexual adventure, and possibly, gender subversion or at least cross-dressing. In addition, the ads capitalize on the semiotic coding of black as hip, trendy, and sensual. Further work on race and identity in advertising is called for, drawing upon theoretical frameworks of the "epidermal schema" (Gordon 1995, 1997).

All of these meanings need not be apparent to any one viewer. Many campaigns build in diverse target markets in a single ad (see Schroeder 2000). The leather corset is employed as a signifier of fetishism, alternative sexuality, or perhaps domination. In other contexts, the corset might signify domination of women. However, given the logic of the ad it is unlikely to be read as a statement about women's oppression, except insofar as women's oppression is fetishized.

Absolut desires the viewer to make a positive connection between the black leather corset and its vodka. Given the way these ads circulate in popular culture, many other associations are possible. For example, it may be that these Absolut Au Kurant are not considered some of the more successful ads, as they are not linked to a famous artist, nor are they part of an established series such as "cities" (Stockholm, Barcelona, New York). Some viewers might merely consider it one more in a vast stock of Absolut images.

The use of tight black leather and stylized stockings implicate the ads in the liminal zone of the fetish. The ads draw upon three fetishism signifiers in visual culture: the hybrid nature of leather and other tight clothing, the exoticization of blackness, and photographic practice of formally reifying objects via technique. Cultural codes such as black leather, garter belts, and the color lavender are bounded by history, place, and identity. In contemporary visual culture, these are strong visual symbols of fetishism and a kind of alternative sexuality. In addition, lavender is the adopted color of the gay and lesbian community, thus for many the association between its use in the Absolut Au Kurant ads and gay culture is readily apparent. Paradoxically, some of these readings may seem to conflict with others, reflecting the flexibility of the ad to appeal to different groups, or target markets, of viewers.

Absolut Kurant is a fairly expensive vodka – indeed it is an icon of affluent consumption where the right image is critical, and name brand use is key. Certain vodka brands signify cosmopolitanism and hipness, and Absolut has played an important role in this trend – the rise of vodka as cultural icon would make an interesting analysis in itself. Of course these ads implicate class and wealth, too. Furthermore, Absolut ads appear in magazines tightly aimed at an upwardly mobile market, eager to learn about the newest exclusive consumer signifiers. Absolut graced the back cover of a recent issue of *Harvard Business Review*.

Marx introduced the commodity fetish concept over a century ago and his analysis of the relationship between consumer goods and the market remains important. Indeed, "fetishism is a term Marx used to characterize the capitalist social process as a whole" (Pietz 1993: 130). Marx did not fully anticipate an economy based on image, one in which the dialectic of the fetish relies less on material things than on symbolic ideas. Advertising's use of photographic technology accelerates this process in a way that seems both readily apparent and unfathomably underscrutinzed. The fetish can function as a tool to understand visual consumption, the type of consumption that is at the heart of contemporary life (Schroeder 2001). Contemporary consumption is highly visual, Websites crave eyeball capture, and advertisers work to break through the clutter, the economy is attention focused (Davenport and Beck 2000). The power of advertising to fetishize objects visually continues this trend in a way that scholars interested in visual culture cannot ignore.

I have focused on body images to develop my arguments, but the function of the fetish need not be confined to bodies, corsets, and stockings. Advertising encourages a fetish-like relationship with things in general. Thus the Nokia phone is imbued with an inordinate amount of attention and concomitant power in the recent "Orange is the new black" ad, and fetish themes are at work in technical products such as Infonet whose ad features an impossibly long pair of legs wearing a similarly high pair of black pumps and black hose. The association apparently is seamless hose=seamless connections, but signifiers abound in what is really a rather complex ad, albeit a sexist use of disembodied legs. In an economy based on images, information, and Internet technology, fetishism – as displacement, as dysfunction, and as deviance – contributes to a larger project of linking products with psychological fulfillment.

Further work would be useful to delineate how the fetish works in a wide variety of ad contexts, and how fetishism has developed as shorthand for various desirable attributes to be associated with the advertised product. Just as art historians and literary scholars have been adept at tracing the history of icons, types, and characters, so could visual studies show how these types migrate into advertising and photography, as well as how advertising creates new type and tropes. The tools of art history come in handy here, for advertising borrows heavily from the iconology and teleology of art history. Advertising no longer merely reflects culture, or only appropriate concepts or images after the art world produced the original idea. Advertising is one of the key engines of visual culture and it requires complex, interdisciplinary analysis, informed by art history, marketing theory, and social psychology.

8 Conclusion

Visual consumption in an attention economy

Toyota Motor Corporation's Website, Gazoo.com, is named after the two Japanese language characters for "visual" (Strom 2000). The Toyota Website is so named to celebrate its ability to bring the showroom to the consumer. The site, like many others, is designed to visually represent the company – its brand, products, dealer showrooms, and customer service. In an article about the company, Akio Toyada, the force behind the site, is shown writing the characters with the phonetic translations below – *ga zoo*. He isn't delivering a PowerPoint presentation, nor is any sophisticated visual equipment present. Curiously, he is using a felt-tip marker to write on a rather nondescript looking whiteboard; he relies on the ancient tradition of writing characters to communicate his message about the latest in information technology – the World Wide Web. Gazoo.com signifies the centrality of vision in today's market, as well as the problems of translating corporate strategy into computer screens.

The Internet, among its many influences, has put a premium on understanding visual consumption. Internet economics consolidates corporate activity into visual displays. Clearly, the look of Web pages is fundamentally related to strategy – visual design has become foregrounded as a key e-commerce tool. The World Wide Web is a visual medium in which consumers navigate through an artificial environment almost entirely dependent upon their sense of sight. Web designers try to "capture eyeballs" with visually interesting, coherent, and easily navigable sites. Although the Web is a contemporary, sophisticated image delivery system, it relies on the visual past to generate meaning. The digital electronic architecture of the Web is based on the classical laws of architecture laid down centuries ago.

Photography provides a large component of Web graphics – and the logic of photographic reproduction informs Internet economics. The economies of scale the Internet affords rely on reproducibility – the ability to digitize and copy information without loss of quality. Photographic technology paved the way for image duplication. Furthermore, visual consumption of the Internet relies on similar principles expounded here – computer screens do not represent an entirely novel visual environment, and basic rules of perception and interpretation apply equally well online. The Web's navigational aesthetics remain open for investigation. The computer screen driven Web limits input from the other senses – it makes visual information primary, and it attenuates other navigational clues such as body position, touch, and sound.

Understanding visual communication

Today's information technologies of television, film, and the Internet are directly connected to the visual past. Research on information technology (IT) or information and communication technology (ICT) usually focuses on complex, sophisticated systems such as mass media, the Internet, telecommunications, or digital satellite transmission arrays. These constitute the basic building blocks of the information society – where information is a crucial corporate competitive advantage as well as a fundamental cultural force. Photography remains a key component of many information technologies – digital incorporation of scanned photographic images helped transform the Internet into what it is today. Photography, in turn, was heavily influenced by the older traditions of painting in its commercial and artistic production, reception, and recognition (Kress and van Leeuwen 1996).

The visual arts are an impressive cultural referent system that the mass media draw upon for their representational power. Themes, subjects, and techniques from art history illuminate contemporary imagery: "Art in all cultures ultimately creates its meaning and vitality by connecting the individual with persons of forces greater than himself or herself" (Pelfrey and Hall-Pelfrey 1993: 309–10). Visual conventions informed by historical practice allowed companies to generate compelling images of products, people, and lifestyles. Advertising connects viewers to products in a personal way, this appeal to identity is why advertising art works so well. Interest in the interconnections between art and marketing are growing, yet the intellectual and cultural gulf between them remains wide (cf. Brown and Patterson 2000).

Associating visual consumption with the art historical world helps to position and understand photography as a global representational system. The approach to consumption affords new perspectives to investigate specific art historical references in consumer behaviors, the gaze, display, and representing identity, to name a few instances. In addition, marketing research can take advantage of useful tools developed in art history and cultural studies to investigate the poetics and politics of advertising as a representational system. Finally, art-centered analyses often generate novel concepts and theories for research on patronage, visual attention, information technology, and fashion, for example.

The connections between advertising, photography, and the Internet center on the image and its role in visual consumption of information technology. Specifically, advertising photography stretches Barthes' influential notion that photography shows "what has been." As consumers we should know that what is shown in ads hasn't really been, it is usually a staged construction designed to sell something. Yet, largely due to photography's realism, combined with technological and artistic expertise, advertising images produce powerful simulations of a real world. Advertising photography exists within culture and can be considered alongside with photography of real life: photojournalism, portrait photography, and fine art photography.

In my research on bank Websites discussed in chapter 5, what truly stood out was the preponderance of human images as graphic elements in the corporate sites. Most were filled with photographs of people, representing customers, employees or managers. As viewers, we cannot know who they really are – if they are models posing for the camera, if they are typical bank employees. In these images, like many advertisements that feature people, "social identity is conveyed primarily through the display of the product in a social context; the people who are inserted into the scene remain undefined, providing only a vague reference to the person code" (Leiss *et al.* 1990: 259). We may assume that they have been selected to portray particular images for the bank – perhaps a diverse workforce, a specific target marketing group, or a photogenic sample of the bank's staff. The photographs stand in for corporate identity. The banks harness the power of photographic images in ways that are almost unnoticed – we are not told what function these pictures serve, nor if the people are paid models, volunteers, or bank spokespeople. A current campaign for Omega watches uses the tagline "Cindy Crawford's choice" to promote a similar relationship between the supermodel and the product. As consumers, surely most of us realize that her choice is not based on personal preference but endorsement fees, yet the ad remains effective in linking her to Omega. Corporate identity and communication relies on photography's representational power to create salient, strategic images – images that may bear only tangential relationships to corporate staffing policies, promotional histories, and board memberships, for example. The visual dimensions of the Web accelerate these trends, and promote a photographic record of corporate composition based on the medium's long relationship with identity and representation.

One might think that the ascendancy of visual images would lead to unprecedented levels of visual literacy; that consumers living in an image-based world might become picture-savvy, accomplished semioticians able to decode and decipher images at will. One colleague argues that post-modern consumers are not "fooled" by images – they know how ads work and resist, embrace, or ignore them at will. Moreover, goes this line of thought, consumers see most ads from an ironic, detached, or playful perspective that dampens their effectiveness as persuasive messages. Another claims that consumers know what advertising is all about, that they "see through" its techniques, and understand its influence upon them. Others have suggested that the visual environment is so heavily saturated with images that advertisements have lost their rhetorical power, thus leading the advertising industry to develop shock ad campaigns in a desperate measure to gain consumer attention.

These pronouncements might seem like obstacles for a visually oriented approach to consumption, so I turn my own attention to clarifying the role of the visual in contemporary culture. Currently, there seem to be four distinct and often contradictory propositions that concern visual consumption. The first proposition suggests that consumers pay little attention to images, including ads. Cognitive capacity, heuristic processing, interest, and motivation limit human attention. I dub this the zapping hypothesis. Consumers "zap" through ads with their handy remote control units, rarely resting their eyes on commercial images. The second proposition holds that today's consumers enjoy high levels of visual literacy – they are successful semioticians of the image economy who understand how images work. This is the savvy consumer, for whom marketing is transparent. In other words, everyone knows ads are designed to sell things. Third, some commentators contend that most consumers are unaware – and thus unaffected by deep meaning in advertising imagery. Whereas close scrutiny of images often reveals semiotic signification, advertising is only skin deep – an ephemeral, playful part of visual culture. This proposition – seemingly the antithesis of the previous claim – revolves around what I call the clueless consumer. Fourth, advertising is doomed by emerging economic phenomena – pricing information on the Web, alternative marketing strategies, and changing media use are combining to alter advertising's role in corporate strategy. Advertising is dead, in other words. The visual landscape will be irrevocably transformed via revolutionary developments in marketing communication technology and market information.

Zapping

In many ways, doubts about how much consumers pay attention to ads – and how effective advertising images are – constitute an empirical question. However, several strands of evidence can be gathered to refute the claim that consumers pay little attention to advertising. First, advertising appears in more forms than ever – on the Internet, within television programs, on bus shelters, in sponsored events – and, as I have argued, the logic of advertising underlies much of visual culture. This type of advertising is difficult to ignore or zap – it is designed to subtly occupy consumer attention within the visual environment. Certainly, the entire corporate world would be reluctant to continue such practices if they did not find them fairly effective. Second, consumers clearly pay attention to some marketing campaigns – certain print ads in particular have become collectors' items, and hundreds of Websites post popular images from CK

One, Absolut, Nike, and other celebrated campaigns. Furthermore, companies like Bare Walls sell poster-sized advertising for home decor. There is little distinction between many celebrity images and advertising – pictures have long been part of the publicity machine. Third, most ads work through repeated exposure – one need not pay much attention to advertising imagery to recognize the dominant figures and images of the ad world.

The savvy consumer

Once during a lecture on the interconnections of art and advertising, I began to describe a painting and its signification system. As the students looked at the image – it was a minor portrait of a nobleman from the eighteenth century – I discussed some basic features of portrait painting; what is shown in the background, pose, clothing, personal effects, and studio props. I pointed out that by including things like globes or maps near the model, painters signified worldliness, scientific knowledge, and possession; and that – like an advertisement – each part of a painting is put there for a reason. One need only consult a dictionary of art to read a paragraph or two about the symbolic significance of globes in art history. Globes are an attribute of truth, fame, and abundance, and commonly appear as an allegorical attribute of still life paintings (e.g., Hall 1979). With a bit of knowledge about mythology, intellectual history, and exploration, objects like a globe's presence in the pantheon of painted objects becomes clearer. The painting we were looking at, for example, showed the sitter's hand resting on some books. I suggested that this is a traditional symbol of education, literacy, and higher learning. I pointed out that few people of the time could read, and that the painter may have added the books on his own – they needn't have been there during the portrait sitting. Thus, the man's hand gently resting on an open book symbolized certain things about his character, in a way that was perhaps more clear when it was painted, but still resonate today.

After this point, one of my students became angry. "You mean that those things in the painting mean something?" he said, his voice rising. "That the painter put those books in there for a reason – they aren't just there in the room?" He was furious. No one had ever taught him about the visual language of images – that painted objects often signify, that things are not always just as they appear, and that seeing is only one part of knowing. "How come no one ever told me this?" he asked. A world of knowledge has passed him by, and once he began to understand this, he realized how much he had been missing – a world had been hidden away from him.

In several years of teaching visual communication courses, I am struck at many student's initial unwillingness to engage seriously with images. In many educational systems, art and art history have been eliminated by budget cuts, usurped by computer graphics courses, or relegated to elective status. Furthermore, much art history is taught as "names and dates" history, a pedagogical style that gives students a poor basis for understanding the power of images in their own lives. Thus, I do not agree that consumers have become visually literate from exposure to images. To me, this is like claiming that someone who eats a lot ultimately becomes a good cook due to exposure to good food.

Some observers imply that some ads "don't make sense." One colleague pointed to the preponderance of stylized, abstracted images in ads to argue that advertising agencies deliberately create campaigns that "deconstruct" advertising. In other words, poststructural ads contain floating images whose meanings are utterly dependent upon viewers' own interpretive biases and predilections. He specifically mentioned ads from companies like Diesel, Benetton, and Calvin Klein, which made my temper flare a bit, as I think these ads contain substantial semiotic material – especially when connected to the visual realm of painting, photography, and graphic art and understood within the circuit of representational production and consumption. Advertising agencies might be surprised that their effects don't mean anything – their business relies on effective communication, after all.

In response to this type of claim, I call forth the CK One ad discussed in chapter 6. With a little effort, I placed this image within the group portrait genre, and pointed to Dutch art as an important genealogical ancestor of group images. Further, if one has a basic knowledge of photographic history – not merely as a technological development, but also as a visual form – CK One imagery might suggest the work of Lewis Hines, who photographed scruffy-looking children and adolescents in miserable circumstances to call attention to child labor and poverty. Hines's work, reified and abstracted from its original context and intention, now hangs in photography collections worldwide as an exemplar of ethically evaluative work that influenced how children's identity is conceived and represented. His group portraits – although far removed in time and purpose, visually correspond to the CK One group portraits. Perhaps most importantly, I could invoke the stunning resemblance between the CK One image and Richard Avedon's photographs of Andy Warhol's Factory gang – well-known images of a famous group of people – which clearly influenced the 1990s ad campaign. Moreover, without venturing into the worlds of art and celebrity, I point to the conventions of the group portrait, which most of us have experienced from family photographs, class photographs, team photographs, or candid shots of friends, colleagues, or office groups. A group of people photographed together form a cognitive set – psychological, visual, and cultural conventions instruct viewers that something meaningful binds people in the same frame together. Even though viewers ought to realize that in CK One's case, the group were posed and paid to appear together; group characteristics are easily ascribed to the models –

they are psychologically united by their (assumed) CK One consumption and by their appearance within the group image. Visual conventions thus link consumers and endorsers within a logic of consumer identity – associating people via consumer habits of others in their group.

Far from void of meaning, celebrated images such as the CK One campaign are filled with powerful associations, interpretations, and historical relevance to the wider world of visual communication. I believe that for most consumers, the growing volume of images militates against understanding how they function. We rarely take the time to thoroughly reflect on advertising imagery, its position as something that comes between programs, articles, or Websites makes it appear ephemeral or at least peripheral to serious consideration. However, given its role in visual culture, advertising clearly commands attention from those interested in visual consumption.

The clueless consumer

I draw on clinical experience – introducing scores of students to visual literacy – to discuss the notion that consumers don't see signification in ads, that interpreters "read in" meanings that are lost in the marketplace. This proposition – which runs counter to the savvy consumer claim – is fairly easily refuted by the literature. When asked, consumers are able to make detailed inferences about imagery and meaning in ads (e.g., Ritson and Elliot 1999; Hirschman and Thompson 1997; McQuarrie and Mick 1999; Mick and Buhl 1992; Zaltman and Coulter 1995). However, this could be a demand artifact – when prompted, for the benefit of the interested interviewer people may be creating meanings on the spot. In my experience, however, most people readily make associations and symbolic connections from ads, using metaphors, images, and semiotics, often without awareness of what they are doing.

For example, one of my students wanted to write about a Salem cigarette ad. The image showed a young woman with greenish skin and black pointed fingernails, wearing a choker of round beads that reflected several images of a man who appeared to be knocking on a door in attempt to get the woman's attention. To me, the image immediately called to mind a witch – and connecting this to the brand Salem completed the semiotic link. Salem, Massachusetts was the site of the notorious seventeenth-century witch trials – made famous by Arthur Miller's play *The Crucible*. My student told me that her roommate thought the image was offensive, but she herself thought it was cool. Resisting the urge to impose my views upon her, I told her that perhaps the image could be both cool and offensive, and that it would make an excellent topic for her term paper. I recommended that she consult a book called *The Painted Witch: How Western Artists have Viewed the Sexuality of Women* (Mullins 1985). She turned in an exceptional paper that examined the image from the historical, social, and semiotic perspective that I have written about here, persuasively connecting the Salem cigarette ad to the larger domains of history, oppression, and target marketing. I think that her strong interest in the image – as built in by the ad's art director – was predicated on these deeper connections that she was vaguely aware of, but lacked the vocabulary to describe. Further, by encouraging her to delve into the significance of the image – without giving her an interpretation – I enabled her to make more sense of the witch's status as a visual icon. I think that considering consumers as clueless vastly underestimates their semiotic ability, interpretive power, and critical thinking potential.

Another version of this stance concerns basic issues of interpretive work – that one interpretation is as good as any other. I don't subscribe to the notion that images "float" – that they can mean anything for anyone. I acknowledge that my image interpretations are one of many – that is what interpretation is all about. Simply because one can generate many interpretations doesn't reduce the usefulness of a carefully considered viewpoint. I often hear complaints that interpretive work "invents" things that "are not there." Calvin Klein, for example, in defending his advertising campaigns often accuses critics of reading in things that he never intended (Churcher and Gaines 1994). It should be clear, however, that the internal content of images is only one part of the interpretive story.

Can images mean anything? Some approaches suggest that images float in the postmodern world – signs disconnected from signifiers – allowing consumers free to generate novel, resistant, and idiosyncratic meaning. Whereas I agree that consumers generate their own meaning, and that they bring their own cognitive, social, and cultural lenses to whatever they see, this does not mean that the historical and political processes that also generate meaning are eliminated. One colleague maintains that images are open to interpretation, with little to anchor or fix them to a particular meaning. However, as I have argued, there are systems of meaning and representational practice that do indeed anchor and fix images, a claim supported by more recent work in cultural studies and art history that is critically opposed to the poststructural notion that signs float free of historical situatedness. This is not to imply that meanings are fixed historically, and that once an image is decoded, interpretive work ceases. Rather, within a theoretical understanding of visual consumption, images exist within cultural and historical frameworks that inform their production, consumption, circulation, and interpretation.

In one class, I showed my students a Chanel shoe advertisement. The image showed a woman's foot about to kick an American football, place-kicker style. The ball rested on a bed of long grass – much longer than convenient for football; the model was wearing high-heeled shoes plainly not designed for most contact sports. Her form was not particularly good – it appeared as if she was going to kick the football with the pointed toe of her Chanel pumps. As this was well into the semester and these students had gained some background in interpreting images, I asked them what they saw. A male student eagerly suggested that this ad showed how durable Chanel shoes are – you can even kick a football in them! The other students howled in protest – they laughed at the idea that the ad was a straightforward product claim. They pointed out how absurd both the image and their fellow student's interpretation appeared. Far from being semiotically postmodern, my student seemed willing to accept the literal, visually apparent surface characteristics of the ad: the football field represented nothing more than a football field and the suggestive act of kicking merely signified product use. Nor did he see the ad as ironic or playful. (I suppose that viewers might make a connection between Chanel's classic pumps, which are durable in terms of fashion cycles and durability from a long-wearing perspective, but I think that interpretation is a stretch.) He didn't really believe that she could play football in the sling-back shoes, yet, as he struggled to make sense of the image, he resorted to an uncritical, unreflective, and distinctly unsavvy interpretation – one encouraged by the abstracted, reified nature of the image.

Without reading much into this ad, most of the students understood the football as a masculine symbol and high-heeled shoes as an icon of femininity. We reminded ourselves that few ads of this type rely on product claims – rather they make associations to other, abstract qualities to create compelling consumer imagery. In this case, I suggested, potential consumers of expensive, elegant, and trendy Chanel shoes are probably not too concerned about being able to play football in them – they are a luxurious lifestyle product that may only be worn for the short period that they are in style. Why then, show the shoes kicking a football? It *is* an arresting image, one that plays with conventions and presents unexpected gender juxtapositions. At the same time, I think Chanel's ad trivializes women's participation in sports – particularly manly, rough sports like football, and it undermines the talents of women athletes everywhere. How does it do this? Female participation in sports has a history – one of exclusion based on spurious science, malicious medicine, and passionate prejudice. Women's athletics is also implicated in wider discussions of equity in government funding, equal opportunity, and political agendas. Thus, the image inadvertently resonates with many issues central to my class full of college-age men and women, several of whom were scholarship athletes.

A female football player – women do play American football – would obviously never attempt to play dressed in high-heels and stockings, nor would she kick the ball in the manner shown in the ad. I suggest that the ad subtly reinforces sexual stereotypes – it is *not* ironic, after all; it promotes Chanel, which has a vested interest in perpetuating notions of femininity and female identity, as well as masculine tastes and turn-ons. Women are routinely teased about their interests in "male" sports and belittled for their athletic ability. To accuse a male of "throwing like a girl" is a tremendous putdown (Young 1990). Until quite recently, women were prevented in participating in many organized sports. Despite equal opportunity legislation in the US and elsewhere, women's sports receive much less athletic funding in schools and universities, women have had less scholarship money available to them, women coaches have traditionally been paid less than men have. Sports, rather than a trivial, silly activity as depicted in the ad, are big business, central to many cultures including the United States. Football, of course, is an important marketing vehicle – the Superbowl game represents the pinnacle of the advertising world. I think my student was a bit embarrassed after several of the other students pointed this out to him – he was able to renegotiate his response to the image and consider their points of view without much effort. He admitted that most ads don't focus on product attributes, and that his interpretation fell flat against his classmates'. But his initial insistence to place the ad within a functional framework is telling – when asked, consumers are able to rationalize abstract images such as this quickly, making expressive, irrational ads appear downright utilitarian. Furthermore, although the ad did not target him, he felt comfortable in making attributions about a product he has little familiarity with, and probably will never buy.

I am not arguing that his interpretation was incorrect, nor do I believe that ads like the Chanel ad generate only one possible meaning. Rather, upon reflection – reflection based on a sophisticated understanding of how the market works, how advertising functions, and the psychological basis of consumer behavior, coupled with more compelling contrasting opinions, my functionalist interpreter retreated to acknowledge the deeper implications of a rather simple image. A female athlete among the students needed no prompting to point out the mixed message of the ad – she had a particularly negative reaction, fueled by her lifelong struggle to be taken seriously as a gifted athlete. Of course, one might object that she does not constitute Chanel's target market. This is beside the point – advertising is the dominant global communication force and its images and logic undergirds most of the world's media. Furthermore, one might point to competing images of women athletes – Nike, for example, portrays women in more flattering ways than Chanel's football ad. However, Nike continues to rely on sexually dualistic conceptions of men and women, they produce sex-typed apparel and athletic shoes, and they promote a vision of sexy athleticism that doesn't stray far from cosmetic advertising imagery (Goldman and Papson 1996). This is not to suggest that advertising imagery is not plural, or to deny that some ads promote positive images or that one ad alone creates problems. Advertising images circulate in culture – their importance and meaning looms far outside narrow target market definitions: it is the cumulative effect of thousands of images over a lifetime that help construct our conceptions of identity, possibility, and difference.

Is advertising dead?

In 1991, marketing guru Regis McKenna predicted the demise of advertising. He argued that marketing relationships and technology will come to replace advertising, which "serves no useful purpose" (McKenna 1991: 8). The "monologue of advertising" cannot accommodate feedback for emerging paradigms such as relationship marketing, McKenna claimed, and most advertising promised more than products could deliver. Others have predicted the downfall of the one-to-many model of traditional media communication, citing the interactivity of the Internet as more effective and efficient. So far, however, Web advertising formally resembles mass media, and advertising imagery dominates many Websites and portals.

A recent article in the *New Yorker* goes further with the claim that one of the most famous ad campaigns in history – for Marlboro cigarettes – was largely ineffective: "people smoked before those ads, and they'll continue to smoke after they're gone. I don't think they sold a single cigarette" (photographer Richard Prince, quoted in Surowiecki 1999). This spectacular assertion seems diametrically opposed to recent court decisions about tobacco advertising that dramatically curtailed cigarette advertising in the US. Remarkably, it was printed without critical commentary in an influential forum.

Another attack on advertising's continued significance comes from pricing enthusiasts. The Web, some claim, will make price transparent, and consumers will be less willing to pay higher premiums for well-known brands. In the information economy, substitutes abound – who needs books when you can download the "information"? (I have always found that people who predict the end of the book don't really like books.) The brand, then, will become less important, hence advertising will come to focus (again) on product utilities. Although the Web does make comparison shopping easier for many products, it is unlikely to uproot consumption behavior developed over the past hundred years. Consumers lack technical know-how to evaluate most products, they lack information about quality, and they often have low motivation to make utilitarian decisions. Consumers use products to meet expressive needs, they want to exert minimize cognitive effort. In general, consumers do not shop around – most consumer behavior is routinized, and despite market fragmentation, many consumers remain brand loyal (Sirgy and Su 2000). The promise of the Web for perfect information and efficient markets may be realized, but it will not completely change consumer behavior.

The continuing prominence of the image

Visual consumption is offered as an alternative approach for marketing scholarship, one that relies on interdisciplinary methods, based on semiotic understandings of signs in contemporary images. Approaching visual representation within consumer research via the interpretive stances presented offers researchers a grounded method that is able to account for political and ethical issues. As art historian Keith Moxey argues:

> Semiotics makes us aware that the cultural values with which we make sense of the world are a tissue of conventions that have been handed down from generation to generation by the members of the culture of which we are a part. It reminds us that there is nothing "natural" about our values; they are social constructs that not only vary enormously in the course of time but differ radically from culture to culture.
>
> (1994: 61)

In connecting images to the external context of consumption, we gain a more thorough – yet never complete – understanding of how images function.

Advertising images are visual spectacles that encourage "*audience participation within a small set of approved responses*" (Peñaloza 1999: 348, emphasis in original). This set of responses rarely includes broader political, social, and historical contexts that might interfere with preferred image decoding. Furthermore, perception depends largely on expectations – what we expect to see we often see. Advertising conventions encourage use of a narrow set of expectations to decode and decipher imagery – positive expectations, generally, which lead to promising conclusions about the advertised item. Contrary to museum going, for instance, looking at ads seem to require checking one's cultural knowledge at the door, so that ads become spectacles of visual consumption. I find visual communication and art history to be an excellent way of developing critical thinking in my students. The mass media provide a multitude of sites that students are engaged and familiar with to work on critical thinking skills. Advertising and photography in particular are of vital interest to students, and mine have enjoyed learning more about a way of apprehending and critiquing visual imagery.

Advertising remains "the privileged discourse for the circulation of messages and social cues about the interplay between persons and objects" (Leiss *et al.* 1990: 50). Certainly, some consumers are savvy, others may indeed be clueless, many people zap commercials when they can, and advertising is changing from its role on the Web. However, the very prominence of images makes it difficult to understand them, marketing appeals work best if "consumers cannot hold their attention, or focus their desire on any object for long; if they are impatient, impetuous, and restive, and above all easily excitable and equally losing interest" (Bauman 1998: 81–2). Given time to unpack and understand advertising imagery, my students often react critically to the messages they began to see in ads. Upon serious reflection, many promises of advertising seem unfulfilled and unfulfillable. Just as the perfect vacation remains an elusive goal, the world of advertising imagery remains always in the future, beyond the reach of today, a wonderful world of whimsy that bears little resemblance to lived experience. Advertising, like travel, carries with it a promise of bliss, of consumer nirvana around the next corner, at the next itinerary stop or the next software version (Bauman 1998).

Traveling – through cyberspace, virtual reality, on business, or as a tourist – structures contemporary life. Photography and travel organize the consumer within the modern market. Visual consumption through showing, displaying, and discussing travel photographs is important in establishing one's identity as a traveler, adventurer, sophisticate, or purist. Travel photographs, then, become chapter headings in the life story, helping to establish setting, character, and mood. Since its invention, photography has been intimately connected with travel and travel photographs have largely replaced travel logs as a method of remembering trips. Moreover, travel has become an excuse to take photographs: "we travel not just to be on the way, but to take pictures along the way" (Time-Life Editorial Staff 1972: 18). Photography provides direction and structure to travel. Often, when observing photographers on vacation, I notice a once-removed quality of their interactions. Each event is experienced as a photo opportunity, every new place a backdrop for a family picture. Postmodern theorists have also noted the spectacle of mediated society (e.g., Debord 1994). We live by the lenses of technology – cameras, video equipment, computer screens – which seem to offer unprecedented visions to us, yet often obscure our sight with dazzling ephemera.

Information technology makes looking at many things possible, but it does not necessarily improve our capacity to *see* – to actively engage our senses in reflective analysis. Photography now dominates how we conceive of people, places, and things. Yet photography is not the truth, it is not a simple record of some reality. I find it useful to think of photography as a consumer behavior as well as a central information technology. Photography's technical ability to reproduce images makes it a central feature of visual consumption. Furthermore, photographs tell us where we have been, who we are, and what we value.

Visual consumption characterizes life in the information age – the computer, the Web, and television structure twentieth-first century lives, commanding time and attention, providing a steady stream of images that appear to bring the world within. Whether images are approached from psychophysiological, semiotic, or art historical perspectives, it is clear that they are critically important for understanding contemporary consumer culture. Visual consumption implicates the image within a multidisciplinary matrix to reinforce their complexity, their connections to ethics and values, and their psychological nature. The image, now as in the past, is the key to understanding how we make sense of our world.

Bibliography

Adam, R. (1990) *Classical Architecture: A Comprehensive Handbook to the Tradition of Classical Style*, New York: Abrams.

Adams, L. S. (1996) *The Methodologies of Art*, New York: HarperCollins.

Allon, J. (1998) "Bank's neo-classical columns get new staying power," *New York Times*, February 15, Section 14: 6.

Alpers, S. (1984) *The Art of Describing: Dutch Art in the Seventeenth Century*, Chicago: University of Chicago Press.

Apter, E. and Pietz, W. (eds) (1993) *Fetishism as Cultural Discourse*, Ithaca, NY: Cornell University Press.

Arnheim, R. (1957) *Film as Art*, Berkeley: University of California Press.

—— (1969) *Visual Thinking*, Berkeley: University of California Press.

—— (1974) *Art and Visual Perception*, Berkeley: University of California Press.

—— (1977) *The Dynamics of Architectural Form*, Berkeley: University of California Press.

Ball, M. S. and Smith, G. W. (1992) *Analyzing Visual Data*, Newbury Park, CA: Sage.

Barleben, K. A. Jr. (1934) *Travel Photography with the Miniature Camera*, Canton, OH: Pomo.

Barnet, S. (1997) *A Short Guide to Writing About Art*, 5th edn, New York: Longman.

Barrett, T. (1990) *Criticizing Photographs: An Introduction to Understanding Images*, Mountain View, CA: Mayfield Press.

—— (1996) *Criticizing Photographs: An Introduction to Understanding Images*, 2nd edition, Mountain View, CA: Mayfield Press.

Barry, A. M. S. (1997) *Visual Intelligence: Perception, Image, and Manipulation in Visual Communication*, Albany: State University of New York Press.

Barthes, R. (1981) *Camera Lucida: Reflections on Photography*, trans. R. Howard, New York: Noonday.

—— (1987) *Criticism and Truth*, trans. K. P. Keuneman, Minneapolis: University of Minnesota Press.

Batchen, G. (1997) *Burning with Desire: The Conception of Photography*, Cambridge, MA: MIT Press.

Bauman, Z. (1998) *Globalization: The Human Consequences*, Cambridge: Polity.

Baxandall, M. (1972) *Painting and Experience in Fifteenth Century Italy*, Oxford: Clarendon Press.

—— (1987) *Patterns of Intention: On the Historical Explanation of Pictures*, New Haven, CT: Yale University Press.

Beatty, S. G. (1995) "Women dislike their reflection in ads," *Wall Street Journal*, December 19: B2.

Belk, R. W. (1988) "Possessions and the extended self," *Journal of Consumer Research*, 15, September: 139–68.

—— (1989) "Visual images of consumption: what you see and what you get," in T. Childers *et al.* (eds) *American Marketing Association Winter Educators" Conference: Marketing Theory and Practice*, Chicago: American Marketing Association, 122.

—— (1990) "The role of possessions in constructing and maintaining a sense of the past," in M. E. Goldberg, G. Gorn and R. W. Pollay (eds) *Advances in Consumer Research*, Vol. 17, Provo, UT: Association for Consumer Research, 669–76.

—— (1995) *Collecting in a Consumer Society*, London: Routledge.

—— (1998) "Multimedia approaches to qualitative data and representations," in B. B. Stern (ed.) *Representing Consumers: Voices, Views, and Visions*, London: Routledge, 308–38.

Belk, R. W and Pollay, R. W. (1985) "Images of ourselves: the good life in twentieth century advertising," *Journal of Consumer Research*, 11, March: 887–97.

Benjamin, W. (1968) *Illuminations*, trans. H. Zohn, New York: Harcourt Brace.

—— (1978) *Reflections*, trans. E. Jephcott, New York: Harcourt Brace.

—— (1980) "A short history of photography," trans. P. Patton, in A. Trachtenberg (ed.) *Classic Essays on Photography*, Stony Creek, CT: Leete's Island Books, 199–216.

Berger, A. A. (1998) *Believing is Seeing: An Introduction to Visual Communication*, Mountain View, CA: Mayfield.

—— (2000) *Ads, Fads and Consumer Culture*, Lanham, MD: Rowman and Littlefield.

Berger, J. (1972) *Ways of Seeing*, London: Penguin/BBC.

Bhabha, H. (1983) "The Other question: the stereotype and colonial discourse," *Screen*, 24, 4: 18–36.

Birnbaum, D. (1999) "Robert Wilson: Stadsteater, Stockholm" [review of *Dream Play*], *Artforum*, New York, February: 92.

Björkman, A. and Hägglund, M. (2000) *The Stockholm Guide*, Vällenby: Svenksa Tryckcentralen.

Bogart, M. H. (1995) *Artists, Advertising, and the Borders of Art*, Chicago: University of Chicago Press.

Booker, J. (1990) *Temples of Mammon: The Architecture of Banking*, Edinburgh: Edinburgh University Press.

Bordo, S. (1997) *Twilight Zones: The Hidden Life of Cultural Images from Plato to O.J.*, Berkeley: University of California Press.

Borgerson, J. L and Schroeder, J. E. (1997) "The ethics of representation – packaging paradise: consuming the 50th state," *Cooley Law Review*, 14: 473–89.

Bornoff, N. (1997) "Araki," *The Face*, July: 98–102

Boulding, K. E. (1956) *The Image: Knowledge in Life and Society*, Ann Arbor: University of Michigan Press.

Bourdieu, P. (1990) *Photography: A Middle-brow Art*, trans. S. Whiteside, Stanford, CA: Stanford University Press.

Boys, J. (1996) "(Mis)representation of society? Problems in the relationships between architectural aesthetics and social meanings", in J. Palmer and

M. Dodson, (eds) *Design and Aesthetics: A Reader*, London: Routledge, 226–47.

Bristor, J. M. and Fischer, E. (1993) "Feminist thought: implications for consumer research," *Journal of Consumer Research*, 19, March: 518–36.

Bristor, J. M., Lee, R. G. and Hunt, M. (1995) "Race and ideology: African American images in television advertising," *Journal of Public Policy & Marketing*, 14, Spring: 1–24.

Brown, S. (1995) *Postmodern Marketing*, London: Routledge.

Brown, S. and Patterson, A. (eds) (2000) *Imagining Marketing: Art, Aesthetics, and the Avant-Garde*, London: Routledge.

Brussat, D. (1997) "A model modern credit union," *Providence Journal-Bulletin*, January 30: B7.

Butler, J. (1990) *Gender Trouble: Feminism and the Subversion of Identity*, New York: Routledge.

Cadava, E. (1999) *Words of Light: Theses on the Photography of History*, Princeton, NJ: Princeton University Press.

Campbell, R. H. (1995) "CK One takes top awards," *Houston Chronicle*, June 29, Fashion Section: 8.

Carley, R. (1994) *The Visual Dictionary of American Domestic Architecture*, New York: Henry Holt.

Carlell, C. (2001) *Technology in Everyday Life: A Study of Consumers and Technology in a Banking Context*, Stockholm: Stockholm University.

Carrier, D. (1991) *Principles of Art History Writing*, University Park: Pennsylvania State University Press.

Cartier-Bresson, H. (1999) *The Mind's Eye: Writings on Photography and Photographers*, New York: Aperture.

Castells, M. (1999) "Flows, networks, and identities: a critical theory of the information society," in Castells, M. *et al.* (eds) *Critical Education in the New Information Age*, Lanham, MD: Rowman and Littlefield, 37–63.

Chajet, C. (1991) *Image by Design*, Reading, MA: Addison-Wesley.

Chambers, S. A. Jr. (1985) "Banks," in D. Maddex (ed.) *Built in the U.S.A.: American Buildings from Airports to Zoos*, Washington, DC: National Trust for Historic Preservation, 20–23.

Chow, R. (1997) *Primitive Passions: Visuality, Sexuality, Ethnography, and Contemporary Chinese Cinema*, New York: Columbia University Press.

Churcher, S. and Gaines, S. S. (1994) *Obsession: The Lives and Times of Calvin Klein*, New York: Carol Publishing Group.

Clarke, G. (1997) *The Photograph*, Oxford: Oxford University Press.

Clifford, J. (1997) *Routes: Travel and Translation in the Late Twentieth Century*, Cambridge, MA: Harvard University Press.

Cole, B. (1991) *Piero della Francesca: Tradition and Innovation in Renaissance Art*, New York: HarperCollins.

Coleman, A. D. (1998) *Depth of Field: Essays on Photography, Mass Media, and Lens Culture*, Albuquerque: University of New Mexico Press.

Conway, H. and Roenisch, R. (1994) *Understanding Architecture*, London: Routledge.

Cortese, A. J. (1999) *Provocateur: Images of Women and Minorities in Advertising*, Lanham, MD: Rowman and Littlefield.

Coulter, R. H. and Zaltman, G. (1994) "Using the Zaltman Metaphor Elicitation Technique to understand brand images," in C. T. Allen and D. Roedder John (eds) *Advances in Consumer Research*, Vol. 21, Provo, UT: Association for Consumer Research, 501–7.

Crary, J. (1990) *Techniques of the Observer: On Vision and Modernity in the Nineteenth Century*, Cambridge, MA: MIT Press.

Csiksentmihalyi, M. and Robinson, R. E. (1990) *The Art of Seeing: An Interpretation of the Aesthetic Encounter*, Malibu, CA: Getty.

Cuno, J. (1997) "Photography and the art museums," *Harvard University Art Museums Review*, 6, Fall: 1.

Daly, S. and Wice, N. (1995) *alt.culture: an a-to-z guide to the '90s – underground, online, and over-the-counter*, New York: HarperPerennial.

Davenport, T. H. and Beck, J. C. (2000) "Getting the attention you need," *Harvard Business Review*, September: 118–28.

Davis, A. Y. (1981) *Women, Race and Class*, New York: Vintage.

Davis, W. (1996) "Gender," in R. S. Nelson and R. Schiff (eds) *Critical Terms for Art History*, Chicago: University of Chicago Press, 220–33.

Debord, G. (1994) *The Society of the Spectacle*, trans. D. Nicholson-Smith, New York: Zone Books.

Desmond, J. (1999) *Staging Tourism: Bodies on Display from Waikiki to Sea World*, Chicago: University of Chicago Press.

Dictionary of Architecture (1995) London: Brockhampton Press.

Dobers, P. and Schroeder, J. (2001) "Representing IT: embodying the electronic economy," Proceedings of the Nordic Academy of Management Conference, Uppsala, Sweden.

Dobers, P. and L. Strannegård (2001) "Lovable networks – a story of affection, attraction and treachery," *Journal of Organizational Change* 14, 1: 8–49.

Drucker, J. (1999) "Who's afraid of visual culture?" *Art Journal*, Winter: 37–47.

du Gay, P. (1997) *Production of Culture/Cultures of Production*, London: Sage/Open University Press.

Edelstein, A. S. (1997) *Total Propaganda: From Mass Culture to Popular Culture*, New York: Lawrence Erlbaum.

Elliot, S. (1994) "Ultrathin models in Coca-Cola and Calvin Klein campaigns draw fire and a boycott call," *New York Times*, April 26: D18.

Fabian, J. (1983) *Time and the Other*, New York: Columbia University Press.

Fernie, E. (ed.) (1995) *Art History and Its Methods: A Critical Anthology*, London: Phaidon.

Fırat, A. F., Dholakia, N. and Venkatesh, A. (1995) "Marketing in a postmodern world," *European Journal of Marketing*: 29: 40–56.

Ford, C. (ed.) (1989) *The Story of Popular Photography*, North Pomfret, VT: Trafalgar Square.

Francis, M. and King, M. (1997) *The Warhol Look: Glamour, Style, Fashion*, Boston: Bulfinch Press.

Frank, T. (1997) *The Conquest of Cool: Business Culture, Counterculture, and the Rise of Hip Consumerism*, Chicago: University of Chicago Press.

Freedberg, D. (1989) *The Power of Images: Studies in the History and Theory of Response*, Chicago: University of Chicago.

Frye, M. (1983) *The Politics of Reality: Essays in Feminist Theory*, Freedom, CA: Crossing Press.

Frye, N. (1957) *Anatomy of Criticism: Four Essays*, Princeton, NJ: Princeton University Press.

Fuchs, R. H. (1978) *Dutch Painting*, London: Thames and Hudson.

Gill, B. (ed.) (1990) *Money Matters: A Critical Look at Bank Architecture*, New York: McGraw-Hill.

Giroux, H. A. (1994) *Disturbing Pleasures: Learning Popular Culture*, New York: Routledge.

Goffman, E. (1979) *Gender Advertisements: Studies in the Anthropology of Visual Communication*, New York: Harper & Row.

Goldberg, V. (1993) *The Power of Photography: How Photographs Changed Our Lives*, New York: Abbeville Press.

—— (1996) "Photographs in history's shifting gaze," *New York Times*, section 2: 1.

Goldman, K. (1995) "Calvin Klein halts jeans ad campaign," *Wall Street Journal*, August 29: B6.

Goldman, R. (1992) *Reading Ads Socially*, New York: Routledge.

Goldman, R. and Papson, S. (1996) *Sign Wars: The Cluttered Landscape of Advertising*, New York: Guilford.

Goldthwaite, R. A. (1993) *Wealth and the Demand for Art in Italy 1300–1600*, Baltimore: Johns Hopkins University Press.

Gordon, L. R. (1995) *Bad Faith and Antiblack Racism*, Atlantic Highlands, NJ: Humanities Press.

—— (1997) *Her Majesty's Other Children: Sketches of Racism from a Neocolonial Age*, Lanham, MD: Rowman and Littlefield.

Gross, L. (1988) "The Ethics of (mis) representation," in L. Gross, J. S. Katz and J. Ruby (eds) *Image Ethics*, Oxford: Oxford University Press, 188–202.

Grosz, E. (1991) "Lesbian fetishism?" *differences*, 3: 39–54.

Guillet de Monthoux, P. (2000) "The art management of aesthetic organizing", in S. Linstead and H. Höpfl (eds) *The Aesthetics of Organization*, London: Sage, 35–60.

Guimond, J. (1991) *American Photography and the American Dream*, Chapel Hill: University of North Carolina Press.

Hall, J. (1979) *Dictionary of Subjects & Symbols in Art*, revised edition, Boulder, CO: Westview.

Hall, S. (ed.) (1997) *Representation: Cultural Representations and Signifying Practices*, London: Open University Press/Sage.

Hamilton, C. (2000) *Absolut: The Biography of a Bottle*, New York: Texere.

Hannerz, U. (1990) "Cosmopolitans and locals in a world culture," *Theory, Culture and Society*, 7, June: 237–51.

Havlena, W. J. and Holak, S. L. (1996) "Exploring nostalgia imagery through the use of consumer collages," in K. P. Corfman and J. G. Lynch (eds) *Advances in Consumer Research*, Vol. 23, Provo: UT: Association for Consumer Research, 35–42.

Heilbrunn, B. (1999) "Brave new brands: marketing paradiso between utopia and a-topia," in S. Brown and A. Patterson (eds) *Proceedings of the Marketing Paradiso Conclave*, Belfast: University of Ulster, 222–35.

Heilemann, J. (1997) "Annals of advertising: all Europeans are not alike," *The New Yorker*, April 28–May 5: 74–81.

Heisley, D. A. and Levy, S. J. (1991) "Autodriving: a photoelicitation technique," *Journal of Consumer Research*, 18, December: 257–73.

Heisley, D. A., McGrath, M. A. and Sherry, J. F. (1991) "'To everything there is a season:' a photoessay of a farmers' market," in R. W. Belk (ed.) *Highways and Buyways: Naturalistic Research from the Consumer Behavior Odyssey*, Provo, UT: Association for Consumer Research, 141–66.

Heller, Scott (1996) "Visual images replace text as focal point for many scholars," *Chronicle of Higher Education*, July 19: A8–A9, A15.

—— (1997) "Race, class, gender, and culture are now part of business history," *Chronicle of Higher Education*, October 17: A15.

Heller, Steven (2000) *Sex Appeal: The Art of Allure in Graphic Design and Advertising*, New York: Allworth Press.

Herbert, Z. (1991) *Still Life with a Bridle*, Hopewell, NJ: Ecco Press.

Hirschman, E. (1986) "Humanistic inquiry in marketing research: philosophy, method, and criteria," *Journal of Marketing Research*, 23: 237–49.

Hirschman, E. and Thompson, C. J. (1997) "Why media matter: advertising and consumers in contemporary communication," *Journal of Advertising*, 26, 1: 43–60.

Holbrook, M. B. (1998) "Journey to Kroywen: an ethnographic stereographic auto-auto-auto driven photo essay," in B. B. Stern (ed.) *Representing Consumers: Voices, Views, and Visions*, London: Routledge, 231–64.

Holt, D. B. (1995a) "How consumers consume: a taxonomy of consumption practices," *Journal of Consumer Research*, 22, June: 1–16.

—— (1995b) "Consumption and society: will Marketing join the conversation?" *Journal of Marketing Research*, 32, November: 487–94.

hooks, b. (1994) *Outlaw Culture: Resisting Representations*, New York: Routledge.

Hudson, L. A. and Ozanne, J. L. (1988) "Alternative ways of seeking knowledge in consumer research," *Journal of Consumer Research*, 14, March: 508–21.

Hupfer, M. (1997) "A pluralistic approach to visual communication: reviewing rhetoric and representation in World War I posters," in D. MacInnis and M. Brucks (eds) *Advances in Consumer Research*, Vol. 24, Provo: Association for Consumer Research.

Hultin, O., Johansson, B. O., Mårtelius, and Wærn, R. (1998) *The Complete Guide to Stockholm Architecture*, Stockholm: Arkitektur Förlag.

James, J. (1994) "Transcending fashion," *ArtNews*, March: 102–7.

Jardine, L. (1996) *Worldly Goods: A New History of the Renaissance*, New York: Nan Talese/Doubleday.

Jay, M. (1993) *Downcast Eyes: The Denigration of Vision in Twentieth-Century French Thought*, Berkeley: University of California Press.

Jensen, R. (1994) *Marketing Modernism in Fin-de-Siècle Europe*, Princeton, NJ: Princeton University Press.

Jhally, S. (1987) *The Codes of Advertising*, New York: St. Martin's Press.

Johnston, F. B. (1966) *The Hampton Album*, New York: Museum of Modern Art/Doubleday.

Johnston, P. (1997) *Real Fantasies: Edward Steichen's Advertising Photography*, Berkeley: University of California Press.

Joy, A. (1993) "The modern Medicis: corporations as consumers of Art," in R. W. Belk (ed.) *Research in Consumer Behavior*, New York: JAI Press, 29–54.

—— (1998) "Framing art: the role of galleries in the circulation of art," in J. F. Sherry, Jr. (ed.) *Servicescapes: The Concept of Place in Contemporary Markets*, Chicago: American Marketing Association, 259–303.

Joy, A. and Venkatesh, A. (1994) "Postmodernism, feminism, and the body: the visible and invisible in consumer research," *International Journal of Research in Marketing*, 11, September: 333–57.

Kaplan, S. and Kaplan, R. (1982) *Cognition and Environment*, New York: Praeger.
Kinosian, J. (1997) "Don't ever change: the message of the new advertising is you're fine just as you are ... and our products can help you stay that way," *Los Angeles Times*, February 4: E2.
Kirstein, L. (1966) "Foreword," in F. B. Johnston, *The Hampton Album*, New York: Museum of Modern Art/Doubleday, 5–11.
Kolbe, R. H. and Albanese, P. J. (1996) "Man to man: a content analysis of sole-male images in male-audience magazines," *Journal of Advertising*, 25, Winter: 1–20.
Kostof, S. (1995) *A History of Architecture*, New York: Oxford University Press.
Kozol, W. (1994) *Life's America: Family and Nation in Postwar Photojournalism*, Philadelphia: Temple University Press.
Krauss, R. (1988) "The impulse to see," in H. Foster (ed.) *Vision and Visuality*, Seattle: Bay Press, 51–78.
Kraut, R., Lundmark, V., Patterson, M., Kiesler, S., Mukopadhyay, T. and Scherlis, W. (1998) "Internet paradox: a social technology that reduces social involvement and psychological well-being?," *American Psychologist*, 5, 9: 1017–31.
Kress, G. and van Leeuwen, T. (1996) *Reading Images: The Grammar of Visual Design*, London and New York: Routledge.
Kruger, B. (1990) *Love For Sale: The Words and Pictures of Barbara Kruger* [Text by K. Linker], New York: Abrams.
—— (1994) *Remote Control: Power, Culture and the World of Appearances*, Cambridge: MIT.
Lalvani, S. (1995) "Consuming the exotic other," *Critical Studies in Mass Communication*, 12, 3: 263–75.
Lears, T. J. J. (1994) *Fables of Abundance: A Cultural History of Advertising in America*, New York: Basic Books.
Leiss, W., Kline, S. and Jhally, S. (1990) *Social Communication in Advertising*, 2nd edn. Scarborough, ON: Nelson Canada.
Lemert, C. and Branaman, A. (eds) (1997) *The Goffman Reader*, Malden, MA: Blackwell.
Leppert, R. (1997) *Art and the Committed Eye: The Cultural Functions of Imagery*, Boulder, CO: Westview/HarperCollins.
Lester, P. M. (1995) *Visual Communication: Images with Messages*, Belmont, CA: Wadsworth.
Lévi-Strauss, C. (1983) *The Raw and the Cooked: Introduction to a Science of Mythology*, trans. J. Weightman and D. Weightman, Chicago: University of Chicago Press.
Lewis, R. W. (1996) *Absolut Book: The Vodka Advertising Story*, New York: Charles Tuttle.
Lin, M. (2000) *Boundaries*, New York: Simon & Schuster.
Lippert, B. (1996) "Sex: both sides now," *Adweek* 37, March 18: 26–8.
Lippke, R. L. (1995) *Radical Business Ethics*, Lanham, MD: Rowman and Littlefield.
Little, K. (1991) "On safari: the visual politics of a tourist representation," in D. Howes (ed.) *The Varieties of Sensory Experience: A Sourcebook in the Anthropology of the Senses*, Toronto: University of Toronto Press, 148–63.
Löfgren, O. (1999) *On Holiday: A History of Vacationing*, Berkeley: University of California Press.

Lutz, C. A. and Collins, J. L. (1993) *Reading National Geographic*, Chicago: University of Chicago Press.

MacCannell, D. (1976) *The Tourist: A New Theory of the Leisure Class*, New York: Schocken.

McCauley, E. A. (1997) "Photography," in S. Barnet *A Short Guide to Writing About Art*, 5th edn. New York: Longman, 61–71.

McCracken, G. (1988) *Culture and Consumption: New Approaches to the Symbolic Character of Consumer Goods and Activities*, Bloomington: Indiana University Press.

McGoun, E. G. (2000) "Form, function, and finance: architecture and rational economics," *Sixth Interdisciplinary Perspectives on Accounting conference*, Manchester, UK, July.

MacKendrick, K. (1998) "Technoflesh, or "didn't that hurt?"," *Fashion Theory, The Journal of Dress, Body & Culture*, 2, 1: 3–24.

McKenna, R. (1991) "Marketing is everything," *Harvard Business Review*, January–February (reprint): 1–10.

McQuarrie, E. F. and Mick, D. G. (1999) "Visual rhetoric in advertising: text-interpretive, experimental, and reader-response analyses, *Journal of Consumer Research*, 26, 1: 37–54.

Malraux, A. (1967) *Museum without Walls*, trans. S. Gilbert and F. Price, Garden City, NY: Doubleday.

Marchand, R. (1985) *Advertising the American Dream: Making Way for Modernity 1920–1940*, Berkeley: University of California.

Mayer, M. (1984) "The banking story," *American Heritage*, April–May: 26–35.

Meamber, L. A. (1997) "The constitution of the arts as cultural production: the role of the consumer, artist, and cultural intermediary as producer/consumer of meaning," Doctoral Dissertation, University of California, Irvine, Department of Management.

Menzel, P. (1994) *Material World: A Global Family Portrait*, San Francisco: Sierra Club Books.

Mercer, K. (1997) "Reading racial fetishism," in S. Hall (ed.) *Representation: Cultural Representations and Signifying Practices*, London: Sage/Open University Press, 285–90.

Messaris, P. (1997) *Visual Persuasion: The Role of Images in Advertising*, Newbury Park, CA: Sage.

Mick, D. G. (1986) "Consumer research and semiotics: exploring the morphology of signs, symbols, and significance," *Journal of Consumer Research*, 13, 3: 196–213

Mick, D. G. and Buhl, C. (1992) "A meaning based model of advertising experiences," *Journal of Consumer Research*, 19 December: 317–38.

Mick, D. G. and Politti, L. G. (1989) "Consumers' interpretations of advertising imagery: a visit to the hell of connotation," in E. C. Hirschman (ed.) *Interpretive Consumer Research*, Provo, UT: Association for Consumer Research, 85–96.

Miles, R. (1989) "Introduction," in University of California, Berkeley Guide to Doctoral Program in Business Administration.

Miller, C. (1992) "Publisher says sexy ads are ok, but sexist ones will sink sales", *Marketing News*, November 23: 8–9.

Miller, D. (1994) "Ontology and style," in J. Friedman (ed.) *Consumption and Identity*, Harwood, Amsterdam, 71–96.

Mingers, J. (1999) "What is it to be critical? Teaching a critical approach to Management undergraduates," Warwick Business School Research Bureau, No. 284.

Minh-Ha, T. T. (1991) *When the Moon Waxes Red: Representation, Gender, and Cultural Politics*, New York: Routledge.

Minor, V. H. (1994) *Art History's History*, Englewood Cliffs, NJ: Prentice-Hall.

Mirzoeff, N. (1999) *An Introduction to Visual Culture*, London: Routledge.

Mitchell, T. (ed.) (2000) *Fetish*, London: Carlton.

Morris, C. (1999) *The Essential Cindy Sherman*, New York: Harry Abrams.

Moxey, K. (1994) *The Practice of Theory: Poststructuralism, Cultural Politics, and Art History*, Ithaca, NY: Cornell University Press.

Mullins, E. (1985) *The Painted Witch: How Western Artists have Viewed the Sexuality of Women*, New York: Carroll & Graf.

Mulvey, L. (1989) *Visual and Other Pleasures: Theories of Representation and Difference*, Bloomington: Indiana University Press.

Murray, S. (2000) "Dull tomes replaced by designer message," *Financial Times*, June 30: 5.

Nava, M., Blake, A., MacRury, I. and Richards, B. (eds) (1996) *Buy This Book: Studies in Advertising and Consumption*, London: Routledge.

Nettis, J. (1965) *Traveling with your Camera: Creative 35mm Photography*, New York: Amphoto.

Newhall, B. (1982) *The History of Photography*, 5th edn, New York: Museum of Modern Art.

Nibbelink, D. D. (1948) *Photography for the Traveler*, Chicago: Ziff-Davis.

Nickel, D. (1998) *Snapshots: The Photography of Everyday Life 1888 to the Present*, San Francisco: San Francisco Museum of Modern Art.

Nisbet, R. (1990) "Men and money: reflections by a Sociologist," in B. Gill (ed.) *Money Matters: A Critical Look at Bank Architecture*, New York: McGraw-Hill, 7–13.

O'Barr, W. M., (1994) *Culture and the Ad: Exploring Otherness in the World of Advertising*, Boulder, CO: Westview.

O'Donohoe, S. (1997) "Leaky boundaries: intertextuality and young adult experiences of advertising," in M. Nava, A. Blake, I. MacRury, and B. Richards (eds) *Buy This Book: Studies in Advertising and Consumption*, London: Routledge, 257–75.

O'Gorman, J. F. (1998) *ABC of Architecture*, Philadelphia: University of Pennsylvania Press.

O'Guinn, T. C. and Shrum, L. J. (1997) "The role of television in the construction of consumer reality," *Journal of Consumer Research*, 23, March: 278–94.

Ohmann, R. (1996) *Selling Culture*, London: Verso.

Olin, M. (1996) "Gaze," in R. S. Nelson and R. Schiff (eds) *Critical Terms for Art History*, Chicago: University of Chicago Press, 208–19.

Onians, J. (1988) *Bearers of Meaning: The Classical Orders in Antiquity, the Middle Ages, and the Renaissance*, Princeton, NJ: Princeton University Press.

Ortner, S. B. (1996) *Making Gender: The Politics and Erotics of Culture*, Boston: Beacon.

Osborne, P. D. (2000) *Travelling Light: Photography, Travel and Visual Culture*, Manchester: Manchester University Press.

Pearce, R. (1999) "Advertising: critical analysis of images," in I. Parker (ed.) *Critical Textwork: An Introduction to Varieties of Discourse and Analysis*, Buckingham: Open University Press, 78–91.

Pelfrey, R. and Hall-Pelfrey, M. (1993) *Art and Mass Media*, New York: Harper & Row.

Pelton, R. Y. (2000) *The World's Most Dangerous Places*, 4th edn, New York: Harper Resource.

Peñaloza, L. (1999) "Just Doing It: a visual ethnographic study of spectacular consumption behavior at Nike Town," *Consumption Markets and Culture* 2, 4: 337–400.

Perkins, D. N. (1994) *The Intelligent Eye: Learning to Think by Looking at Art*, Los Angeles, CA: Getty Center for Education in the Arts.

Peters, Tom (2001) "Rule #3: leadership is confusing as hell," *Fast Company*, March: 124–40.

Pevsner, N. (1976) *A History of Building Types*, Princeton, NJ: Princeton University Press.

Pietz, W. (1993) "Fetishism and materialism: the limits of theory in Marx," in E. Apter, and W. Pietz (eds) *Fetishism as Cultural Discourse*, Ithaca, NY: Cornell University Press, 119–51.

Pinkel, S., Chen, D., Lawson, Z., Long, M., and Sugarman, J. (1995) "Queer representations in mass popular culture," online: http:/www.pomona.edu/REPRES/GAYS/GAYIN.HTML

Poe, E. A. (1980/1840) "The Daguerreotype," in A. Trachtenberg (ed.) *Classic Essays on Photography*, Stony Creek, CT: Leete's Island Books, 37–38.

Poiesz, T. B. C. (1989) "The image concept: its place in consumer psychology," *Journal of Economic Psychology*, 10: 457–72.

Polan, D. (1986) "Brief encounters: mass culture and the evacuation of sense," in Tania Modleski (ed.) *Studies in Entertainment: Critical Approaches to Mass Culture*, Bloomington: Indiana University Press, 167–87.

Pratt, M. L. (1992) *Imperial Eyes: Travel Writing and Transculturation*, New York: Routledge.

Prown, J. D. (1982) "Mind in matter: an introduction to material culture theory and method," *Winterthur Portfolio*, 17: 1–19.

Ramamurthy, A. (1997) "Constructions of illusion: photography and commodity culture," in L. Wells (ed.) *Photography: A Critical Introduction*, London: Routledge, 151–99.

Rasmussen, S. E. (1959) *Experiencing Architecture*, Cambridge, MA: MIT Press.

Reynolds, T. J. and Gutman, J. (1984) "Advertising is image management," *Journal of Advertising Research*, 24: 27–37.

Richins, M. L. (1994) "Special possessions and the expression of material values," *Journal of Consumer Research*, 21, 4: 522–33.

Ritson, M. and Elliot, R. (1999) "The social uses of advertising: an ethnographic study of adolescent advertising audiences," *Journal of Consumer Research*, 26, 3: 260–77.

Rosenblum, N. (1994) *A History of Women Photographers*, New York: Abbeville Press.

—— (1997) *A World History of Photography*, 3rd edn, New York: Abbeville Press.

Roskill, M. (1989) *The Interpretation of Pictures*, Amherst: University of Massachusetts Press.

Rosler, M. (1989) "In, around, and afterthoughts (on documentary photography)," in R. Bolton (ed.) *The Contest of Meaning: Critical Histories of Photography*, Cambridge: MIT Press, 303–42.

Rugg, L. H. (1997) *Picturing Ourselves: Photography & Autobiography*, Chicago: University of Chicago Press.

Ruskin, J. (1961/1849) *The Seven Lamps of Architecture*, New York: The Noonday Press.

Sandelands, L. (1998) *Feeling and Form in Social Life*, Lanham, MD: Rowman and Littlefield.

Savedoff, B. E. (2000) *Transforming Images: How Photography Complicates the Picture*, Ithaca, NY: Cornell University Press.

Schama, S. (1988) *The Embarrassment of Riches: An Interpretation of Dutch Culture in the Golden Age*, Berkeley: University of California Press.

Scholes, R. (1989) *Protocols of Reading*, New Haven, CT: Yale University Press.

Schroeder, J. E. (1992) "Materialism and modern art," in F. Rudmin and M. Richins (eds) *Meaning, Measure, and Morality of Materialism*, Provo, UT: Association for Consumer Research, 10–14.

—— (1995) Essay review: *Fables of Abundance: A Cultural History of Advertising in America* by Jackson Lears, *Marketing Modernism in Fin-de-Siècle Europe* by Robert Jensen, and *Privacy and Publicity: Modern Architecture as Mass Media* by Beatriz Colomina, *Design Issues*, 11: 76–81.

—— (1997a) "Andy Warhol: consumer researcher," in D. MacInnis and M. Brucks (eds) *Advances in Consumer Research*, Vol. 24, Provo: Association for Consumer Research, 476–82.

—— (1997b) "Roots of modern marketing in Italian Renaissance Art," in A. Falkenberg and T. Rittenberg (eds) *Proceedings of the Macromarketing Seminar*, Bergen, Norway: Norwegian School of Economics and Business Administration.

—— (1998) "Consuming representation: a visual approach to consumer research," in B. B. Stern (ed.) *Representing Consumers: Voices, Views, and Visions*, London and New York: Routledge, 193–230.

—— (1999) "Consuming representation: insights from Dutch Art of the Golden Age," in E. Arnould and L. Scott (eds) *Advances in Consumer Research*, Vol. 26, Provo: Association for Consumer Research, 641–3.

—— (2000) "The consumer in society: utopian visions revisited," *Marketing Intelligence and Planning*, 6/7: 376–81.

—— (2001) "Édouard Manet, Calvin Klein and the strategic use of scandal," in S. Brown and A. Patterson (eds) *Imagining Marketing: Art, Aesthetics, and the Avant-Garde*, London: Routledge, 36–51.

Schroeder, J. E. and Borgerson, J. L. (1998) "Marketing images of gender: a visual analysis," *Consumption Markets & Culture*, 2: 161–201.

—— (1999) "Packaging paradise: consuming Hawaiian music," in E. Arnould and L. Scott (eds) *Advances in Consumer Research*, Vol. 26, Provo: Association for Consumer Research, 46–50.

—— (2001) "Innovations in information technology: insights into consumer culture from Italian Renaissance Art," *Consumption Markets and Culture*, forthcoming.

—— (2002) "Dark desires: fetishism, ontology and representation in contemporary advertising," in T. Reichert and J. Lambiase (eds) *Sex in Advertising: Multidisciplinary Perspectives on the Erotic Appeal*, New York: Lawrence Erlbaum Associates.

Schroeder, J. E. and Zwick, D. (1999) "Consuming masculinity: advertising, the gaze, and male bodies," paper presented at the Association for Consumer Research Conference, Columbus, Ohio.

Scott, J. W. (1988) *Gender and the Politics of History*, New York: Columbia University Press.

Scott, L. A. (1994a) "Images of advertising: the need for a theory of visual rhetoric," *Journal of Consumer Research*, 21, September: 252–73.

—— (1994b) "The bridge from text to mind: adapting reader-response theory to consumer research," *Journal of Consumer Research*, 21, December: 461–80.

Scully, V. (1991) *Architecture: The Natural and the Manmade*, New York: St Martin's.

Sennett, R. (1990) *The Conscience of the Eye: The Design and Social Life of Cities*, New York: Norton.

Seo, D. (1998) "A new obsession: Calvin Klein ads with a wholesome bent? Yes, he says but critics unsure," *Los Angeles Times*, February 5: D4.

Sharoff, R. (1997) "World bank: architecture as diplomacy," *New York Times*, March 6: 43.

Sherry, J. F. Jr. (ed.) (1998) *Servicescapes: The Concept of Place in Contemporary Markets*, Chicago: American Marketing Association.

Simmel, G. (1978) *The Philosophy of Money*, trans. T. Bottomore and D. Frisby, London: Routledge and Kegan Paul.

Sirgy, M. J. and Su, C. (2000) "The ethics of consumer sovereignty in an age of high tech," *Journal of Business Ethics*, 28: 1–14.

Slater, D. (1997) *Consumer Culture and Modernity*, Cambridge, England: Polity Press.

Sloan, P. (1994) "Calvin Klein spins scent to music stores," *Marketing News*, 65: 24.

—— (1996) "Real people suit Calvin Klein in CK B, jeans and boxers ads," *Advertising Age*, 67, August 19, 3.

Solomon, D. (1994) "A career behind the camera," *Wall Street Journal*, March 25: 31.

Solomon-Godeau, A. (1991) *Photography at the Dock: Essays on Photographic History, Institutions, and Practices*, University of Minnesota Press, Minneapolis.

—— (1993) "The legs of the Countess," in E. Apter and W. Pietz. (eds) *Fetishism as Cultural Discourse*, Ithaca, NY: Cornell University Press, 266–306.

Sontag, S. (1977) *On Photography*, New York: Noonday.

Spiggle, S. (1985) "7-Up Art, Pepsi Art, and Sunkist Art: the representation of brand symbols in Art," in *Advances in Consumer Research*, Vol. 12, Provo, UT: Association for Consumer Research, 11–16.

Staniszewski, M. A. (1995) *Believing is Seeing: Creating the Culture of Art*, New York: Penguin.

Stern, B. B. (1988) "Medieval allegory: roots of advertising strategy for the mass market," *Journal of Marketing*, 52: 84–94.

—— (1989) "Literary criticism and consumer research: overview and illustrative analysis," *Journal of Consumer Research*, 16, 4: 322–34.

—— (1994) "Classical and vignette television advertising dramas: structural models, formal analysis, and consumer effects," *Journal of Consumer Research*, 20, 1: 601–15.

—— (1996) "Textual analysis in advertising research: construction and deconstruction of meanings," *Journal of Advertising*, 25, 3: 61–73.

—— (1998) "Introduction: the problematics of representation," in B. B. Stern (ed.)

Representing Consumers: Voices, Views, and Visions, New York: Routledge, 1–23.

Stern, B. B. and Schroeder, J. E. (1994) "Interpretive methodology from art and literary criticism: a humanistic approach to advertising imagery," *European Journal of Marketing*, 28, 3: 114–32.

Stokstad, M. (1995) *Art History*, New York: Abrams.

Strindberg, J. A. (1982) *Plays: Two,* trans. M. Meyer, London: Methuen.

Strom, S. (2000) "In Japan, an established company is transformed," *New York Times*, December 20: 19.

Suder, M. (2001) "Photography market: classic or contemporary?" *Wall Street Journal Europe*, March 2–3: 30.

Sullivan, R. (1995) "Denim and desire," *Vogue*, [US edition] November: 166–70.

Summers, D. (1996) "Representation," in R. S. Nelson and R. Schiff (eds) *Critical Terms for Art History*, Chicago: University of Chicago, 3–16.

Summerson, J. (1963) *The Classical Language of Architecture*, Cambridge, MA: MIT Press.

Surowiecki, J. (1999) "A cowboy is gone from the highway, but he rides on in the art world," *The New Yorker*, May 10: 37–8.

Szarkowski, J. (1988) *Winogrand: Figments from the Real World*, New York: Museum of Modern Art.

—— (1989) *Photography Until Now*, New York: Museum of Modern Art.

Tagg, J. (1989) *The Burden of Representation: Essays on Photographies and Histories*, Minneapolis: University of Minnesota.

Taylor, J. C. (1981) *Learning to Look: A Handbook for the Visual Arts*, 2nd edn, Chicago: University of Chicago Press.

Teather, D. (1995) "Hidden gender: androgyny in advertising," *Marketing,* November 30, 18.

Thompson, C. J. (1996) "Caring consumers: gendered consumption meanings and the juggling lifestyle," *Journal of Consumer Research*, 22, 1: 388–407.

Thompson, C. J. and Haytko, D. L. (1997) "Speaking of fashion: consumers' uses of fashion discourses and the appropriation of countervailing cultural meanings," *Journal of Consumer Research*, 24, 2: 15–42.

Thompson, C. J. and Hirschman, E. C. (1995) "Understanding the socialized body: a poststructuralist analysis of consumers' self-conceptions, body images, and self-care practices," *Journal of Consumer Research*, 22, 3: 139–53.

Thompson, C. J. and Tambyah, S. K. (1999) "Trying to be cosmopolitan," *Journal of Consumer Research*, 26, 3: 214–59.

Time-Life Editorial Staff (1972) *Travel Photography*, New York: Time-Life.

Torgovnick, M. (1991) *Gone Primitive*, Chicago: University of Chicago Press.

Triggs, E. (1995) "Visual rhetoric and semiotics," in T. Triggs, (ed.) *Communicating Design: Essays in Visual Communication*, London: Batsford, 81–6.

Tzonis, A. and Lefaivre, L. (1986) *Classical Architecture: The Poetics of Order*, Cambridge, MA: MIT Press.

Upton, D. (1998) *Architecture in the United States*, Oxford: Oxford University Press.

Urry, J. (1990) *The Tourist Gaze: Leisure and Travel in Contemporary Societies*, London: Sage.

—— (1995) *Consuming Places,* London: Routledge.

Venkatesh, A., Sherry, J. F., and Fırat, A. F. (1993) "Postmodernism and the marketing imaginary," *International Journal of Research in Marketing*, 10: 215–23.

Wagstaff, J. (2001) "Web navigation proves difficult to get right," *Wall Street Journal Europe*, March 8: 25.

Walker, M. U. (1998) *Moral Understandings: Feminist Studies in Ethics*, New York: Routledge.

Watson, P. (1992) *From Manet to Manhattan: The Rise of the Modern Art Market*, New York: Random House.

Weissberg, L. (1997) "Circulating images: notes on the photographic exchange," in J.-M. Rabaté (ed.) *Writing the Image After Roland Barthes*, Philadelphia: University of Pennsylvania Press, 109–31.

Wells Fargo Bank (2000) *Annual Report 1999*, San Francisco: Well Fargo Bank.

Wells, L. (ed.) 1997) *Photography: A Critical Introduction*, Routledge: London.

West, S. (ed.) (1996) *The Bulfinch Guide to Art History*, Boston: Bulfinch Press.

White, L. (1994) "Small wonder: the Kate Moss phenomenon," *Vogue* [British edition], August: 90–5.

Williamson, J. (1978) *Decoding Advertisements*, London: Marion Boyers.

—— (1986) *Consuming Passions: The Dynamics of Popular Culture*, London: Marion Boyers.

Willis, S. (1991) *A Primer for Everyday Life*, New York: Routledge.

Witkowski, T. H. (1996) "Farmers bargaining: buying and selling as a subject in American genre painting, 1835–1868," *Journal of Macromarketing*, 17, Fall: 84–101.

—— (1999) "The art of consumption," in E. Arnould and L. Scott (eds) *Advances in Consumer Research*, Vol. 26, Provo, UT: Association for Consumer Research, 640–7.

Wood, H. (1999) *Displacing Natives: The Rhetorical Production of Hawaii*, Boulder, CO: Rowman & Littlefield.

Woodford, S. (1983) *Looking at Pictures*, Cambridge: Cambridge University Press.

Wooley, A. E. (1965) *Traveling with your Camera*, New York: A. S. Barnes and Co.

Young, I. M. (1990) *Throwing Like a Girl and Other Essays in Feminist Philosophy and Social Theory*, Bloomington, IN: Indiana University Press.

Zajonc, R. B. (1968) "Attitudinal effects of mere exposure," *Journal of Personality and Social Psychology*, 9: 52–80.

Zaltman, G. (1997) "Rethinking market research: putting people back in," *Journal of Marketing Research*, 34: 424–37.

Zaltman, G. and Coulter, R. A. (1995) "Seeing the voice of the customer: metaphor-based advertising research," *Journal of Advertising Research*, 35, July–August: 35–51.

Zim, H. S. and Burnett, R. W. (1956) *Photography: The Amateur's Guide to Better Pictures*, New York: Simon and Schuster.

Zwick, D. (2001) *The Speed of Money: Investment as Consumption in the Age of Computer-Mediated Communication*, Doctoral Dissertation, University of Rhode Island.

Index

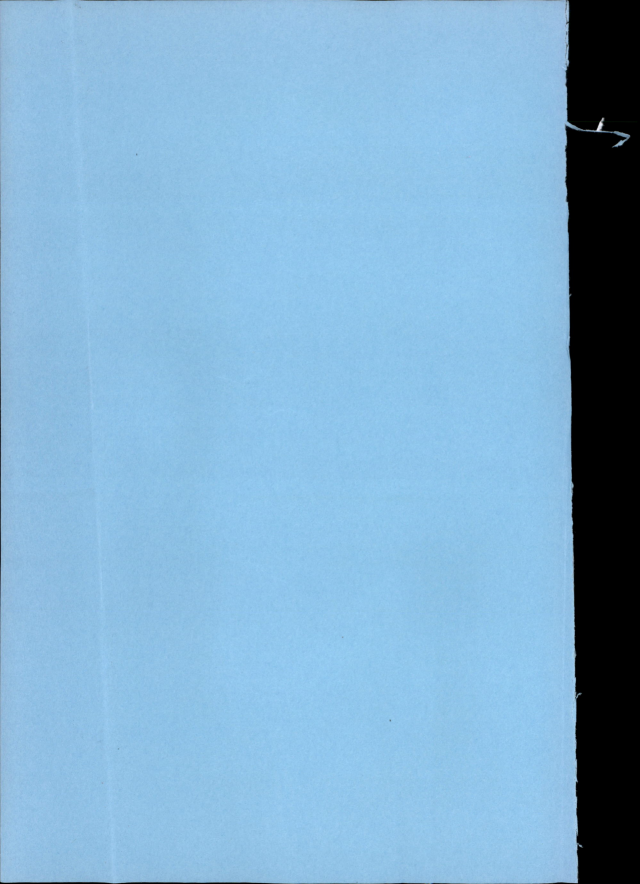